C-4957 CAREER EXAMINATION SERIES

This is your
PASSBOOK® for...

Financial Services Examiner II, III, IV, V

Test Preparation Study Guide
Questions & Answers

COPYRIGHT NOTICE

This book is SOLELY intended for, is sold ONLY to, and its use is RESTRICTED to individual, bona fide applicants or candidates who qualify by virtue of having seriously filed applications for appropriate license, certificate, professional and/or promotional advancement, higher school matriculation, scholarship, or other legitimate requirements of education and/or governmental authorities.

This book is NOT intended for use, class instruction, tutoring, training, duplication, copying, reprinting, excerption, or adaptation, etc., by:

1) Other publishers
2) Proprietors and/or Instructors of "Coaching" and/or Preparatory Courses
3) Personnel and/or Training Divisions of commercial, industrial, and governmental organizations
4) Schools, colleges, or universities and/or their departments and staffs, including teachers and other personnel
5) Testing Agencies or Bureaus
6) Study groups which seek by the purchase of a single volume to copy and/or duplicate and/or adapt this material for use by the group as a whole without having purchased individual volumes for each of the members of the group
7) Et al.

Such persons would be in violation of appropriate Federal and State statutes.

PROVISION OF LICENSING AGREEMENTS – Recognized educational, commercial, industrial, and governmental institutions and organizations, and others legitimately engaged in educational pursuits, including training, testing, and measurement activities, may address request for a licensing agreement to the copyright owners, who will determine whether, and under what conditions, including fees and charges, the materials in this book may be used them. In other words, a licensing facility exists for the legitimate use of the material in this book on other than an individual basis. However, it is asseverated and affirmed here that the material in this book CANNOT be used without the receipt of the express permission of such a licensing agreement from the Publishers. Inquiries re licensing should be addressed to the company, attention rights and permissions department.

All rights reserved, including the right of reproduction in whole or in part, in any form or by any means, electronic or mechanical, including photocopying, recording, or by any information storage and retrieval system, without permission in writing from the Publisher.

Copyright © 2025 by
National Learning Corporation

212 Michael Drive, Syosset, NY 11791
(516) 921-8888 • www.passbooks.com
E-mail: info@passbooks.com

PASSBOOK® SERIES

THE *PASSBOOK® SERIES* has been created to prepare applicants and candidates for the ultimate academic battlefield – the examination room.

At some time in our lives, each and every one of us may be required to take an examination – for validation, matriculation, admission, qualification, registration, certification, or licensure.

Based on the assumption that every applicant or candidate has met the basic formal educational standards, has taken the required number of courses, and read the necessary texts, the *PASSBOOK® SERIES* furnishes the one special preparation which may assure passing with confidence, instead of failing with insecurity. Examination questions – together with answers – are furnished as the basic vehicle for study so that the mysteries of the examination and its compounding difficulties may be eliminated or diminished by a sure method.

This book is meant to help you pass your examination provided that you qualify and are serious in your objective.

The entire field is reviewed through the huge store of content information which is succinctly presented through a provocative and challenging approach – the question-and-answer method.

A climate of success is established by furnishing the correct answers at the end of each test.

You soon learn to recognize types of questions, forms of questions, and patterns of questioning. You may even begin to anticipate expected outcomes.

You perceive that many questions are repeated or adapted so that you can gain acute insights, which may enable you to score many sure points.

You learn how to confront new questions, or types of questions, and to attack them confidently and work out the correct answers.

You note objectives and emphases, and recognize pitfalls and dangers, so that you may make positive educational adjustments.

Moreover, you are kept fully informed in relation to new concepts, methods, practices, and directions in the field.

You discover that you are actually taking the examination all the time: you are preparing for the examination by "taking" an examination, not by reading extraneous and/or supererogatory textbooks.

In short, this PASSBOOK®, used directedly, should be an important factor in helping you to pass your test.

FINANCIAL SERVICES EXAMINER II, III, IV, V

DUTIES
As a Financial Services Examiner II, you would monitor various types of financial services activities in accordance with the statutory responsibilities of the agency; function as an advanced performance level; may supervise Financial Services Examiners I, and lower-level staff; serve as commissioned examiner on an assignment of increased size and complexity; administer financial services examination/regulatory programs; develop examination plans; conduct financial services examinations, forensic accounting reviews, and examinations of alleged money-laundering activities as necessary; and independently handle difficult and complex assignments or regulatory matters.

As a Financial Services Examiner III, you would supervise lower-lever Financial Services Examiners; function as a team leader; perform the duties of lower-level Financial Services Examiners and direct lower-level staff engaged in programmatic activities; serve as the lead examiner on a larger and more complex assignment; manage assignment of increasing complexity, difficulty, and sensitivity; and oversee staff in the development of financial services policies, and implementation of new financial services initiatives, including regulatory programs, insurance, examination procedures, management and administration.

As a Financial Services Examiner IV, you would function as a section head; direct staff engaged in programmatic activities; oversee section activities and staff; serve as the lead examiner on the largest assignment; oversee the most complex, difficult, and sensitive assignments and regulatory matters; conduct special studies; and represent the agency as a liaison with other governmental entities on a local, State, or federal level, or with field units for program, project, or policy areas as assigned.

As a Financial Services Examiner V, you would plan and organize examinations and assign subordinate examiners to specific segments of the examination; supervise all phases of examinations and the analysis of an institution's overall financial and operational condition; analyze the adequacy of institution's audit department; examine affiliate relationships with emphasis on potential conflicts of interest or unsound policies; assemble individual reports into a coherent examination report; meet with management during the examination and discuss examination findings; submit comprehensive report of examination with recommendations on corrective measures; make on-site visits to ongoing field examinations to determine progress, provide supervision, and solve problems encountered by lower-level staff; and conduct examinations of a highly complex nature or special investigations requiring a high degree of technical knowledge.

SCOPE OF THE EXAMINATION
The written test is designed to test for knowledge, skills, and/or abilities in such areas as:

1. **Preparing reports and official documents** - These questions test for the ability to prepare reports and other official documents for use within and among governmental agencies, in legal or regulatory settings, or for dissemination to the public. Some questions test for a knowledge of grammar, usage, punctuation, and sentence structure. Others test for the ability to present information clearly and accurately, to use the proper tone, and to organize paragraphs logically and comprehensibly.
2. **Understanding and interpreting tabular material** - These questions test your ability to understand, analyze, and use the internal logic of data presented in tabular form. You may be asked to perform tasks such as completing tables, drawing conclusions from them,

analyzing data trends or interrelationships, and revising or combining data sets. The concepts of rate, ratio, and proportion are tested. Mathematical operations are simple, and computational speed is not a major factor in the test.

3. **Evaluating conclusions based on factual information** - These questions test your ability to evaluate and draw conclusions from factual information presented. Each question consists of a set of factual statements and a conclusion. You will be asked to determine whether the conclusion can be proven to be true by the facts, proven to be false by the facts, or if the facts are inadequate to prove the conclusion.

4. **Ensuring effective inter/intra agency communications** - These questions test for understanding of techniques for interacting effectively with individuals and agencies, to educate and inform them about topics of concern, to clarify agency programs or policies, to negotiate conflicts or resolve complaints, and to represent one's agency or program in a manner in keeping with good public relations practices. Questions may also cover interacting with the staff of one's own agency and/or that of other agencies in cooperative efforts of public outreach or service.

5. **Supervising a project** - These questions test for the ability to conduct and supervise the activities necessary to achieve the goals and deadlines of a specific project. The questions cover such topics as setting up the project, developing the workplan for the project, assigning and reviewing work, evaluating performance and progress, coordinating phases of the project, handling problems as they arise, and meeting deadlines.

6. **Working and interacting with others** - These questions test for knowledge of how to effectively approach work and maintain professional relationships with others in the workplace. Each question presents a situation and a number of possible approaches for handling it. Question topics may include working with supervisors and coworkers, interacting with members of the public, handling conflict, and managing workplace demands and priorities. The questions are not specific to any job title or place of work.

7. **Supervision** - These questions test for knowledge of the principles and practices employed in planning, organizing, and controlling the activities of a work unit toward predetermined objectives. The concepts covered, usually in a situational question format, include such topics as assigning and reviewing work; evaluating performance; maintaining work standards; motivating and developing subordinates; implementing procedural change; increasing efficiency; and dealing with problems of absenteeism, morale, and discipline.

8. **Analyzing and evaluating information** - These questions test for the ability to analyze, interpret, and draw reasonable conclusions from information presented in text, data, images or symbols. This may involve identifying a significant problem or issue; focusing on relevant data and text; identifying trends, relationships, and significant features; assessing relevant alternatives; suggesting or evaluating possible conclusions; and applying logical principles to information provided.

9. **Administrative supervision** - These questions test for knowledge of the principles and practices involved in directing the activities of a large subordinate staff, including subordinate supervisors. Questions relate to the personal interactions between an upper-level supervisor and their subordinate supervisors in the accomplishment of objectives. These questions cover such areas as assigning work to and coordinating the activities of several units, establishing and guiding staff development programs, evaluating the performance of subordinate supervisors, and maintaining relationships with other organizational sections.

10. **Understanding and applying administrative principles** - These questions test for knowledge of how to effectively manage and direct an organization or an organizational segment. These questions cover developing objectives, formulating policies, making decisions, forecasting and planning, developing personnel, organizing and coordinating work, communicating information, providing leadership, and delegating authority and responsibility.

HOW TO TAKE A TEST

I. YOU MUST PASS AN EXAMINATION

A. WHAT EVERY CANDIDATE SHOULD KNOW

Examination applicants often ask us for help in preparing for the written test. What can I study in advance? What kinds of questions will be asked? How will the test be given? How will the papers be graded?

As an applicant for a civil service examination, you may be wondering about some of these things. Our purpose here is to suggest effective methods of advance study and to describe civil service examinations.

Your chances for success on this examination can be increased if you know how to prepare. Those "pre-examination jitters" can be reduced if you know what to expect. You can even experience an adventure in good citizenship if you know why civil service exams are given.

B. WHY ARE CIVIL SERVICE EXAMINATIONS GIVEN?

Civil service examinations are important to you in two ways. As a citizen, you want public jobs filled by employees who know how to do their work. As a job seeker, you want a fair chance to compete for that job on an equal footing with other candidates. The best-known means of accomplishing this two-fold goal is the competitive examination.

Exams are widely publicized throughout the nation. They may be administered for jobs in federal, state, city, municipal, town or village governments or agencies.

Any citizen may apply, with some limitations, such as the age or residence of applicants. Your experience and education may be reviewed to see whether you meet the requirements for the particular examination. When these requirements exist, they are reasonable and applied consistently to all applicants. Thus, a competitive examination may cause you some uneasiness now, but it is your privilege and safeguard.

C. HOW ARE CIVIL SERVICE EXAMS DEVELOPED?

Examinations are carefully written by trained technicians who are specialists in the field known as "psychological measurement," in consultation with recognized authorities in the field of work that the test will cover. These experts recommend the subject matter areas or skills to be tested; only those knowledges or skills important to your success on the job are included. The most reliable books and source materials available are used as references. Together, the experts and technicians judge the difficulty level of the questions.

Test technicians know how to phrase questions so that the problem is clearly stated. Their ethics do not permit "trick" or "catch" questions. Questions may have been tried out on sample groups, or subjected to statistical analysis, to determine their usefulness.

Written tests are often used in combination with performance tests, ratings of training and experience, and oral interviews. All of these measures combine to form the best-known means of finding the right person for the right job.

II. HOW TO PASS THE WRITTEN TEST

A. NATURE OF THE EXAMINATION

To prepare intelligently for civil service examinations, you should know how they differ from school examinations you have taken. In school you were assigned certain definite pages to read or subjects to cover. The examination questions were quite detailed and usually emphasized memory. Civil service exams, on the other hand, try to discover your present ability to perform the duties of a position, plus your potentiality to learn these duties. In other words, a civil service exam attempts to predict how successful you will be. Questions cover such a broad area that they cannot be as minute and detailed as school exam questions.

In the public service similar kinds of work, or positions, are grouped together in one "class." This process is known as *position-classification*. All the positions in a class are paid according to the salary range for that class. One class title covers all of these positions, and they are all tested by the same examination.

B. FOUR BASIC STEPS

1) Study the announcement

How, then, can you know what subjects to study? Our best answer is: "Learn as much as possible about the class of positions for which you've applied." The exam will test the knowledge, skills and abilities needed to do the work.

Your most valuable source of information about the position you want is the official exam announcement. This announcement lists the training and experience qualifications. Check these standards and apply only if you come reasonably close to meeting them.

The brief description of the position in the examination announcement offers some clues to the subjects which will be tested. Think about the job itself. Review the duties in your mind. Can you perform them, or are there some in which you are rusty? Fill in the blank spots in your preparation.

Many jurisdictions preview the written test in the exam announcement by including a section called "Knowledge and Abilities Required," "Scope of the Examination," or some similar heading. Here you will find out specifically what fields will be tested.

2) Review your own background

Once you learn in general what the position is all about, and what you need to know to do the work, ask yourself which subjects you already know fairly well and which need improvement. You may wonder whether to concentrate on improving your strong areas or on building some background in your fields of weakness. When the announcement has specified "some knowledge" or "considerable knowledge," or has used adjectives like "beginning principles of..." or "advanced ... methods," you can get a clue as to the number and difficulty of questions to be asked in any given field. More questions, and hence broader coverage, would be included for those subjects which are more important in the work. Now weigh your strengths and weaknesses against the job requirements and prepare accordingly.

3) Determine the level of the position

Another way to tell how intensively you should prepare is to understand the level of the job for which you are applying. Is it the entering level? In other words, is this the position in which beginners in a field of work are hired? Or is it an intermediate or advanced level? Sometimes this is indicated by such words as "Junior" or "Senior" in the class title. Other jurisdictions use Roman numerals to designate the level – Clerk I, Clerk II, for example. The word "Supervisor" sometimes appears in the title. If the level is not indicated by the title, check the description of duties. Will you be working under very close supervision, or will you have responsibility for independent decisions in this work?

4) Choose appropriate study materials

Now that you know the subjects to be examined and the relative amount of each subject to be covered, you can choose suitable study materials. For beginning level jobs, or even advanced ones, if you have a pronounced weakness in some aspect of your training, read a modern, standard textbook in that field. Be sure it is up to date and has general coverage. Such books are normally available at your library, and the librarian will be glad to help you locate one. For entry-level positions, questions of appropriate difficulty are chosen – neither highly advanced questions, nor those too simple. Such questions require careful thought but not advanced training.

If the position for which you are applying is technical or advanced, you will read more advanced, specialized material. If you are already familiar with the basic principles of your field, elementary textbooks would waste your time. Concentrate on advanced textbooks and technical periodicals. Think through the concepts and review difficult problems in your field.

These are all general sources. You can get more ideas on your own initiative, following these leads. For example, training manuals and publications of the government agency which employs workers in your field can be useful, particularly for technical and professional positions. A letter or visit to the government department involved may result in more specific study suggestions, and certainly will provide you with a more definite idea of the exact nature of the position you are seeking.

III. KINDS OF TESTS

Tests are used for purposes other than measuring knowledge and ability to perform specified duties. For some positions, it is equally important to test ability to make adjustments to new situations or to profit from training. In others, basic mental abilities not dependent on information are essential. Questions which test these things may not appear as pertinent to the duties of the position as those which test for knowledge and information. Yet they are often highly important parts of a fair examination. For very general questions, it is almost impossible to help you direct your study efforts. What we can do is to point out some of the more common of these general abilities needed in public service positions and describe some typical questions.

1) General information

Broad, general information has been found useful for predicting job success in some kinds of work. This is tested in a variety of ways, from vocabulary lists to questions about current events. Basic background in some field of work, such as sociology or economics, may be sampled in a group of questions. Often these are principles which have become familiar to most persons through exposure rather than through formal training. It is difficult to advise you how to study for these questions; being alert to the world around you is our best suggestion.

2) Verbal ability

An example of an ability needed in many positions is verbal or language ability. Verbal ability is, in brief, the ability to use and understand words. Vocabulary and grammar tests are typical measures of this ability. Reading comprehension or paragraph interpretation questions are common in many kinds of civil service tests. You are given a paragraph of written material and asked to find its central meaning.

3) Numerical ability

Number skills can be tested by the familiar arithmetic problem, by checking paired lists of numbers to see which are alike and which are different, or by interpreting charts and graphs. In the latter test, a graph may be printed in the test booklet which you are asked to use as the basis for answering questions.

4) Observation

A popular test for law-enforcement positions is the observation test. A picture is shown to you for several minutes, then taken away. Questions about the picture test your ability to observe both details and larger elements.

5) Following directions

In many positions in the public service, the employee must be able to carry out written instructions dependably and accurately. You may be given a chart with several columns, each column listing a variety of information. The questions require you to carry out directions involving the information given in the chart.

6) Skills and aptitudes

Performance tests effectively measure some manual skills and aptitudes. When the skill is one in which you are trained, such as typing or shorthand, you can practice. These tests are often very much like those given in business school or high school courses. For many of the other skills and aptitudes, however, no short-time preparation can be made. Skills and abilities natural to you or that you have developed throughout your lifetime are being tested.

Many of the general questions just described provide all the data needed to answer the questions and ask you to use your reasoning ability to find the answers. Your best preparation for these tests, as well as for tests of facts and ideas, is to be at your physical and mental best. You, no doubt, have your own methods of getting into an exam-taking mood and keeping "in shape." The next section lists some ideas on this subject.

IV. KINDS OF QUESTIONS

Only rarely is the "essay" question, which you answer in narrative form, used in civil service tests. Civil service tests are usually of the short-answer type. Full instructions for answering these questions will be given to you at the examination. But in case this is your first experience with short-answer questions and separate answer sheets, here is what you need to know:

1) Multiple-choice Questions

Most popular of the short-answer questions is the "multiple choice" or "best answer" question. It can be used, for example, to test for factual knowledge, ability to solve problems or judgment in meeting situations found at work.

A multiple-choice question is normally one of three types—

- It can begin with an incomplete statement followed by several possible endings. You are to find the one ending which *best* completes the statement, although some of the others may not be entirely wrong.
- It can also be a complete statement in the form of a question which is answered by choosing one of the statements listed.

- It can be in the form of a problem – again you select the best answer.

Here is an example of a multiple-choice question with a discussion which should give you some clues as to the method for choosing the right answer:

When an employee has a complaint about his assignment, the action which will *best* help him overcome his difficulty is to
  A. discuss his difficulty with his coworkers
  B. take the problem to the head of the organization
  C. take the problem to the person who gave him the assignment
  D. say nothing to anyone about his complaint

In answering this question, you should study each of the choices to find which is best. Consider choice "A" – Certainly an employee may discuss his complaint with fellow employees, but no change or improvement can result, and the complaint remains unresolved. Choice "B" is a poor choice since the head of the organization probably does not know what assignment you have been given, and taking your problem to him is known as "going over the head" of the supervisor. The supervisor, or person who made the assignment, is the person who can clarify it or correct any injustice. Choice "C" is, therefore, correct. To say nothing, as in choice "D," is unwise. Supervisors have and interest in knowing the problems employees are facing, and the employee is seeking a solution to his problem.

2) True/False Questions

The "true/false" or "right/wrong" form of question is sometimes used. Here a complete statement is given. Your job is to decide whether the statement is right or wrong.

SAMPLE: A roaming cell-phone call to a nearby city costs less than a non-roaming call to a distant city.

This statement is wrong, or false, since roaming calls are more expensive.

This is not a complete list of all possible question forms, although most of the others are variations of these common types. You will always get complete directions for answering questions. Be sure you understand *how* to mark your answers – ask questions until you do.

V. RECORDING YOUR ANSWERS

Computer terminals are used more and more today for many different kinds of exams.
For an examination with very few applicants, you may be told to record your answers in the test booklet itself. Separate answer sheets are much more common. If this separate answer sheet is to be scored by machine – and this is often the case – it is highly important that you mark your answers correctly in order to get credit.
An electronic scoring machine is often used in civil service offices because of the speed with which papers can be scored. Machine-scored answer sheets must be marked with a pencil, which will be given to you. This pencil has a high graphite content which responds to the electronic scoring machine. As a matter of fact, stray dots may register as answers, so do not let your pencil rest on the answer sheet while you are pondering the correct answer. Also, if your pencil lead breaks or is otherwise defective, ask for another.

Since the answer sheet will be dropped in a slot in the scoring machine, be careful not to bend the corners or get the paper crumpled.

The answer sheet normally has five vertical columns of numbers, with 30 numbers to a column. These numbers correspond to the question numbers in your test booklet. After each number, going across the page are four or five pairs of dotted lines. These short dotted lines have small letters or numbers above them. The first two pairs may also have a "T" or "F" above the letters. This indicates that the first two pairs only are to be used if the questions are of the true-false type. If the questions are multiple choice, disregard the "T" and "F" and pay attention only to the small letters or numbers.

Answer your questions in the manner of the sample that follows:

32. The largest city in the United States is
    A. Washington, D.C.
    B. New York City
    C. Chicago
    D. Detroit
    E. San Francisco

1) Choose the answer you think is best. (New York City is the largest, so "B" is correct.)
2) Find the row of dotted lines numbered the same as the question you are answering. (Find row number 32)
3) Find the pair of dotted lines corresponding to the answer. (Find the pair of lines under the mark "B.")
4) Make a solid black mark between the dotted lines.

VI. BEFORE THE TEST

Common sense will help you find procedures to follow to get ready for an examination. Too many of us, however, overlook these sensible measures. Indeed, nervousness and fatigue have been found to be the most serious reasons why applicants fail to do their best on civil service tests. Here is a list of reminders:

- Begin your preparation early – Don't wait until the last minute to go scurrying around for books and materials or to find out what the position is all about.
- Prepare continuously – An hour a night for a week is better than an all-night cram session. This has been definitely established. What is more, a night a week for a month will return better dividends than crowding your study into a shorter period of time.
- Locate the place of the exam – You have been sent a notice telling you when and where to report for the examination. If the location is in a different town or otherwise unfamiliar to you, it would be well to inquire the best route and learn something about the building.
- Relax the night before the test – Allow your mind to rest. Do not study at all that night. Plan some mild recreation or diversion; then go to bed early and get a good night's sleep.
- Get up early enough to make a leisurely trip to the place for the test – This way unforeseen events, traffic snarls, unfamiliar buildings, etc. will not upset you.
- Dress comfortably – A written test is not a fashion show. You will be known by number and not by name, so wear something comfortable.

- Leave excess paraphernalia at home – Shopping bags and odd bundles will get in your way. You need bring only the items mentioned in the official notice you received; usually everything you need is provided. Do not bring reference books to the exam. They will only confuse those last minutes and be taken away from you when in the test room.
- Arrive somewhat ahead of time – If because of transportation schedules you must get there very early, bring a newspaper or magazine to take your mind off yourself while waiting.
- Locate the examination room – When you have found the proper room, you will be directed to the seat or part of the room where you will sit. Sometimes you are given a sheet of instructions to read while you are waiting. Do not fill out any forms until you are told to do so; just read them and be prepared.
- Relax and prepare to listen to the instructions
- If you have any physical problem that may keep you from doing your best, be sure to tell the test administrator. If you are sick or in poor health, you really cannot do your best on the exam. You can come back and take the test some other time.

VII. AT THE TEST

The day of the test is here and you have the test booklet in your hand. The temptation to get going is very strong. Caution! There is more to success than knowing the right answers. You must know how to identify your papers and understand variations in the type of short-answer question used in this particular examination. Follow these suggestions for maximum results from your efforts:

1) Cooperate with the monitor

The test administrator has a duty to create a situation in which you can be as much at ease as possible. He will give instructions, tell you when to begin, check to see that you are marking your answer sheet correctly, and so on. He is not there to guard you, although he will see that your competitors do not take unfair advantage. He wants to help you do your best.

2) Listen to all instructions

Don't jump the gun! Wait until you understand all directions. In most civil service tests you get more time than you need to answer the questions. So don't be in a hurry. Read each word of instructions until you clearly understand the meaning. Study the examples, listen to all announcements and follow directions. Ask questions if you do not understand what to do.

3) Identify your papers

Civil service exams are usually identified by number only. You will be assigned a number; you must not put your name on your test papers. Be sure to copy your number correctly. Since more than one exam may be given, copy your exact examination title.

4) Plan your time

Unless you are told that a test is a "speed" or "rate of work" test, speed itself is usually not important. Time enough to answer all the questions will be provided, but this does not mean that you have all day. An overall time limit has been set. Divide the total time (in minutes) by the number of questions to determine the approximate time you have for each question.

5) Do not linger over difficult questions

If you come across a difficult question, mark it with a paper clip (useful to have along) and come back to it when you have been through the booklet. One caution if you do this – be sure to skip a number on your answer sheet as well. Check often to be sure that you have not lost your place and that you are marking in the row numbered the same as the question you are answering.

6) Read the questions

Be sure you know what the question asks! Many capable people are unsuccessful because they failed to *read* the questions correctly.

7) Answer all questions

Unless you have been instructed that a penalty will be deducted for incorrect answers, it is better to guess than to omit a question.

8) Speed tests

It is often better NOT to guess on speed tests. It has been found that on timed tests people are tempted to spend the last few seconds before time is called in marking answers at random – without even reading them – in the hope of picking up a few extra points. To discourage this practice, the instructions may warn you that your score will be "corrected" for guessing. That is, a penalty will be applied. The incorrect answers will be deducted from the correct ones, or some other penalty formula will be used.

9) Review your answers

If you finish before time is called, go back to the questions you guessed or omitted to give them further thought. Review other answers if you have time.

10) Return your test materials

If you are ready to leave before others have finished or time is called, take ALL your materials to the monitor and leave quietly. Never take any test material with you. The monitor can discover whose papers are not complete, and taking a test booklet may be grounds for disqualification.

VIII. EXAMINATION TECHNIQUES

1) Read the general instructions carefully. These are usually printed on the first page of the exam booklet. As a rule, these instructions refer to the timing of the examination; the fact that you should not start work until the signal and must stop work at a signal, etc. If there are any *special* instructions, such as a choice of questions to be answered, make sure that you note this instruction carefully.

2) When you are ready to start work on the examination, that is as soon as the signal has been given, read the instructions to each question booklet, underline any key words or phrases, such as *least, best, outline, describe* and the like. In this way you will tend to answer as requested rather than discover on reviewing your paper that you *listed without describing*, that you selected the *worst* choice rather than the *best* choice, etc.

3) If the examination is of the objective or multiple-choice type – that is, each question will also give a series of possible answers: A, B, C or D, and you are called upon to select the best answer and write the letter next to that answer on your answer paper – it is advisable to start answering each question in turn. There may be anywhere from 50 to 100 such questions in the three or four hours allotted and you can see how much time would be taken if you read through all the questions before beginning to answer any. Furthermore, if you come across a question or group of questions which you know would be difficult to answer, it would undoubtedly affect your handling of all the other questions.

4) If the examination is of the essay type and contains but a few questions, it is a moot point as to whether you should read all the questions before starting to answer any one. Of course, if you are given a choice – say five out of seven and the like – then it is essential to read all the questions so you can eliminate the two that are most difficult. If, however, you are asked to answer all the questions, there may be danger in trying to answer the easiest one first because you may find that you will spend too much time on it. The best technique is to answer the first question, then proceed to the second, etc.

5) Time your answers. Before the exam begins, write down the time it started, then add the time allowed for the examination and write down the time it must be completed, then divide the time available somewhat as follows:
   - If 3-1/2 hours are allowed, that would be 210 minutes. If you have 80 objective-type questions, that would be an average of 2-1/2 minutes per question. Allow yourself no more than 2 minutes per question, or a total of 160 minutes, which will permit about 50 minutes to review.
   - If for the time allotment of 210 minutes there are 7 essay questions to answer, that would average about 30 minutes a question. Give yourself only 25 minutes per question so that you have about 35 minutes to review.

6) The most important instruction is to *read each question* and make sure you know what is wanted. The second most important instruction is to *time yourself properly* so that you answer every question. The third most important instruction is to *answer every question*. Guess if you have to but include something for each question. Remember that you will receive no credit for a blank and will probably receive some credit if you write something in answer to an essay question. If you guess a letter – say "B" for a multiple-choice question – you may have guessed right. If you leave a blank as an answer to a multiple-choice question, the examiners may respect your feelings but it will not add a point to your score. Some exams may penalize you for wrong answers, so in such cases *only*, you may not want to guess unless you have some basis for your answer.

7) Suggestions
   a. Objective-type questions
      1. Examine the question booklet for proper sequence of pages and questions
      2. Read all instructions carefully
      3. Skip any question which seems too difficult; return to it after all other questions have been answered
      4. Apportion your time properly; do not spend too much time on any single question or group of questions

5. Note and underline key words – *all, most, fewest, least, best, worst, same, opposite,* etc.
6. Pay particular attention to negatives
7. Note unusual option, e.g., unduly long, short, complex, different or similar in content to the body of the question
8. Observe the use of "hedging" words – *probably, may, most likely,* etc.
9. Make sure that your answer is put next to the same number as the question
10. Do not second-guess unless you have good reason to believe the second answer is definitely more correct
11. Cross out original answer if you decide another answer is more accurate; do not erase until you are ready to hand your paper in
12. Answer all questions; guess unless instructed otherwise
13. Leave time for review

b. Essay questions
1. Read each question carefully
2. Determine exactly what is wanted. Underline key words or phrases.
3. Decide on outline or paragraph answer
4. Include many different points and elements unless asked to develop any one or two points or elements
5. Show impartiality by giving pros and cons unless directed to select one side only
6. Make and write down any assumptions you find necessary to answer the questions
7. Watch your English, grammar, punctuation and choice of words
8. Time your answers; don't crowd material

8) Answering the essay question

Most essay questions can be answered by framing the specific response around several key words or ideas. Here are a few such key words or ideas:

M's: manpower, materials, methods, money, management
P's: purpose, program, policy, plan, procedure, practice, problems, pitfalls, personnel, public relations

  a. Six basic steps in handling problems:
    1. Preliminary plan and background development
    2. Collect information, data and facts
    3. Analyze and interpret information, data and facts
    4. Analyze and develop solutions as well as make recommendations
    5. Prepare report and sell recommendations
    6. Install recommendations and follow up effectiveness

  b. Pitfalls to avoid
    1. *Taking things for granted* – A statement of the situation does not necessarily imply that each of the elements is necessarily true; for example, a complaint may be invalid and biased so that all that can be taken for granted is that a complaint has been registered

2. *Considering only one side of a situation* – Wherever possible, indicate several alternatives and then point out the reasons you selected the best one
3. *Failing to indicate follow up* – Whenever your answer indicates action on your part, make certain that you will take proper follow-up action to see how successful your recommendations, procedures or actions turn out to be
4. *Taking too long in answering any single question* – Remember to time your answers properly

IX. AFTER THE TEST

Scoring procedures differ in detail among civil service jurisdictions although the general principles are the same. Whether the papers are hand-scored or graded by machine we have described, they are nearly always graded by number. That is, the person who marks the paper knows only the number – never the name – of the applicant. Not until all the papers have been graded will they be matched with names. If other tests, such as training and experience or oral interview ratings have been given, scores will be combined. Different parts of the examination usually have different weights. For example, the written test might count 60 percent of the final grade, and a rating of training and experience 40 percent. In many jurisdictions, veterans will have a certain number of points added to their grades.

After the final grade has been determined, the names are placed in grade order and an eligible list is established. There are various methods for resolving ties between those who get the same final grade – probably the most common is to place first the name of the person whose application was received first. Job offers are made from the eligible list in the order the names appear on it. You will be notified of your grade and your rank as soon as all these computations have been made. This will be done as rapidly as possible.

People who are found to meet the requirements in the announcement are called "eligibles." Their names are put on a list of eligible candidates. An eligible's chances of getting a job depend on how high he stands on this list and how fast agencies are filling jobs from the list.

When a job is to be filled from a list of eligibles, the agency asks for the names of people on the list of eligibles for that job. When the civil service commission receives this request, it sends to the agency the names of the three people highest on this list. Or, if the job to be filled has specialized requirements, the office sends the agency the names of the top three persons who meet these requirements from the general list.

The appointing officer makes a choice from among the three people whose names were sent to him. If the selected person accepts the appointment, the names of the others are put back on the list to be considered for future openings.

That is the rule in hiring from all kinds of eligible lists, whether they are for typist, carpenter, chemist, or something else. For every vacancy, the appointing officer has his choice of any one of the top three eligibles on the list. This explains why the person whose name is on top of the list sometimes does not get an appointment when some of the persons lower on the list do. If the appointing officer chooses the second or third eligible, the No. 1 eligible does not get a job at once, but stays on the list until he is appointed or the list is terminated.

X. HOW TO PASS THE INTERVIEW TEST

The examination for which you applied requires an oral interview test. You have already taken the written test and you are now being called for the interview test – the final part of the formal examination.

You may think that it is not possible to prepare for an interview test and that there are no procedures to follow during an interview. Our purpose is to point out some things you can do in advance that will help you and some good rules to follow and pitfalls to avoid while you are being interviewed.

What is an interview supposed to test?

The written examination is designed to test the technical knowledge and competence of the candidate; the oral is designed to evaluate intangible qualities, not readily measured otherwise, and to establish a list showing the relative fitness of each candidate – as measured against his competitors – for the position sought. Scoring is not on the basis of "right" and "wrong," but on a sliding scale of values ranging from "not passable" to "outstanding." As a matter of fact, it is possible to achieve a relatively low score without a single "incorrect" answer because of evident weakness in the qualities being measured.

Occasionally, an examination may consist entirely of an oral test – either an individual or a group oral. In such cases, information is sought concerning the technical knowledges and abilities of the candidate, since there has been no written examination for this purpose. More commonly, however, an oral test is used to supplement a written examination.

Who conducts interviews?

The composition of oral boards varies among different jurisdictions. In nearly all, a representative of the personnel department serves as chairman. One of the members of the board may be a representative of the department in which the candidate would work. In some cases, "outside experts" are used, and, frequently, a businessman or some other representative of the general public is asked to serve. Labor and management or other special groups may be represented. The aim is to secure the services of experts in the appropriate field.

However the board is composed, it is a good idea (and not at all improper or unethical) to ascertain in advance of the interview who the members are and what groups they represent. When you are introduced to them, you will have some idea of their backgrounds and interests, and at least you will not stutter and stammer over their names.

What should be done before the interview?

While knowledge about the board members is useful and takes some of the surprise element out of the interview, there is other preparation which is more substantive. It *is* possible to prepare for an oral interview – in several ways:

1) Keep a copy of your application and review it carefully before the interview

This may be the only document before the oral board, and the starting point of the interview. Know what education and experience you have listed there, and the sequence and dates of all of it. Sometimes the board will ask you to review the highlights of your experience for them; you should not have to hem and haw doing it.

2) Study the class specification and the examination announcement

Usually, the oral board has one or both of these to guide them. The qualities, characteristics or knowledges required by the position sought are stated in these documents. They offer valuable clues as to the nature of the oral interview. For example, if the job involves supervisory responsibilities, the announcement will usually indicate that knowledge of modern supervisory methods and the qualifications of the candidate as a supervisor will be tested. If so, you can expect such questions, frequently in the form of a hypothetical situation which you are expected to solve. NEVER go into an oral without knowledge of the duties and responsibilities of the job you seek.

3) Think through each qualification required

Try to visualize the kind of questions you would ask if you were a board member. How well could you answer them? Try especially to appraise your own knowledge and background in each area, *measured against the job sought*, and identify any areas in which you are weak. Be critical and realistic – do not flatter yourself.

4) Do some general reading in areas in which you feel you may be weak

For example, if the job involves supervision and your past experience has NOT, some general reading in supervisory methods and practices, particularly in the field of human relations, might be useful. Do NOT study agency procedures or detailed manuals. The oral board will be testing your understanding and capacity, not your memory.

5) Get a good night's sleep and watch your general health and mental attitude

You will want a clear head at the interview. Take care of a cold or any other minor ailment, and of course, no hangovers.

What should be done on the day of the interview?

Now comes the day of the interview itself. Give yourself plenty of time to get there. Plan to arrive somewhat ahead of the scheduled time, particularly if your appointment is in the fore part of the day. If a previous candidate fails to appear, the board might be ready for you a bit early. By early afternoon an oral board is almost invariably behind schedule if there are many candidates, and you may have to wait. Take along a book or magazine to read, or your application to review, but leave any extraneous material in the waiting room when you go in for your interview. In any event, relax and compose yourself.

The matter of dress is important. The board is forming impressions about you – from your experience, your manners, your attitude, and your appearance. Give your personal appearance careful attention. Dress your best, but not your flashiest. Choose conservative, appropriate clothing, and be sure it is immaculate. This is a business interview, and your appearance should indicate that you regard it as such. Besides, being well groomed and properly dressed will help boost your confidence.

Sooner or later, someone will call your name and escort you into the interview room. *This is it.* From here on you are on your own. It is too late for any more preparation. But remember, you asked for this opportunity to prove your fitness, and you are here because your request was granted.

What happens when you go in?

The usual sequence of events will be as follows: The clerk (who is often the board stenographer) will introduce you to the chairman of the oral board, who will introduce you to the other members of the board. Acknowledge the introductions before you sit down. Do not be surprised if you find a microphone facing you or a stenotypist sitting by. Oral interviews are usually recorded in the event of an appeal or other review.

Usually the chairman of the board will open the interview by reviewing the highlights of your education and work experience from your application – primarily for the benefit of the other members of the board, as well as to get the material into the record. Do not interrupt or comment unless there is an error or significant misinterpretation; if that is the case, do not hesitate. But do not quibble about insignificant matters. Also, he will usually ask you some question about your education, experience or your present job – partly to get you to start talking and to establish the interviewing "rapport." He may start the actual questioning, or turn it over to one of the other members. Frequently, each member undertakes the questioning on a particular area, one in which he is perhaps most competent, so you can expect each member to participate in the examination. Because time is limited, you may also expect some rather abrupt switches in the direction the questioning takes, so do not be upset by it. Normally, a board member will not pursue a single line of questioning unless he discovers a particular strength or weakness.

After each member has participated, the chairman will usually ask whether any member has any further questions, then will ask you if you have anything you wish to add. Unless you are expecting this question, it may floor you. Worse, it may start you off on an extended, extemporaneous speech. The board is not usually seeking more information. The question is principally to offer you a last opportunity to present further qualifications or to indicate that you have nothing to add. So, if you feel that a significant qualification or characteristic has been overlooked, it is proper to point it out in a sentence or so. Do not compliment the board on the thoroughness of their examination – they have been sketchy, and you know it. If you wish, merely say, "No thank you, I have nothing further to add." This is a point where you can "talk yourself out" of a good impression or fail to present an important bit of information. Remember, *you close the interview yourself*.

The chairman will then say, "That is all, Mr. _____, thank you." Do not be startled; the interview is over, and quicker than you think. Thank him, gather your belongings and take your leave. Save your sigh of relief for the other side of the door.

How to put your best foot forward

Throughout this entire process, you may feel that the board individually and collectively is trying to pierce your defenses, seek out your hidden weaknesses and embarrass and confuse you. Actually, this is not true. They are obliged to make an appraisal of your qualifications for the job you are seeking, and they want to see you in your best light. Remember, they must interview all candidates and a non-cooperative candidate may become a failure in spite of their best efforts to bring out his qualifications. Here are 15 suggestions that will help you:

1) Be natural – Keep your attitude confident, not cocky

If you are not confident that you can do the job, do not expect the board to be. Do not apologize for your weaknesses, try to bring out your strong points. The board is interested in a positive, not negative, presentation. Cockiness will antagonize any board member and make him wonder if you are covering up a weakness by a false show of strength.

2) Get comfortable, but don't lounge or sprawl

Sit erectly but not stiffly. A careless posture may lead the board to conclude that you are careless in other things, or at least that you are not impressed by the importance of the occasion. Either conclusion is natural, even if incorrect. Do not fuss with your clothing, a pencil or an ashtray. Your hands may occasionally be useful to emphasize a point; do not let them become a point of distraction.

3) Do not wisecrack or make small talk

This is a serious situation, and your attitude should show that you consider it as such. Further, the time of the board is limited – they do not want to waste it, and neither should you.

4) Do not exaggerate your experience or abilities

In the first place, from information in the application or other interviews and sources, the board may know more about you than you think. Secondly, you probably will not get away with it. An experienced board is rather adept at spotting such a situation, so do not take the chance.

5) If you know a board member, do not make a point of it, yet do not hide it

Certainly you are not fooling him, and probably not the other members of the board. Do not try to take advantage of your acquaintanceship – it will probably do you little good.

6) Do not dominate the interview

Let the board do that. They will give you the clues – do not assume that you have to do all the talking. Realize that the board has a number of questions to ask you, and do not try to take up all the interview time by showing off your extensive knowledge of the answer to the first one.

7) Be attentive

You only have 20 minutes or so, and you should keep your attention at its sharpest throughout. When a member is addressing a problem or question to you, give him your undivided attention. Address your reply principally to him, but do not exclude the other board members.

8) Do not interrupt

A board member may be stating a problem for you to analyze. He will ask you a question when the time comes. Let him state the problem, and wait for the question.

9) Make sure you understand the question

Do not try to answer until you are sure what the question is. If it is not clear, restate it in your own words or ask the board member to clarify it for you. However, do not haggle about minor elements.

10) Reply promptly but not hastily

A common entry on oral board rating sheets is "candidate responded readily," or "candidate hesitated in replies." Respond as promptly and quickly as you can, but do not jump to a hasty, ill-considered answer.

11) Do not be peremptory in your answers

A brief answer is proper – but do not fire your answer back. That is a losing game from your point of view. The board member can probably ask questions much faster than you can answer them.

12) Do not try to create the answer you think the board member wants

He is interested in what kind of mind you have and how it works – not in playing games. Furthermore, he can usually spot this practice and will actually grade you down on it.

13) Do not switch sides in your reply merely to agree with a board member

Frequently, a member will take a contrary position merely to draw you out and to see if you are willing and able to defend your point of view. Do not start a debate, yet do not surrender a good position. If a position is worth taking, it is worth defending.

14) Do not be afraid to admit an error in judgment if you are shown to be wrong

The board knows that you are forced to reply without any opportunity for careful consideration. Your answer may be demonstrably wrong. If so, admit it and get on with the interview.

15) Do not dwell at length on your present job

The opening question may relate to your present assignment. Answer the question but do not go into an extended discussion. You are being examined for a *new* job, not your present one. As a matter of fact, try to phrase ALL your answers in terms of the job for which you are being examined.

Basis of Rating

Probably you will forget most of these "do's" and "don'ts" when you walk into the oral interview room. Even remembering them all will not ensure you a passing grade. Perhaps you did not have the qualifications in the first place. But remembering them will help you to put your best foot forward, without treading on the toes of the board members.

Rumor and popular opinion to the contrary notwithstanding, an oral board wants you to make the best appearance possible. They know you are under pressure – but they also want to see how you respond to it as a guide to what your reaction would be under the pressures of the job you seek. They will be influenced by the degree of poise you display, the personal traits you show and the manner in which you respond.

ABOUT THIS BOOK

This book contains tests divided into Examination Sections. Go through each test, answering every question in the margin. We have also attached a sample answer sheet at the back of the book that can be removed and used. At the end of each test look at the answer key and check your answers. On the ones you got wrong, look at the right answer choice and learn. Do not fill in the answers first. Do not memorize the questions and answers, but understand the answer and principles involved. On your test, the questions will likely be different from the samples. Questions are changed and new ones added. If you understand these past questions you should have success with any changes that arise. Tests may consist of several types of questions. We have additional books on each subject should more study be advisable or necessary for you. Finally, the more you study, the better prepared you will be. This book is intended to be the last thing you study before you walk into the examination room. Prior study of relevant texts is also recommended. NLC publishes some of these in our Fundamental Series. Knowledge and good sense are important factors in passing your exam. Good luck also helps. So now study this Passbook, absorb the material contained within and take that knowledge into the examination. Then do your best to pass that exam.

EXAMINATION SECTION

REPORT WRITING

EXAMINATION SECTION

TEST 1

DIRECTIONS: Each question or incomplete statement is followed by several suggested answers or completions. Select the one that BEST answers the question or completes the statement. *PRINT THE LETTER OF THE CORRECT ANSWER IN THE SPACE AT THE RIGHT.*

Questions 1-4.

DIRECTIONS: Answer Questions 1 through 4 on the basis of the following report which was prepared by a supervisor for inclusion in his agency's annual report.

Line #
1   On Oct. 13, I was assigned to study the salaries paid.
2   to clerical employees in various titles by the city and by
3   private industry in the area.
4   In order to get the data I needed, I called Mr. Johnson at
5   the Bureau of the Budget and the payroll officers at X Corp.—
6   a brokerage house, Y Co. —an insurance company, and Z Inc. —
7   a publishing firm. None of them was available and I had to call
8   all of them again the next day.
9   When I finally got the information I needed, I drew up a
10 chart, which is attached. Note that not all of the companies I
11 contacted employed people at all the different levels used in the
12 city service.
13 The conclusions I draw from analyzing this information is
14 as follows: The city's entry-level salary is about average for
15 the region; middle-level salaries are generally higher in the
16 city government plan than in private industry; but salaries at the
17 highest levels in private industry are better than city em-
18 ployees' pay.

1. Which of the following criticisms about the style in which this report is written is MOST valid?   1.____
   A. It is too informal.   B. It is too concise.
   C. It is too choppy.   D. The syntax is too complex.

2. Judging from the statements made in the report, the method followed by this employee in performing his research was   2.____
   A. *good*; he contacted a representative sample of businesses in the area
   B. *poor*; he should have drawn more definite conclusions
   C. *good*; he was persistent in collecting information
   D. *poor*; he did not make a thorough study

3. One sentence in this report contains a grammatical error. This sentence begins on line number
   A. 4   B. 7   C. 10   D. 14

4. The type of information given in this report which should be presented in footnotes or in an appendix is the
   A. purpose of the study
   B. specifics about the businesses contacted
   C. reference to the chart
   D. conclusions drawn by the author

5. The use of a graph to show statistical data in a report is SUPERIOR to a table because it
   A. features approximations
   B. emphasizes facts and relationships more dramatically
   C. presents data more accurately
   D. is easily understood by the average reader

6. Of the following, the degree of formality required of a written report in tone is MOST likely to depend on the
   A. subject matter of the report
   B. frequency of its occurrence
   C. amount of time available for its preparation
   D. audience for whom the report is intended

7. Of the following, a distinguishing characteristic of a written report intended for the head of your agency as compared to a report prepared for a lower-echelon staff member is that the report for the agency head should USUALLY include
   A. considerably more detail, especially statistical data
   B. the essential details in an abbreviated form
   C. all available source material
   D. an annotated bibliography

8. Assume that you are asked to write a lengthy report for use by the administrator of your agency, the subject of which is "The Impact of Proposed New Data Processing Operation on Line Personnel" in your agency. You decide that the *most* appropriate type of report for you to prepare is an analytical report, including recommendations.
   The MAIN reason for your decision is that
   A. the subject of the report is extremely complex
   B. large sums of money are involved
   C. the report is being prepared for the administrator
   D. you intend to include charts and graphs

9. Assume that you are preparing a report based on a survey dealing with the attitudes of employees in Division X regarding proposed new changes in compensating employees for working overtime. Three percent of the respondents to the survey voluntarily offer an unfavorable opinion on the method of assigning overtime work, a question not specifically asked of the employees.
   On the basis of this information, the MOST appropriate and significant of the following comments for you to make in the report with regard to employees' attitudes on assigning overtime work is that
   A. an insignificant percentage of employees dislike the method of assigning overtime work
   B. three percent of the employees in Division X dislike the method of assigning overtime work
   C. three percent of the sample selected for the survey voiced an unfavorable opinion on the method of assigning overtime work
   D. some employees voluntarily voiced negative feelings about the method of assigning overtime work, making it impossible to determine the extent of this attitude

10. A supervisor should be able to prepare a report that is well-written and unambiguous.
    Of the following sentences that might appear in a report, select the one which communicates MOST clearly the intent of its author.
    A. When your subordinates speak to a group of people, they should be well-informed.
    B. When he asked him to leave, SanMan King told him that he would refuse the request.
    C. Because he is a good worker, Foreman Jefferson assigned Assistant Foreman D'Agostino to replace him.
    D. Each of us is responsible for the actions of our subordinates.

11. In some reports, especially longer ones, a list of the resources (books, papers, magazines, etc.) used to prepare it is included. This list is called the
    A. accreditation   B. bibliography
    C. summary   D. glossary

12. Reports are usually divided into several sections, some of which are more necessary than others.
    Of the following, the section which is ABSOLUTELY necessary to include in a report is
    A. a table of contents   B. the body
    C. an index   D. a bibliography

13. Suppose you are writing a report on an interview you have just completed with a particularly hostile applicant.
Which of the following BEST describes what you should include in this report?
    A. What you think caused the applicant's hostile attitude during the interview
    B. Specific examples of the applicant's hostile remarks and behavior
    C. The relevant information uncovered during the interview
    D. A recommendation that the applicant's request be denied because of his hostility

13._____

14. When including recommendations in a report to your supervisor, which of the following is MOST important for you to do?
    A. Provide several alternative courses of action for each recommendation
    B. First present the supporting evidence, then the recommendations
    C. First present the recommendations, then the supporting evidence
    D. Make sure the recommendations arise logically out of the information in the report

14._____

15. It is often necessary that the writer of a report present facts and sufficient arguments to gain acceptance of the points, conclusions, or recommendations set forth in the report.
Of the following, the LEAST advisable step to take in organizing a report, when such argumentation is the important factor, is a(n)
    A. elaborate expression of personal belief
    B. businesslike discussion of the problem as a whole
    C. orderly arrangement of convincing data
    D. reasonable explanation of the primary issues

15._____

16. In some types of reports, visual aids add interest, meaning, and support. They also provide an essential means of effectively communicating the message of the report.
Of the following, the selection of the suitable visual aids to use with a report is LEAST dependent on the
    A. nature and scope of the report
    B. way in which the aid is to be used
    C. aid used in other reports
    D. prospective readers of the report

16._____

17. Visual aids used in a report may be placed either in the text material or in the appendix.
Deciding where to put a chart, table, or any such aid should depend on the
    A. title of the report   B. purpose of the visual aid
    C. title of the visual aid   D. length of the report

17._____

18. A report is often revised several times before final preparation and distribution in an effort to make certain the report meets the needs of the situation for which it is designed.
Which of the following is the BEST way for the author to be sure that a report covers the areas he intended?

18._____

A. Obtain a coworker's opinion
B. Compare it with a content checklist
C. Test it on a subordinate
D. Check his bibliography

19. In which of the following situations is an oral report preferable to a written report? When a(n)
    A. recommendation is being made for a future plan of action
    B. department head requests immediate information
    C. long-standing policy change is made
    D. analysis of complicated statistical data is involved

20. When an applicant is approved, the supervisor must fill in standard forms with certain information.
    The GREATEST advantage of using standard forms in this situation rather than having the supervisor write the report as he sees fit is that
    A. the report can be acted on quickly
    B. the report can be written without directions from a supervisor
    C. needed information is less likely to be left out of the report
    D. information that is written up this way is more likely to be verified

21. Assume that it is part of your job to prepare a monthly report for your unit head that eventually goes to the director. The report contains information on the number of applicants you have interviewed that have been approved and the number of applicants you have interviewed that have been turned down.
    Errors on such reports are serious because
    A. you are expected to be able to prove how many applicants you have interviewed each month
    B. accurate statistics are needed for effective management of the department
    C. they may not be discovered before the report is transmitted to the director
    D. they may result in loss to the applicants left out of the report

22. The frequency with which job reports are submitted should depend MAINLY on
    A. how comprehensive the report has to be
    B. the amount of information in the report
    C. the availability of an experienced man to write the report
    D. the importance of changes in the information included in the report

23. The CHIEF purpose in preparing an outline for a report is usually to insure that
    A. the report will be grammatically correct
    B. every point will be given equal emphasis
    C. principal and secondary points will be properly integrated
    D. the language of the report will be of the same level and include the same technical terms

24. The MAIN reason for requiring written job reports is to 24.____
    A. avoid the necessity of oral orders
    B. develop better methods of doing the work
    C. provide a permanent record of what was done
    D. increase the amount of work that can be done

25. Assume you are recommending in a report to your supervisor that a radical 25.____
    change in a standard maintenance procedure should be adopted.
    Of the following, the MOST important information to be included in this report is
    A. a list of the reasons for making this change
    B. the names of others who favor the change
    C. a complete description of the present procedure
    D. amount of training time needed for the new procedure

KEY (CORRECT ANSWERS)

1.	A		11.	B
2.	D		12.	B
3.	D		13.	C
4.	B		14.	D
5.	B		15.	A
6.	D		16.	C
7.	B		17.	B
8.	A		18.	B
9.	D		19.	B
10.	D		20.	C

21. B
22. D
23. C
24. C
25. A

TEST 2

DIRECTIONS: Each question or incomplete statement is followed by several suggested answers or completions. Select the one that BEST answers the question or completes the statement. *PRINT THE LETTER OF THE CORRECT ANSWER IN THE SPACE AT THE RIGHT.*

1. It is often necessary that the writer of a report present facts and sufficient arguments to gain acceptance of the points, conclusions, or recommendations set forth in the report.
   Of the following, the LEAST advisable step to take in organizing a report, when such argumentation is the important factor, is a(n)
   A. elaborate expression of personal belief
   B. businesslike discussion of the problem as a whole
   C. orderly arrangement of convincing data
   D. reasonable explanation of the primary issues

   1.____

2. Of the following, the factor which is generally considered to be LEAST characteristic of a good control report is that it
   A. stresses performance that adheres to standard rather than emphasizing the exception
   B. supplies information intended to serve as the basis for corrective action
   C. provides feedback for the planning process
   D. includes data that reflect trends as well as current status

   2.____

3. An administrative assistant has been asked by his superior to write a concise, factual report with objective conclusions and recommendations based on facts assembled by other researchers.
   Of the following factors, the administrative assistant should give LEAST consideration to
   A. the educational level of the person or persons for whom the report is being prepared
   B. the use to be made of the report
   C. the complexity of the problem
   D. his own feelings about the importance of the problem

   3.____

4. When making a written report, it is often recommended that the findings or conclusions be presented near the beginning of the report.
   Of the following, the MOST important reason for doing this is that it
   A. facilitates organizing the material clearly
   B. assures that all the topics will be covered
   C. avoids unnecessary repetition of ideas
   D. prepares the reader for the facts that will follow

   4.____

5. You have been asked to write a report on methods of hiring and training new employees. Your report is going to be about ten pages long.
   For the convenience of your readers, a brief summary of your findings should
   A. appear at the beginning of your report
   B. be appended to the report as a postscript
   C. be circulated in a separate memo
   D. be inserted in tabular form in the middle of your report

6. In preparing a report, the MAIN reason for writing an outline is usually to
   A. help organize thoughts in a logical sequence
   B. provide a guide for the typing of the report
   C. allow the ultimate user to review the report in advance
   D. ensure that the report is being prepared on schedule

7. The one of the following which is MOST appropriate as a reason for including footnotes in a report is to
   A. correct capitalization   B. delete passages
   C. improve punctuation   D. cite references

8. A completed formal report may contain all of the following EXCEPT
   A. a synopsis   B. a preface
   C. marginal notes   D. bibliographical references

9. Of the following, the MAIN use of proofreaders' marks is to
   A. explain corrections to be made
   B. indicate that a manuscript has been read and approved
   C. let the reader know who proofread the report
   D. indicate the format of the report

10. Informative, readable, and concise reports have been found to observe the following rules:
    Rule I.   Keep the report short and easy to understand
    Rule II. Vary the length of sentences.
    Rule III. Vary the style of sentences so that, for example, they are not all just subject-verb, subject-verb.
    Consider this hospital laboratory report: The experiment was started in January. The apparatus was put together in six weeks. At that time, the synthesizing process was begun. The synthetic chemicals were separated. Then they were used in tests on patients.
    Which one of the following choices MOST accurately classifies the above rules into those which are violated by this report ad those which are not?
    A. II is violated, but I and III are not.
    B. III is violated, but I and II are not.
    C. II and III are violated, but I is not.
    D. I, II, and III are violated,

Questions 11-13.

DIRECTIONS: Questions 11 through 13 are based on the following example of a report. The report consists of eight numbered sentences, some of which are not consistent with the principles of good report writing.

(1) I interviewed Mrs. Loretta Crawford in Room 424 of County Hospital. (2) She had collapsed on the street and been brought into emergency. (3) She is an attractive woman with many friends judging by the cards she had received. (4) She did not know what her husband's last job had been, or what their present income was. (5) The first thing that Mrs. Crawford said was that she had never worked and that her husband was presently unemployed. (6) She did not know if they had any medical coverage or if they could pay the bill. (7) She said that her husband could not be reached by telephone but that he would be in to see her that afternoon. (8) I left word at the nursing station to be called when he arrived.

11. A good report should be arranged in logical order.
 Which of the following sentences from the report does NOT appear in its proper sequence in the report?
 A. 1 B. 4 C. 7 D. 8

12. Only material that is relevant to the main thought of a report should be included. Which of the following sentences from the report contains material which is LEAST relevant to this report? Sentence
 A. 3 B. 4 C. 6 D. 8

13. Reports should include all essential information.
 Of the following, the MOST important fact that is missing from this report is:
 A. Who was involved in the interview
 B. What was discovered at the interview
 C. When the interview took place
 D. Where the interview took place

Questions 14-15.

DIRECTIONS: Each of Questions 14 and 15 consists of four numbered sentences which constitute a paragraph in a report. They are not in the right order. Choose the numbered arrangement appearing after letter A, B, C, or D which is MOST logical and which BEST expresses the thought of the paragraph.

14. I. Congress made the commitment explicit in the Housing Act of 1949, establishing as a national goal the realization of a decent home and suitable environment for every American family.
 II. The result has been that the goal of decent home and suitable environment is still as far distant as ever for the disadvantaged urban family
 III. In spite of this action by Congress, federal housing programs have continued to be fragmented and grossly under-funded.
 IV. The passage of the National Housing Act signaled a new federal commitment to provide housing for the nation's citizens.

The CORRECT answer is:
A. I, IV, III, II   B. IV, I, III, II   C. IV, I, III, II   D. II, IV, I, III

15. I. The greater expense does not necessarily involve "exploitation," but it is often perceived as exploitative and unfair by those who are aware of the price differences involved, but unaware of operating costs.
    II. Ghetto residents believe they are "exploited" by local merchants, and evidence substantiates some of these beliefs.
    III. However, stores in low-income areas were more likely to be small independents, which could not achieve the economies available to supermarket chains and were, therefore, more likely to charge higher prices, and the customers were more likely to buy smaller-sized packages which are more expensive per unit of measure.
    IV. A study conducted in one city showed that distinctly higher prices were charged for goods sold in ghetto stores than in other areas.

    The CORRECT answer is:
    A. IV, II, I, III   B. IV, I, III, II   C. II, IV, III, I   D. II, III, IV, I

15.___

16. In organizing data to be presented in a formal report, the FIRST of the following steps should be
    A. determining the conclusions to be drawn
    B. establishing the time sequence of the data
    C. sorting and arranging like data into groups
    D. evaluating how consistently the data support the recommendations

16.___

17. All reports should be prepared with at least one copy so that
    A. there is one copy for your file
    B. there is a copy for your supervisor
    C. the report can be sent to more than one person
    D. the person getting the report can forward a copy to someone else

17.___

18. Before turning in a report of an investigation he has made, a supervisor discovers some additional information he did not include in this report. Whether he rewrites this report to include this additional information should PRIMARILY depend on the
    A. importance of the report itself
    B. number of people who will eventually review this report
    C. established policy covering the subject matter of the report
    D. bearing this new information has on the conclusions of the report

18.___

KEY (CORRECT ANSWERS)

1.	A	11.	B
2.	A	12.	A
3.	D	13.	C
4.	D	14.	B
5.	A	15.	C
6.	A	16.	C
7.	D	17.	A
8.	C	18.	D
9.	A		
10.	C		

INTERPRETING STATISTICAL DATA GRAPHS, CHARTS AND TABLES

EXAMINATION SECTION

TEST 1

DIRECTIONS: Questions 1 through 7 are to be answered SOLELY on the basis of the following graph. *PRINT THE LETTER OF THE CORRECT ANSWER IN THE SPACE AT THE RIGHT.*

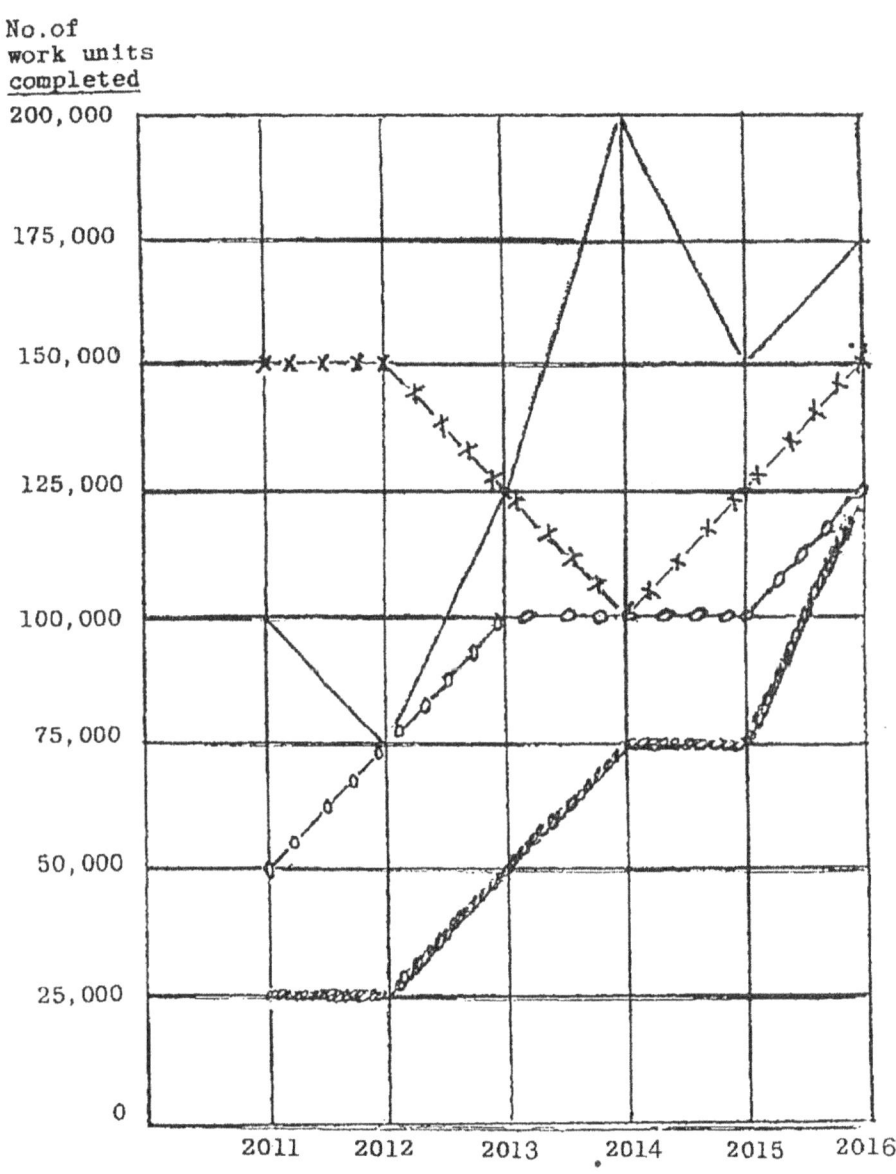

2 (#1)

Units of each type of work completed by a public agency from 2011 to 2016.
Letters Written ━━━━━━━━━━━━━━━━━━━━━
Documents Filed ━━X━━X━━X━━X
Applications Processed ━━━━0━━0━━0━━0
Inspections Made ooooooooooooooooooooooooo

1. The year for which the number of units of one type of work completed was *less* than it was for the previous year while the number of each of the other types of work completed was *more* than it was for the previous year was
   A. 2012   B. 2013   C. 2014   D. 2015

2. The number of letters written EXCEEDED the number of applications processed by the *same* amount in _____ of the years.
   A. two   B. three   C. four   D. five

3. The year in which the number of each type of work completed was *greater* than in the preceding year was
   A. 2013   B. 2014   C. 2015   D. 2016

4. The number of applications processed and the number of documents filed were the SAME in
   A. 2012   B. 2013   C. 2014   D. 2015

5. The TOTAL number of units of work completed by the agency
   A. increased in each year after 2011
   B. decreased from the prior year in two of the years after 2011
   C. was the same in two successive years from 2011 to 2016
   D. was less in 2011 than in any of the following years

6. For the year in which the number of letters written was twice as high as it was in 2011, the number of documents FILED was _____ it was in 2011.
   A. the same as   B. two-thirds of what
   C. five-sixths of what   D. one and one-half times what

7. The variable which was the MOST stable during the period 2011 through 2016 was
   A. Inspections Made   B. Letters Written
   C. Documents Filed   D. Applications Processed

KEY (CORRECT ANSWERS)

1. B   5. C
2. B   6. B
3. D   7. B
4. C

TEST 2

DIRECTIONS: Questions 1 through 8 are to be answered SOLELY on the basis of the following graph. *PRINT THE LETTER OF THE CORRECT ANSWER IN THE SPACE AT THE RIGHT.*

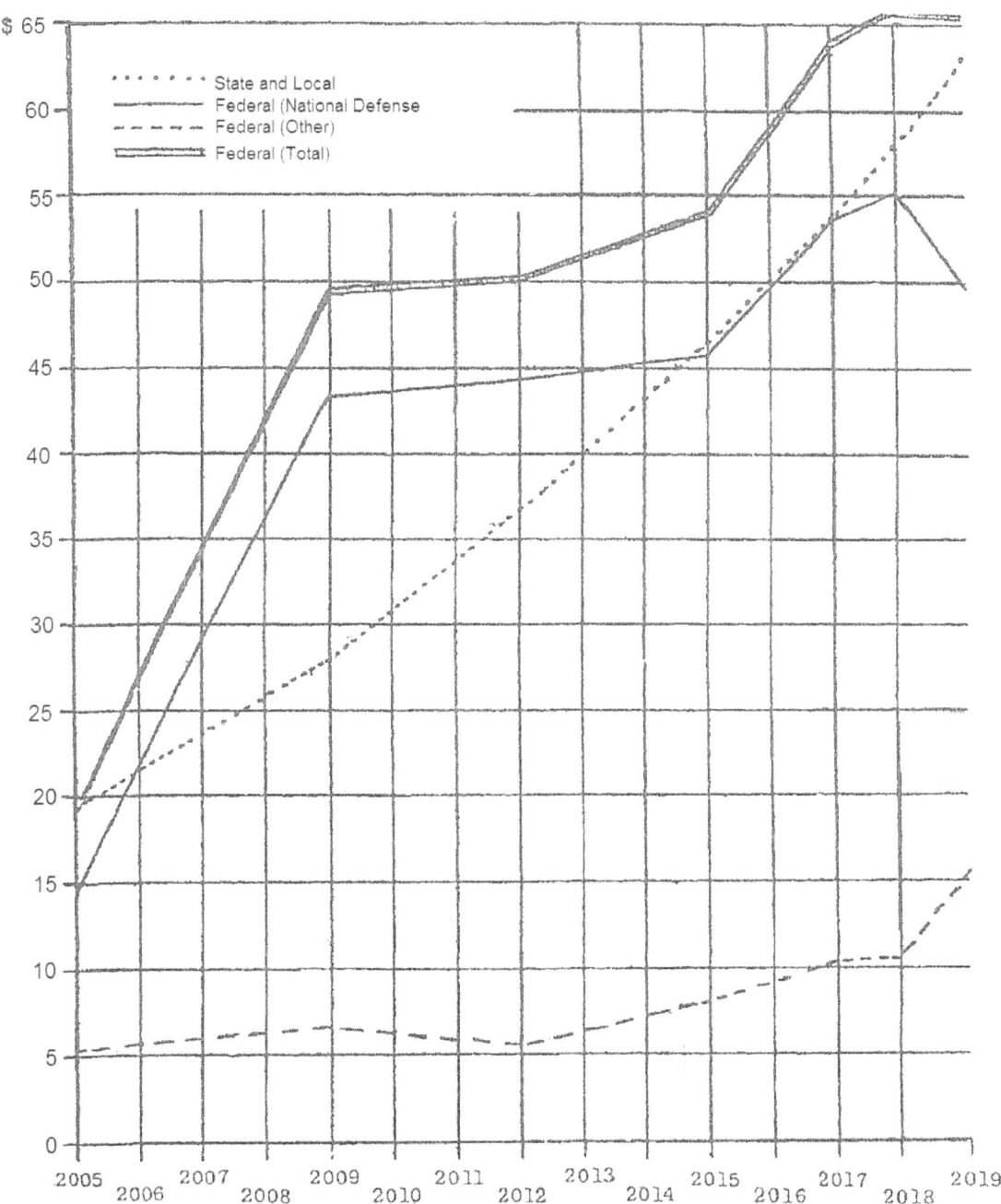

2 (#2)

1. Purchases by the Federal government for non-defense purposes, and purchases by State and Local governments comprised the smallest proportion of the total government purchases of goods and services for all purposes in which of the following years?
   A. 2005   B. 2009   C. 2012   D. 2015

1.____

2. Which one of the following MOST closely approximates the percentage increase in State and Local purchases of goods and services in 2019 as compared to 2005?
   A. 110%   B. 150%   C. 220%   D. 350%

2.____

3. Total government purchases of goods and services in 2019 was MOST NEARLY _____ billion dollars.
   A. 80   B. 110   C. 128   D. 144

3.____

4. In 2015, purchases made by State and Local governments
   A. exceeded Federal government total purchases
   B. exceeded purchases made by them in 2009 by more than 50%
   C. increased less than 10% over 2012
   D. were less than 50% of purchases made by them in 2018

4.____

5. Purchases of goods and services for national defense in 2009 by the Federal government was MOST NEARLY
   A. 15% less than the total spent by Federal, State and Local governments for all purposes in 2005
   B. 50% of the total spent by Federal, State, and Local governments for all purposes in 2012
   C. four times the amount spent in 2005 for National Defense
   D. ten times the amount spent in 2009 by the Federal government for purposes other than National Defense

5.____

6. In which one of the following years did State and Local purchases of goods and services comprise the GREATEST proportion of the total spent by government jurisdictions?
   A. 2005   B. 2009   C. 2012   D. 2017

6.____

7. The dollar increase in purchases of goods and services was LEAST for which one of the following?
   A. State and Local governments between 2005 and 2009
   B. State and Local governments between 2012 and 2015
   C. Total Federal government between 2015 and 2017
   D. Federal government other than National Defense between 2015 and 2018

7.____

8. The rate of increase in Federal purchases of goods and services for National Defense was GREATEST between which of the following periods?
   A. From 2009 to 2012   B. From 2012 and 2015
   C. From 2015 to 2017   D. From 2017 to 2019

8.____

KEY (CORRECT ANSWERS)

1. B
2. C
3. C
4. B
5. B
6. A
7. D
8. C

TEST 3

DIRECTIONS: Questions 1 through 10 are to be answered SOLELY on the basis of the following table showing the amounts purchased by various purchasing units during 2015. *PRINT THE LETTER OF THE CORRECT ANSWER IN THE SPACE AT THE RIGHT.*

DOLLAR VOLUME PURCHASED BY EACH PURCHASING UNIT
DURING EACH QUARTER OF 2015
(Figures Shown Represent Thousands of Dollars)

Purchasing Unit	First Quarter	Second Quarter	Third Quarter	Fourth Quarter
A	578	924	698	312
B	1,426	1,972	1,586	1,704
C	366	494	430	716
D	1,238	1,708	1,884	1,546
E	730	742	818	774
F	948	1,118	1,256	788

1. The TOTAL dollar volume purchased by *all* of the purchasing units during 2015 approximated MOST NEARLY
   A. $2,000,000   B. $4,000,000   C. $20,000,000   D. $40,000,000

2. During which quarter was the GREATEST total dollar amount of purchases made?
   A. First   B. Second   C. Third   D. Fourth

3. Assume that the dollar volume purchased by Unit F during 2015 exceeded the dollar volume purchased by Unit F during 2014 was 50%
   Then, the dollar volume purchased by Unit F during 2014 was
   A. $2,055,000   B. $2,550,000   C. $2,740,000   D. $6,165,000

4. Which one of the following purchasing units showed the SHARPEST decrease in the amount purchased during the *fourth* quarter as compared with the *third* quarter?
   A. A   B. B   C. D   D. E

5. Comparing the dollar volume purchased in the *second* quarter with the dollar volume purchased in the *third* quarter, the decrease in the dollar volume during the third quarter was PRIMARILY due to the decrease in the dollar volume purchased by Units
   A. A and B   B. C and D   C. C and E   D. C and F

6. Of the following, the unit which had the LARGEST number of dollars of increased purchases from any one quarter to the next following quarter was Unit
   A. A   B. B   C. C   D. D

1.____

2.____

3.____

4.____

5.____

6.____

3 (#3)

7. Of the following, the unit with the LARGEST dollar volume of purchases during the second half of 2015 was Unit
   A. A   B. B   C. D   D. F

   7._____

8. Which one of the following MOST closely approximates the percentage which Unit B's total 2015 purchases represents of the total 2015 purchases of all units, including Unit B?
   A. 10%   B. 15%   C. 25%   D. 45%

   8._____

9. Assume that research showed that each ten thousand dollars ($10,000) of purchases by Unit D during 2015 required an average of thirteen (13) man-hours of buyers' staff time.
   On that basis, which one of the following MOST closely approximates the number of man-hours of buyers' staff time required by Unit D during 2015?
   A. 1,800   B. 8,000   C. 68,000   D. 78,000

   9._____

10. Assume that research showed that each ten thousand dollars ($10,000) of purchases by Unit C during 2015 required an average of ten (10) man-hours of buyers' staff time. This research also showed that during 2015 the average man-hours of buyers' staff time per ten thousand dollars of purchases required by Unit C exceeded by 25% of the average man-hours of buyers' staff time per ten thousand dollars of purchases required by Unit E.
    On that basis, which one of the following MOST closely approximates the number of buyer's staff man-hours required by Unit E during 2015?
    A. 2,200   B. 2,400   C. 3,000   D. 3,700

    10._____

KEY (CORRECT ANSWERS)

1.	C		6.	B
2.	B		7.	C
3.	C		8.	C
4.	A		9.	B
5.	A		10.	B

TEST 4

DIRECTIONS: Questions 1 through 6 are to be answered SOLELY on the basis of the following table and graph and the accompanying notes. *PRINT THE LETTER OF THE CORRECT ANSWER IN THE SPACE AT THE RIGHT.*

CONSUMER PROTECTION DIVISION-METROPOLITAN CITY
Number and Kinds of Violations (2017-2019)

NATURE OF VIOLATION	2017 District						2018 District						2019 District					
	A	B	C	D	E	Total	A	B	C	D	E	Total	A	B	C	D	E	Total
Scales	27	31	42	16	12	128	18	34	36	15	19	122	20	28	31	12	10	101
Gasoline sales	12	9	17	6	3	47	9	4	19			32	6	5	16	3	6	36
Illegal meat coloring	9	8	13	4		34	10	12	21	9	2	54	8	6	5	2	1	22
Fat content-chopped meat	21	19	40	7	1	88	20	17	31	3	3	74	16	12	18	4	3	53
Checkout counter errors	12	9	10	2		33	12	8	21			41	16	21	9	2	2	50
Fuel oil sales	6	5	4		16	31			2		6	8	5	6	6		18	35
Fraudulent labels	18	29	39	14	14	114	21	36	31	12	18	118	12	25	19	15	25	96
TOTALS	105	110	165	49	46	475	90	111	161	39	48	449	83	103	104	38	65	393

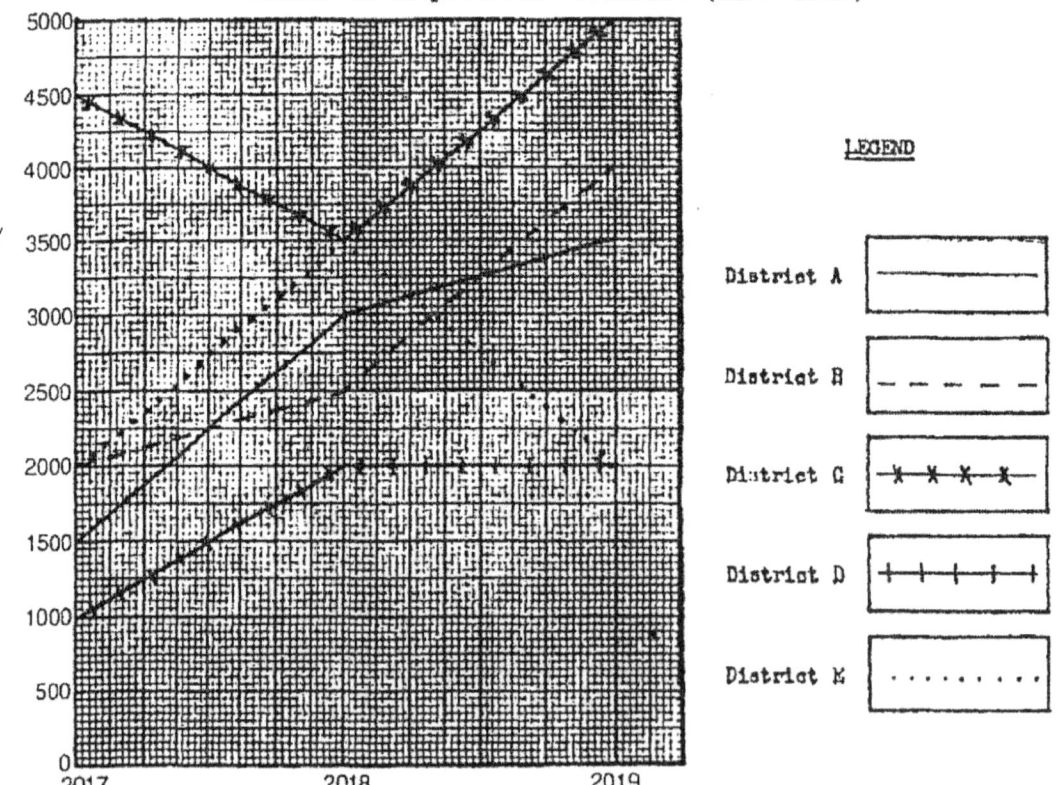

NOTES: The Consumer Protection Division of Metropolitan City is divided into five districts designated A, B, C, D and E.

Number of establishments in each district:
District A – 26,000   District C – 27,000   District E – 12,000
District B – 30,000   District D – 15,000

Number of field inspectors assigned to each district in 2017 and 2018
District A – 20   District C – 25   District E – 11
District B – 24   District D – 21

At the beginning of 2019 there was a general reassignment of field inspectors and the staff of field inspectors was increased. This resulted in assignments of field inspectors as follows:
District A – 20   District C – 32   District E – 16
District B – 26   District D - 16

1. Of the following districts, the one in which the ratio of meat coloring violations to total number of violations in the district was GREATEST in 2018 is District
   A. A   B. B   C. C   D. D

2. In 2018, the number of violations uncovered per field inspector for the entire city was MOST NEARLY
   A. 3.9   B. 4.1   C. 4.4   D. 4.8

3. In 2017, the number of violations per 1,000 establishments in District C was MOST NEARLY
   A. 3.9   B. 6.1   C. 10.4   D. 16.5

4. The number of inspections performed by the Consumer Protection Division in 2018 was MOST NEARLY
   A. 449   B. 12,000   C. 13,500   D. 14,500

5. In 2017, the number of violations uncovered per 100 inspections for the entire city was MOST NEARLY
   A. 23   B. 3.2   C. 4.3   D. 48.0

6. If it had been decided at the beginning of 2019 to assign inspectors so that the ratio of the number of inspectors in each district to the total number of inspectors would be the same as the ratio of the number of establishments in the district to the total number of establishments in the city, the number of inspectors assigned to District A would have been
   A. 24   B. 25   C. 26   D. 17

KEY (CORRECT ANSWERS)

1.	D	4.	D
2.	C	5.	C
3.	B	6.	C

TEST 5

DIRECTIONS: Questions 1 through 4 are to be answered SOLELY on the basis of the following graph and the accompanying notes. *PRINT THE LETTER OF THE CORRECT ANSWER IN THE SPACE AT THE RIGHT.*

NOTES: The graph shows space allocation in three municipal food markets in a certain city. The five columns for each market represent the total amount of each market's space. The miscellaneous column accounts for all non-rental space allocated to shopping aisles, loading facilities, etc.

Assume that during 2019 there was no tenant turnover and that the amount of space rented and unrented remained constant.
The rental charges in 2019 for all types of business were as follows:
  Jefferson Market: $10.00 per square foot
  Jackson Market: $17.50 per square foot
  Lincoln Market: $15.00 per square foot

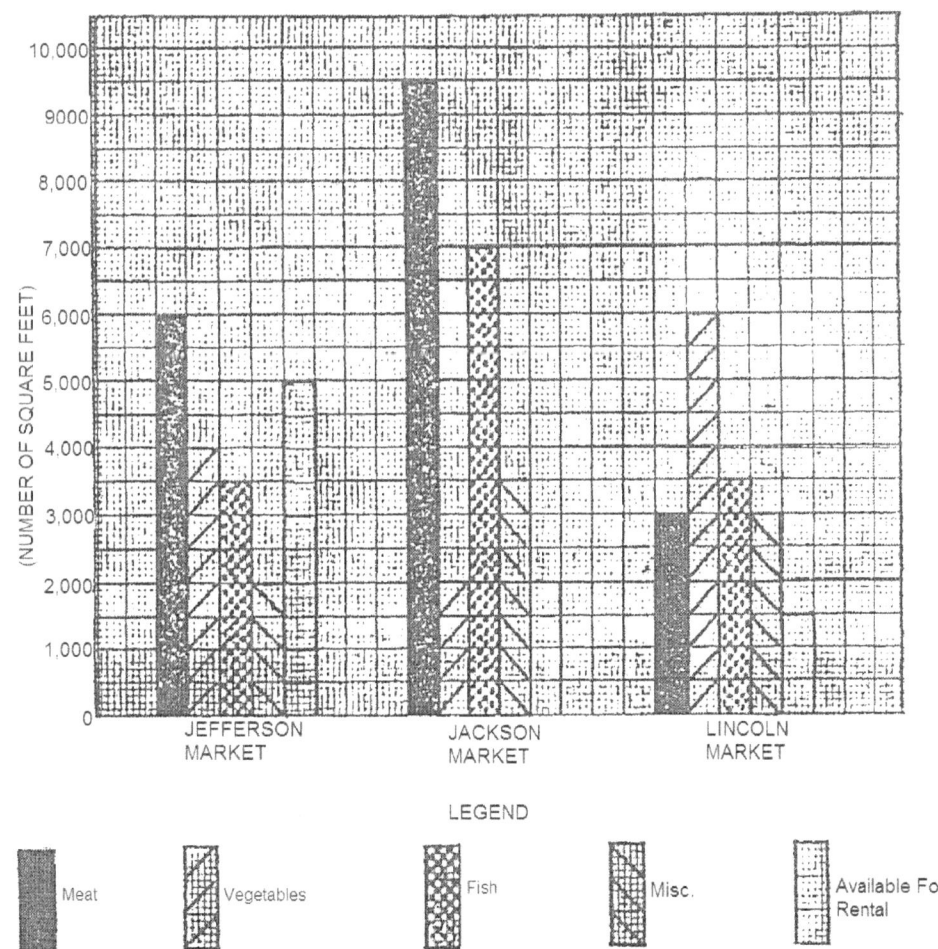

2019 SPACE ALLOCATIONS IN THE JEFFERSON, JACKSON AND LINCOLN MUNICIPAL FOOD MARKETS
(According to Type of Business)

LEGEND: Meat, Vegetables, Fish, Misc., Available For Rental

23

1. The percentage of overall space in the Lincoln Market leased to fish dealers in 2019 is, MOST NEARLY,
   A. 17%   B. 19%   C. 21%   D. 23%

2. The total amount of space in all three municipal food markets devoted to the meat business EXCEEDED the amount of space in these markets devoted to the fish business by ____ square feet.
   A. 2,500   B. 4,500   C. 14,000   D. 18,500

3. If all of the space in the Lincoln Market available for rental in 2019 had been rented, the income received from this market would have INCREASED by
   A. 6%   B. 12%   C. 18%   D. 24%

4. Approximately what percent of the 2019 rental income of the Jackson Market was derived from vegetable dealers?
   A. 8.3%
   B. 9.1%
   C. 10.8%
   D. A percent which cannot be determined from the data given

1.____
2.____
3.____
4.____

KEY (CORRECT ANSWERS)

1. C
2. B
3. B
4. C

TEST 6

DIRECTIONS: Questions 1 through 5 involve calculation of annual grade averages for college students who have just completed their junior year. These averages are to be based on the following table showing the number of credit hours for each student during the year at each of the grade levels: A, B, C, D, and F. How these letter grades may be translated into numerical grades is indicated in the first column of the table. *PRINT THE LETTER OF THE CORRECT ANSWER IN THE SPACE AT THE RIGHT.*

	Grade Value	Credit Hours – Junior Year					
		King	Lewis	Martin	Norris	Ott	Perry
A =	95	12	12	9	15	6	3
B =	85	9	12	9	12	18	6
C =	75	6	6	9	3	3	21
D =	65	3	3	3	3	-	-
F =	0	-	-	33	-	-	-

NOTES: Calculating a grade average for an individual student is a 4-step process:
    I. Multiply each grade value by the number of credit hours for which the student received that grade.
    II. Add these multiplication products for each student.
    III. Add the student's total credit hours.
    IV. Divide the multiplication product total by the total number of credit hours.
    V. Round the result, if there is a decimal place, to the nearest whole number. A number ending in .5 would be rounded to the next higher number.

EXAMPLE: Using student King's grades as an example, his grade average can be calculated by going through the following four steps:

    I. 95 × 12 = 1140   III. 12
        85 × 9 = 765   9
        75 × 6 = 450   6
        65 × 3 = 195   3
        0 × 0 = 0   0
    II. TOTAL = 2550   30 TOTAL credit hours
                              IV. Divide 2550 by 30: 2550/30 = 85

King's grade average is 85.
Now answer Questions 1 through 5 on the basis of the information given above.

1. The grade average of Lewis is   1.____
    A. 83   B. 84   C. 85   D. 86

2. The grade average of Martin is   2.____
    A. 72   B. 73   C. 74   D. 75

3. The grade average of Norris is   3.____
    A. 85   B. 86   C. 87   D. 88

4. Student Ott must attain a grade average of 90 in each of his years in college to be accepted into the graduate school of his choice.
If, in summer school during his junior year, he takes two 3-credit courses and receives a grade of 95 in each one, his grade average for his junior year will then be MOST NEARLY
   A. 87   B. 88   C. 89   D. 90

5. If Perry takes an additional 3-credit course during the year and receives a grade of 95, his grade average will be increased to APPROXIMATELY
   A. 79   B. 80   C. 89   D. 82

KEY (CORRECT ANSWERS)

1. C
2. D
3. C
4. B
5. B

TEST 7

DIRECTIONS: Questions 1 through 5 are to be answered SOLELY on the basis of the chart below which relates to the increase in taxes. *PRINT THE LETTER OF THE CORRECT ANSWER IN THE SPACE AT THE RIGHT.*

INCREASE IN STATE AND LOCAL TAXES PER PERSON							
	2017	2019	Percent Increase		2017	2019	Percent Increase
Delaware	$138	$372	170	Iowa	$180	$389	116
Maryland	162	411	156	Tennessee	118	252	114
New York	227	576	153	Arkansas	103	221	114
Nebraska	144	362	151	Wyoming	193	414	114
Kentucky	111	278	150	New Mexico	151	324	114
Rhode Island	153	379	148	Idaho	156	328	110
Virginia	128	314	145	Pennsylvania	162	340	109
Arizona	163	387	135	South Dakota	169	353	108
Indiana	141	334	137	Illinois	179	373	108
New Jersey	173	406	135	South Carolina	108	225	108
Wisconsin	187	439	135	Maine	149	308	106
California	232	540	133	Ohio	149	306	105
Michigan	184	428	132	Colorado	189	386	104
Missouri	132	301	128	Nevada	232	466	101
North Carolina	115	259	125	Connecticut	196	392	100
Vermont	173	384	123	Kansas	173	346	100
Minnesota	183	406	122	Texas	139	276	99
West Virginia	119	263	120	Utah	166	327	98
Massachusetts	206	453	119	New Hampshire	152	299	97
Alabama	103	224	118	North Dakota	176	338	92
Washington	189	410	117	Oregon	204	387	90
Florida	153	330	116	Oklahoma	152	287	89
Georgia	125	270	116	Louisiana	160	298	86
Mississippi	112	242	116	Montana	189	351	86

1. The dollar increase per person in taxes between 2017-2019 was GREATEST in which state?   1.____
   A. New York	B. California	C. Wisconsin
   D. New Jersey	E. Delaware

2. The state whose people paid the LOWEST amount per person in taxes in 2019 was   2.____
   A. Montana	B. Mississippi	C. Alabama
   D. Arkansas	E. South Carolina

3. Which of the following states DOUBLED its taxes from 2017 to 2019?   3.____
   A. Kentucky	B. North Carolina	C. Kansas
   D. Texas	E. None of the above

27

4. Which state had the SMALLEST increase in taxes from 2017 to 2019?　　4.____
   A. Montana　　B. Alabama　　C. Arkansas
   D. Mississippi　　E. South Carolina

5. In which of the following states was the per capita tax the GREATEST in 2017?　　5.____
   A. Massachusetts　　B. New York　　C. Nevada
   D. Delaware　　E. Oregon

KEY (CORRECT ANSWERS)

1. A
2. D
3. C
4. E
5. C

TEST 8

DIRECTIONS: Questions 1 through 6 are to be answered SOLELY on the basis of the chart below which relates to the Distribution of Minority Groups by Pay Category. *PRINT THE LETTER OF THE CORRECT ANSWER IN THE SPACE AT THE RIGHT.*

TABLE 1- DISTRIBUTION OF ALL MINORITY GROUPS COMBINED, BY PAY CATEGORY AS OF NOVEMBER 30, 2019 AND MAY 31, 2020					
	November 2019		May 2020		Percent Change
Pay System	Number	Percent	Number	Percent	
All Pay Systems	500,508	100.0	501,871	100.0	0.3
General Schedule and Similar	181,725	36.3	186,170	37.1	2.4
Wage Systems	155,744	31.1	151,919	30.3	-2.5
Postal Field Service	158,945	31.8	159,211	31.7	0.2
All Other	4,094	0.8	4,571	0.9	11.7

1. From the table, what was the TOTAL of government workers in *all pay* systems in November 2019?
   A. 155,744   B. 181,725   C. 186,170
   D. 500,508   E. None of the above

1.____

2. What was the percentage difference between Wage Systems and All Pay Systems in November 2019 and Postal Field Service and All Pay Systems in May 2020?
   A. .2%   B. .6%   C. 1.1%   D. 1.7%   E. 2.5%

2.____

3. How many more minority group members were employed by the Postal Field Service in May 2020 than in November 2019?
   A. .2%   B. 256   C. 266   D. 1,246   E. 1,266

3.____

4. In which of the pay systems did the percentage of minority workers decline?
   A. General Schedule and Similar   B. Wage Systems
   C. Postal Field Service   D. All Other
   E. None of the above

4.____

5. In which system was the percentage gain of minority members from 2019 to 2020 the GREATEST?
   A. General Schedule and Similar
   B. Wage Systems
   C. Postal Field Service
   D. All Other Systems
   E. One cannot tell from the information given

5.____

6. Which system reflects the GREATEST percentage increase from 2019 to 2020 to the total minority work force?
   A. General Schedule and Similar
   B. Wage Systems
   C. Postal Field Service
   D. All Other
   E. One cannot tell from the information given

6._____

KEY (CORRECT ANSWERS)

1. E   4. B
2. B   5. D
3. C   6. A

EVALUATING CONCLUSIONS BASED ON FACTUAL INFORMATION

Test material will be presented in a multiple-choice question format.

Test Task: You will be given a set of statements and a conclusion based on the statements. You are to assume the statements are true. The conclusion is reached from these statements *only* not on what you may happen to know about the subject discussed. Each question has three possible answers. You must then select the correct answer in the following manner:

    Select A, if the statements prove that the conclusion is true.
    Select B, if the statements prove that the conclusion is false.
    Select C, if the statements are inadequate to prove the conclusion either true or false.

SAMPLE QUESTION #1:

STATEMENTS: All uniforms are cleaned by the Conroy Company. Blue uniforms are cleaned on Mondays or Fridays; green or brown uniforms are cleaned on Wednesdays. Alan and Jean have blue uniforms, Gary has green uniforms, and Ryan has brown uniforms.

CONCLUSION: Jean's uniforms are cleaned on Wednesdays.
    A statements prove the conclusion TRUE
    B statements prove the conclusion FALSE
    C statements are INADEQUATE to prove the conclusion

The correct answer to this sample question is Choice B.

SOLUTION: The last sentence of the statements says that Jean has blue uniforms. The second sentence of the statements says that blue uniforms are cleaned on Monday or Friday. The conclusion says Jean's uniforms are cleaned on Wednesday. Wednesday is neither Monday nor Friday. Therefore, the conclusion must be false (choice B).

SAMPLE QUESTION #2

STATEMENTS: If Beth works overtime, the assignment will be completed. If the assignment is completed, then all unit employees will receive a bonus. Beth works overtime.

CONCLUSION: A bonus will be given to all employees in the unit.
    A. statements prove the conclusion TRUE.
    B. statements prove the conclusion FALSE.
    C. statements are INADEQUATE to prove the conclusion

The correct answer to this sample question is Choice A.

SOLUTION: The conclusion follows necessarily from the statements. Beth works overtime. The assignment is completed. Therefore, all unit employees will receive a bonus.

SAMPLE QUESTION #3

STATEMENTS: Bill is older than Wanda. Edna is older than Bill. Sarah is twice as old as Wanda.

CONCLUSION: Sarah is older than Edna.
- A. statements prove the conclusion TRUE
- B. statements prove the conclusion FALSE
- C. statements are INADEQUATE to prove the conclusion

The correct answer to this sample question is Choice C.

SOLUTION: We know from the statements that both Sarah and Edna are older than Wanda. We do not have any other information about Sarah and Edna. Therefore, no conclusion about whether or not Sarah is older than Edna can be made.

EVALUATING CONCLUSIONS IN LIGHT OF KNOWN FACTS
EXAMINATION SECTION
TEST 1

DIRECTIONS: Each question or incomplete statement is followed by several suggested answers or completions. Select the one that BEST answers the question or completes the statement. *PRINT THE LETTER OF THE CORRECT ANSWER IN THE SPACE AT THE RIGHT.*

Questions 1-9.

DIRECTIONS: In Questions 1 through 9, you will read a set of facts and a conclusion drawn from them. The conclusion may be valid or invalid, based on the facts—it's your task to determine the validity of the conclusion.

For each question, select the letter before the statement that BEST expresses the relationship between the given facts and the conclusion that has been drawn from them. Your choices are:
    A. The facts prove the conclusion;
    B. The facts disprove the conclusion; or
    C. The facts neither prove nor disprove the conclusion.

1. FACTS: If the supervisor retires, James, the assistant supervisor, will not be transferred to another department. James will be promoted to supervisor if he is not transferred. The supervisor retired.

   CONCLUSION: James will be promoted to supervisor.
       A. The facts prove the conclusion.
       B. The facts disprove the conclusion.
       C. The facts neither prove nor disprove the conclusion.

   1.____

2. FACTS: In the town of Luray, every player on the softball team works at Luray National Bank. In addition, every player on the Luray softball team wear glasses.

   CONCLUSIONS: At least some of the people who work at Luray National Bank wear glasses.
       A. The facts prove the conclusion.
       B. The facts disprove the conclusion.
       C. The facts neither prove nor disprove the conclusion.

   2.____

3. FACTS: The only time Henry and June go out to dinner is on an evening when they have childbirth classes. Their childbirth classes meet on Tuesdays and Thursdays.

   3.____

2 (#1)

CONCLUSION: Henry and June never go out to dinner on Friday or Saturday.
  A. The facts prove the conclusion.
  B. The facts disprove the conclusion.
  C. The facts neither prove nor disprove the conclusion.

4. FACTS: Every player on the field hockey team has at least one bruise. Everyone on the field hockey team also has scarred knees.

CONCLUSION: Most people with both bruises and scarred knees are field hockey players.
  A. The facts prove the conclusion.
  B. The facts disprove the conclusion.
  C. The facts neither prove nor disprove the conclusion.

4._____

5. FACTS: In the chess tournament, Lance will win his match against Jane if Jane wins her match against Mathias. If Lance wins his match against Jane, Christine will not win her match against Jane.

CONCLUSION: Christine will not win her match against Jane if Jane wins her match against Mathias.
  A. The facts prove the conclusion.
  B. The facts disprove the conclusion.
  C. The facts neither prove nor disprove the conclusion.

5._____

6. FACTS: No green lights on the machine are indicators for the belt drive status. Not all of the lights on the machine's upper panel are green. Some lights on the machine's lower panel are green.

CONCLUSION: The green lights on the machine's lower panel may be indicators for the belt drive status.
  A. The facts prove the conclusion.
  B. The facts disprove the conclusion.
  C. The facts neither prove nor disprove the conclusion.

6._____

7. FACTS: At a small, one-room country school, there are eight students: Amy, Ben, Carla, Dan, Elliot, Francine, Greg, and Hannah. Each student is in either the 6th, 7th, or 8th grade. Either two or three students are in each grade. Amy, Dan, and Francine are all in different grades. Ben and Elliot are both in the 7th grade. Hannah and Carl are in the same grade.

CONCLUSION: Exactly three students are in the 7th grade.
  A. The facts prove the conclusion.
  B. The facts disprove the conclusion.
  C. The facts neither prove nor disprove the conclusion.

7._____

8. FACTS: Two married couples are having lunch together. Two of the four people are German and two are Russian, but in each couple the nationality of the spouse is not necessarily the same as the other's. One person in the group is a teacher, the other a lawyer, one an engineer, and the other a writer. The teacher is a Russian man. The writer is Russian, and her husband is an engineer. One of the people, Mr. Stern, is German.

   CONCLUSION: Mr. Stern's wife is a writer.
   A. The facts prove the conclusion.
   B. The facts disprove the conclusion.
   C. The facts neither prove nor disprove the conclusion.

   8.____

9. FACTS: The flume ride at the county fair is open only to children who are at least 36 inches tall. Lisa is 30 inches tall. John is shorter than Henry, but more than 10 inches taller than Lisa.

   CONCLUSION: Lisa is the only one who can't ride the flume ride.
   A. The facts prove the conclusion.
   B. The facts disprove the conclusion.
   C. The facts neither prove nor disprove the conclusion.

   9.____

Questions 10-17.

DIRECTIONS: Questions 10 through 17 are based on the following reading passage. It is not your knowledge of the particular topic that is being tested, but your ability to reason based on what you have read. The passage is likely to detail several proposed courses of action and factors affecting these proposals. The reading passage is followed by a conclusion or outcome based on the facts in the passage, or a description of a decision taken regarding the situation. The conclusion is followed by a number of statements that have a possible connection to the conclusion. For each statement, you are to determine whether:
   A. The statement proves the conclusion.
   B. The statement supports the conclusion but does not prove it.
   C. The statement disproves the conclusion.
   D. The statement weakens the conclusion but does not disprove it.
   E. The statement has no relevance to the conclusion.

Remember that the conclusion after the passage is to be accepted as the outcome of what actually happened, and that you are being asked to evaluate the impact each statement would have had on the conclusion.

PASSAGE:

The Grand Army of Foreign Wars, a national veteran's organization, is struggling to maintain its National Home, where the widowed spouses and orphans of deceased members are housed together in a small village-like community. The Home is open to spouses and children who are bereaved for any reason, regardless of whether the member's death was related to military service, but a new global conflict has led to a dramatic surge in the number of members' deaths: many veterans who re-enlisted for the conflict have been killed in action.

The Grand Army of Foreign Wars is considering several options for handling the increased number of applications for housing at the National Home, which has been traditionally supported by membership due. At its national convention, it will choose only one of the following:

The first idea is a one-time $50 tax on all members, above and beyond the dues they pay already. Since the organization has more than a million member, this tax should be sufficient for the construction and maintenance of new housing for applicants on the existing grounds of the National Home. The idea is opposed, however, by some older members who live on fixed incomes. These members object in principle to the taxation of Grand Army members. The Grand Army has never imposed a tax on its members.

The second idea is to launch a national fundraising drive the public relations campaign that will attract donations for the National Home. Several national celebrities are members of the organization, and other celebrities could be attracted to the cause. Many Grand Army members are wary of this approach, however: in the past, the net receipts of some fundraising efforts have been relatively insignificant, given the costs of staging them.

A third approach, suggested by many of the younger members, is to have new applicants share some of the costs of construction and maintenance. The spouses and children would pay an up-front "enrollment" fee, based on a sliding scale proportionate to their income and assets, and then a monthly fee adjusted similarly to contribute to maintenance costs. Many older members are strongly opposed to this idea, as it is in direct contradiction to the principles on which the organization was founded more than a century ago.

The fourth option is simply to maintain the status quo, focus the organization's efforts on supporting the families who already live at the National Home, and wait to accept new applicants based on attrition.

CONCLUSION: At its annual national convention, the Grand Army of Foreign Wars votes to impose a one-time tax of $10 on each member for the purpose of expanding and supporting the National Home to welcome a larger number of applicants. The tax is considered to be the solution most likely to produce the funds needed to accommodate the growing number of applicants.

10. Actuarial studies have shown that because the Grand Army's membership consists mostly of older veterans from earlier wars, the organization's membership will suffer a precipitous decline in numbers in about five years.
    A. The statement proves the conclusion.
    B. The statement supports the conclusion but does not prove it.
    C. The statement disproves the conclusion.
    D. The statement weakens the conclusion but does not disprove it.
    E. The statement has no relevance to the conclusion.

10._____

11. After passage of the funding measure, a splinter group of older members appeals for the "sliding scale" provision to be applied to the tax, so that some members may be allowed to contribute less based on their income.
    A. The statement proves the conclusion.
    B. The statement supports the conclusion but does not prove it.
    C. The statement disproves the conclusion.
    D. The statement weakens the conclusion but does not disprove it.
    E. The statement has no relevance to the conclusion.

11._____

5 (#1)

12. The original charter of the Grand Army of Foreign Wars specifically states that the organization will not levy taxes or duties on its members beyond its modest annual dues. It takes a super-majority of attending delegates at the national convention to make alterations to the charter.
    A. The statement proves the conclusion.
    B. The statement supports the conclusion but does not prove it.
    C. The statement disproves the conclusion.
    D. The statement weakens the conclusion but does not disprove it.
    E. The statement has no relevance to the conclusion.

    12.____

13. Six months before Grand Army of Foreign Wars' national convention, the Internal Revenue Service rules that because it is an organization that engages in political lobbying, the Grand Army must no longer enjoy its own federal tax-exempt status.
    A. The statement proves the conclusion.
    B. The statement supports the conclusion but does not prove it.
    C. The statement disproves the conclusion.
    D. The statement weakens the conclusion but does not disprove it.
    E. The statement has no relevance to the conclusion.

    13.____

14. Two months before the national convention, Dirk Rockwell, arguably the country's most famous film actor, announces in a nationally televised interview that he has been saddened to learn of the plight of the National Home, and that he is going to make it his own personal crusade to see that it is able to house and support a greater number of widowed spouses and orphans in the future.
    A. The statement proves the conclusion.
    B. The statement supports the conclusion but does not prove it.
    C. The statement disproves the conclusion.
    D. The statement weakens the conclusion but does not disprove it.
    E. The statement has no relevance to the conclusion.

    14.____

15. The Grand Army's final estimate is that the cost of expanding the National Home to accommodate the increased number of applicants will be about $61 million.
    A. The statement proves the conclusion.
    B. The statement supports the conclusion but does not prove it.
    C. The statement disproves the conclusion.
    D. The statement weakens the conclusion but does not disprove it.
    E. The statement has no relevance to the conclusion.

    15.____

16. Just before the national convention, the Federal Department of Veterans Affairs announces steep cuts in the benefits package that is currently offered to the widowed spouses and orphans of veterans.
    A. The statement proves the conclusion.
    B. The statement supports the conclusion but does not prove it.
    C. The statement disproves the conclusion.
    D. The statement weakens the conclusion but does not disprove it.
    E. The statement has no relevance to the conclusion.

    16.____

17. After the national convention, the Grand Army of Foreign Wars begins charging a modest "start-up" fee to all families who apply for residence at the national home.
    A. The statement proves the conclusion.
    B. The statement supports the conclusion but does not prove it.
    C. The statement disproves the conclusion.
    D. The statement weakens the conclusion but does not disprove it.
    E. The statement has no relevance to the conclusion.

17.____

Questions 18-25.

DIRECTIONS: Questions 18 through 25 each provide four factual statements and a conclusion based on these statements. After reading the entire question, you will decide whether:
    A. The conclusion is proved by statements I-IV;
    B. The conclusion is disproved by statements I-IV.
    C. The facts are not sufficient to prove or disprove the conclusion.

18. FACTUAL STATEMENTS:
    I. In the Field Day high jump competition, Martha jumped higher than Frank.
    II. Carl jumped higher than Ignacio.
    III. Ignacio jumped higher than Frank.
    IV. Dan jumped higher than Carl.

    CONCLUSION: Frank finished last in the high jump competition.
    A. The conclusion is proved by statements I-IV;
    B. The conclusion is disproved by statements I-IV.
    C. The facts are not sufficient to prove or disprove the conclusion.

18.____

19. FACTUAL STATEMENTS:
    I. The door to the hammer mill chamber is locked if light 6 is red.
    II. The door to the hammer mill chamber is locked only when the mill is operating.
    III. If the mill is not operating, light 6 is blue.
    IV. Light 6 is blue.

    CONCLUSION: The door to the hammer mill chamber is locked.
    A. The conclusion is proved by statements I-IV;
    B. The conclusion is disproved by statements I-IV.
    C. The facts are not sufficient to prove or disprove the conclusion.

19.____

20. FACTUAL STATEMENTS:
    I. Ziegfried, the lion tamer at the circus, has demanded ten additional minutes of performance time during each show.
    II. If Ziegfried is allowed his ten additional minutes per show, he will attempt to teach Kimba the tiger to shoot a basketball.
    III. If Kimba learns how to shoot a basketball, then Ziegfried was not given his ten additional minutes.
    IV. Ziegfried was given his ten additional minutes.

20.____

7 (#1)

CONCLUSION: Despite Ziegfried's efforts, Kimba did not learn how to shoot a basketball.
   A. The conclusion is proved by statements I-IV;
   B. The conclusion is disproved by statements I-IV.
   C. The facts are not sufficient to prove or disprove the conclusion.

21. FACTUAL STATEMENTS:
   I. If Stan goes to counseling, Sara won't divorce him.
   II. If Sara divorces Stan, she'll move back to Texas.
   III. If Sara doesn't divorce Stan, Irene will be disappointed.
   IV. Stan goes to counseling.

   CONCLUSION: Irene will be disappointed.
   A. The conclusion is proved by statements I-IV;
   B. The conclusion is disproved by statements I-IV.
   C. The facts are not sufficient to prove or disprove the conclusion.

22. FACTUAL STATEMENTS:
   I. If Delia is promoted to district manager, Claudia will have to be promoted to team leader.
   II. Delia will be promoted to district manager unless she misses her fourth-quarter sales quota.
   III. If Claudia is promoted to team leader, Thomas will be promoted to assistant team leader.
   IV. Delia meets her fourth-quarter sales quota.

   CONCLUSION: Thomas is promoted to assistant team leader.
   A. The conclusion is proved by statements I-IV;
   B. The conclusion is disproved by statements I-IV.
   C. The facts are not sufficient to prove or disprove the conclusion.

23. FACTUAL STATEMENTS:
   I. Clone D is identical to Clone B.
   II. Clone B is not identical to Clone A.
   III. Clone D is not identical to Clone C.
   IV. Clone E is not identical to the clones that are identical to Clone B.

   CONCLUSION: Clone E is identical to Clone D.
   A. The conclusion is proved by statements I-IV;
   B. The conclusion is disproved by statements I-IV.
   C. The facts are not sufficient to prove or disprove the conclusion.

24. FACTUAL STATEMENTS:
   I. In the Stafford Tower, each floor is occupied by a single business.
   II. Big G Staffing is on a floor between CyberGraphics and MainEvent.
   III. Gasco is on the floor directly below CyberGraphics and three floors above Treehorn Audio.
   IV. MainEvent is five floors below EZ Tax and four floors below Treehorn Audio.

8 (#1)

CONCLUSION: EZ Tax is on a floor between Gasco and MainEvent.
   A. The conclusion is proved by statements I-IV;
   B. The conclusion is disproved by statements I-IV.
   C. The facts are not sufficient to prove or disprove the conclusion.

25. FACTUAL STATEMENTS: 25.____
   I. Only county roads lead to Nicodemus.
   II. All the roads from Hill City to Graham County are federal highways.
   III. Some of the roads from Plainville lead to Nicodemus.
   IV. Some of the roads running from Hill City lead to Strong City.

   CONCLUSION: Some of the roads from Plainville are county roads.
   A. The conclusion is proved by statements I-IV;
   B. The conclusion is disproved by statements I-IV.
   C. The facts are not sufficient to prove or disprove the conclusion.

KEY (CORRECT ANSWERS)

1.	A		11.	A
2.	A		12.	D
3.	A		13.	E
4.	C		14.	D
5.	A		15.	B
6.	B		16.	B
7.	A		17.	C
8.	A		18.	A
9.	A		19.	B
10.	E		20.	A

21.	A
22.	A
23.	B
24.	A
25.	A

SOLUTIONS TO PROBLEMS

1. CORRECT ANSWER: A
   Given Statement 3, we deduce that James will not be transferred to another department. By Statement 2, we can conclude that James will be promoted.

2. CORRECT ANSWER: A
   Since every player on the softball team wears glasses, these individuals compose some of the people who work at the bank. Although not every person who works at the bank plays softball, those bank employees who do play softball wear glasses.

3. CORRECT ANSWER: A
   If Henry and June go out to dinner, we conclude that it must be on Tuesday or Thursday, which are the only two days when they have childbirth classes. This implies that if it is not Tuesday or Thursday, then this couple does not go out to dinner.

4. CORRECT ANSWER: C
   We can only conclude that if a person plays on the field hockey team, then he or she has both bruises and scarred knees. But there are probably a great number of people who have both bruises and scarred knees but do not play on the field hockey team. The given conclusion can neither be proven or disproven.

5. CORRECT ANSWER: A
   From statement 1, if Jane beats Mathias, then Lance will beat Jane. Using statement 2, we can then conclude that Christine will not win her match against Jane.

6. CORRECT ANSWER: B
   Statement 1 tells us that no green light can be an indicator of the belt drive status. Thus, the given conclusion must be false.

7. CORRECT ANSWER: A
   We already know that Ben and Elliot are in the 7th grade. Even though Hannah and Carl are in the same grade, it cannot be the 7th grade because we would then have at least four students in this 7th grade. This would contradict the third statement, which states that either two or three students are in each grade. Since Amy, Dan, and Francine are in different grade, exactly one of them must be in the 7th grade. Thus, Ben, Elliot, and exactly one of Amy, Dan, and Francine are the three students in the 7th grade.

8. CORRECT ANSWER: A
   One man is a teacher, who is Russian. We know that the writer is female and is Russian. Since her husband is an engineer, he cannot be the Russian teacher. Thus, her husband is of German descent, namely Mr. Stern. This means that Mr. Stern's wife is the writer. Note that one couple consists of a male Russian teacher and a female German lawyer. The other couple consists of a male German engineer and a female Russian writer.

9. CORRECT ANSWER: A
Since John is more than 10 inches taller than Lisa, his height is at least 46 inches. Also, John is shorter than Henry, so Henry's height must be greater than 46 inches. Thus, Lisa is the only one whose height is less than 36 inches. Therefore, she is the only one who is not allowed on the flume ride.

18. CORRECT ANSWER: A
Dan jumped higher than Carl, who jumped higher than Ignacio, who jumped higher than Frank. Since Martha jumped higher than Frank, every person jumped higher than Frank. Thus, Frank finished last.

19. CORRECT ANSWER: B
If the light is red, then the door is locked. If the door is locked, then the mill is operating. Reversing the logical sequence of these statements, if the mill is not operating, then the door is not locked, which means that the light is blue. Thus, the given conclusion is disproved.

20. CORRECT ANSWER: A
Using the contrapositive of statement III, Ziegfried was given his ten additional minutes, then Kimba did not learn how to shoot a basketball. Since statement IV is factual, the conclusion is proved.

21. CORRECT ANSWER: A
From Statements IV and I, we conclude that Sara doesn't divorce Stan. Then statement III reveals that Irene will be disappointed. Thus, the conclusion is proved.

22. CORRECT ANSWER: A
Statement II can be rewritten as "Delia is promoted to district manager or she misses her sales quota." Furthermore, this statement is equivalent to "If Delia makes her sales quota, then she is promoted to district manager." From statement I, we conclude that Claudia is promoted to team leader. Finally, by statement III, Thomas is promoted to assistant team leader.

23. CORRECT ANSWER: B
By statement IV, Clone E is not identical to any clones identical to Clone B. Statement I tells us that Clones B and D are identical. Therefore, Clone E cannot be identical to Clone D. The conclusion is disproved.

24. CORRECT ANSWER: A
Based on all four statements, CyberGraphics is somewhere below MainEvent. Gasco is one floor below CyberGraphics. EZ Tax is two floors below Gasco. Treehorn Audio is one floor below EZ Tax. MainEvent is four floors below Treehorn Audio. Thus, EZ Tax is two floors below Gasco and five floors above MainEvent. The conclusion is proved.

25. CORRECT ANSWER: A
From statement III, we know that some of the roads from Plainville lead to Nicodemus. But statement I tells us that only county roads lead to Nicodemus. Therefore, some of the roads from Plainville must be county roads. The conclusion is proved.

TEST 2

DIRECTIONS: Each question or incomplete statement is followed by several suggested answers or completions. Select the one that BEST answers the question or completes the statement. *PRINT THE LETTER OF THE CORRECT ANSWER IN THE SPACE AT THE RIGHT.*

Questions 1-9.

DIRECTIONS: In Questions 1 through 9, you will read a set of facts and a conclusion drawn from them. The conclusion may be valid or invalid, based on the facts—it's your task to determine the validity of the conclusion.

For each question, select the letter before the statement that BEST expresses the relationship between the given facts and the conclusion that has been drawn from them. Your choices are:
  A. The facts prove the conclusion;
  B. The facts disprove the conclusion; or
  C. The facts neither prove nor disprove the conclusion.

1. FACTS: Some employees in the testing department are statisticians. Most of the statisticians who work in the testing department are projection specialists. Tom Wilks works in the testing department.

    CONCLUSION: Tom Wilks is a statistician.
      A. The facts prove the conclusion.
      B. The facts disprove the conclusion.
      C. The facts neither prove nor disprove the conclusion.

   1.____

2. FACTS: Ten coins are split among Hank, Lawrence, and Gail. If Lawrence gives his coins to Hank, then Hank will have more coins than Gail. If Gail gives her coins to Lawrence, then Lawrence will have more coins than Hank.

    CONCLUSION: Hank has six coins.
      A. The facts prove the conclusion.
      B. The facts disprove the conclusion.
      C. The facts neither prove nor disprove the conclusion.

   2.____

3. FACTS: Nobody loves everybody. Janet loves Ken. Ken loves everybody who loves Janet.

    CONCLUSION: Everybody loves Janet.
      A. The facts prove the conclusion.
      B. The facts disprove the conclusion.
      C. The facts neither prove nor disprove the conclusion.

   3.____

4. FACTS: Most of the Torres family lives in East Los Angeles. Many people in East Los Angeles celebrate Cinco de Mayo. Joe is a member of the Torres family.

   CONCLUSION: Joe lives in East Los Angeles.
   A. The facts prove the conclusion.
   B. The facts disprove the conclusion.
   C. The facts neither prove nor disprove the conclusion.

   4.____

5. FACTS: Five professionals each occupy one story of a five-story office building. Dr. Kane's office is above Dr. Assad's. Dr. Johnson's office is between Dr. Kane's and Dr. Conlon's. Dr. Steen's office is between Dr. Conlon's and Dr. Assad's. Dr. Johnson is on the fourth story.

   CONCLUSION: Dr. Kane occupies the top story.
   A. The facts prove the conclusion.
   B. The facts disprove the conclusion.
   C. The facts neither prove nor disprove the conclusion.

   5.____

6. FACTS: To be eligible for membership in the Yukon Society, a person must be able to either tunnel through a snowbank while wearing only a T-shirt and short, or hold his breath for two minutes under water that is 50°F. Ray can only hold his breath for a minute and a half.

   CONCLUSION: Ray can still become a member of the Yukon Society by tunneling through a snowbank while wearing a T-shirt and shorts.
   A. The facts prove the conclusion.
   B. The facts disprove the conclusion.
   C. The facts neither prove nor disprove the conclusion.

   6.____

7. FACTS: A mark is worth five plunks. You can exchange four sharps for a tinplot. It takes eight marks to buy a sharp.

   CONCLUSION: A sharp is the most valuable.
   A. The facts prove the conclusion.
   B. The facts disprove the conclusion.
   C. The facts neither prove nor disprove the conclusion.

   7.____

8. FACTS: There are gibbons, as well as lemurs, who like to play in the trees at the monkey house. All those who like to play in the trees at the monkey house are fed lettuce and bananas.

   CONCLUSION: Lemurs and gibbons are types of monkeys.
   A. The facts prove the conclusion.
   B. The facts disprove the conclusion.
   C. The facts neither prove nor disprove the conclusion.

   8.____

9. FACTS: None of the Blackfoot tribes is a Salishan Indian tribe. Salishan Indians 9.____
came from the northern Pacific Coast. All Salishan Indians live each of the
Continental Divide.

CONCLUSION: No Blackfoot tribes live east of the Continental Divide.
- A. The facts prove the conclusion.
- B. The facts disprove the conclusion.
- C. The facts neither prove nor disprove the conclusion.

Questions 10-17.

DIRECTIONS: Questions 10 through 17 are based on the following reading passage. It is not your knowledge of the particular topic that is being tested, but your ability to reason based on what you have read. The passage is likely to detail several proposed courses of action and factors affecting these proposals. The reading passage is followed by a conclusion or outcome based on the facts in the passage, or a description of a decision taken regarding the situation. The conclusion is followed by a number of statements that have a possible connection to the conclusion. For each statement, you are to determine whether:
- A. The statement proves the conclusion.
- B. The statement supports the conclusion but does not prove it.
- C. The statement disproves the conclusion.
- D. The statement weakens the conclusion but does not disprove it.
- E. The statement has no relevance to the conclusion.

Remember that the conclusion after the passage is to be accepted as the outcome of what actually happened, and that you are being asked to evaluate the impact each statement would have had on the conclusion.

PASSAGE:

On August 12, Beverly Willey reported that she was in the elevator late on the previous evening after leaving her office on the 16th floor of a large office building. In her report, she states that a man got on the elevator at the 11th floor, pulled her off the elevator, assaulted her, and stole her purse. Ms. Willey reported that she had seen the man in the elevators and hallways of the building before. She believes that the man works in the building. Her description of him is as follows: he is tall, unshaven, with wavy brown hair and a scar on his left cheek. He walks with a pronounced limp, often dragging his left foot behind his right.

CONCLUSION: After Beverly Willey makes her report, the police arrest a 43-year-old man, Barton Black, and charge him with her assault.

4 (#2)

10. Barton Black is a former Marine who served in Vietnam, where he sustained shrapnel wounds to the left side of his face and suffered nerve damage in his left leg.
    A. The statement proves the conclusion.
    B. The statement supports the conclusion but does not prove it.
    C. The statement disproves the conclusion.
    D. The statement weakens the conclusion but does not disprove it.
    E. The statement has no relevance to the conclusion.

10.____

11. When they arrived at his residence to question him, detectives were greeted at the door by Barton Black, who was tall and clean-shaven.
    A. The statement proves the conclusion.
    B. The statement supports the conclusion but does not prove it.
    C. The statement disproves the conclusion.
    D. The statement weakens the conclusion but does not disprove it.
    E. The statement has no relevance to the conclusion.

11.____

12. Barton Black was booked into the county jail several days after Beverly Willey's assault.
    A. The statement proves the conclusion.
    B. The statement supports the conclusion but does not prove it.
    C. The statement disproves the conclusion.
    D. The statement weakens the conclusion but does not disprove it.
    E. The statement has no relevance to the conclusion.

12.____

13. Upon further investigation, detectives discover that Beverly Willey does not work at the office building.
    A. The statement proves the conclusion.
    B. The statement supports the conclusion but does not prove it.
    C. The statement disproves the conclusion.
    D. The statement weakens the conclusion but does not disprove it.
    E. The statement has no relevance to the conclusion.

13.____

14. Upon further investigation, detectives discover that Barton Black does not work at the office building.
    A. The statement proves the conclusion.
    B. The statement supports the conclusion but does not prove it.
    C. The statement disproves the conclusion.
    D. The statement weakens the conclusion but does not disprove it.
    E. The statement has no relevance to the conclusion.

14.____

15. In the spring of the following year, Barton Black is convicted of assaulting Beverly Willey on August 11.
    A. The statement proves the conclusion.
    B. The statement supports the conclusion but does not prove it.
    C. The statement disproves the conclusion.
    D. The statement weakens the conclusion but does not disprove it.
    E. The statement has no relevance to the conclusion.

15.____

16. During their investigation of the assault, detectives determine that Beverly Willey was assaulted on the 12th floor of the office building.   16.____
    A. The statement proves the conclusion.
    B. The statement supports the conclusion but does not prove it.
    C. The statement disproves the conclusion.
    D. The statement weakens the conclusion but does not disprove it.
    E. The statement has no relevance to the conclusion.

17. The day after Beverly Willey's assault, Barton Black fled the area and was never seen again.   17.____
    A. The statement proves the conclusion.
    B. The statement supports the conclusion but does not prove it.
    C. The statement disproves the conclusion.
    D. The statement weakens the conclusion but does not disprove it.
    E. The statement has no relevance to the conclusion.

Questions 18-25.

DIRECTIONS: Questions 18 through 25 each provide four factual statements and a conclusion based on these statements. After reading the entire question, you will decide whether:
   A. The conclusion is proved by statements I-IV;
   B. The conclusion is disproved by statements I-IV.
   C. The facts are not sufficient to prove or disprove the conclusion.

18. FACTUAL STATEMENTS: 18.____
    I. Among five spice jars on the shelf, the sage is to the right of the parsley.
    II. The pepper is to the left of the basil.
    III. The nutmeg is between the sage and the pepper.
    IV. The pepper is the second spice from the left.

    CONCLUSION: The safe is the farthest to the right.
       A. The conclusion is proved by statements I-IV;
       B. The conclusion is disproved by statements I-IV.
       C. The facts are not sufficient to prove or disprove the conclusion.

19. FACTUAL STATEMENTS: 19.____
    I. Gear X rotates in a clockwise direction if Switch C is in the OFF position.
    II. Gear X will rotate in a counter-clockwise direction is Switch C is ON.
    III. If Gear X is rotating in a clockwise direction, then Gear Y will not be rotating at all.
    IV. Switch C is ON.

    CONCLUSION: Gear X is rotating in a counter-clockwise direction.
       A. The conclusion is proved by statements I-IV;
       B. The conclusion is disproved by statements I-IV.
       C. The facts are not sufficient to prove or disprove the conclusion.

20. FACTUAL STATEMENTS:
    I. Lane will leave for the Toronto meeting today only if Terence, Rourke, and Jackson all file their marketing reports by the end of the work day.
    II. Rourke will file her report on time only if Ganz submits last quarter's data.
    III. If Terence attends the security meeting, he will attend it with Jackson, and they will not file their marketing reports by the end of the work day.

    CONCLUSION: Lane will leave for the Toronto meeting today.
    A. The conclusion is proved by statements I-IV;
    B. The conclusion is disproved by statements I-IV.
    C. The facts are not sufficient to prove or disprove the conclusion.

21. FACTUAL STATEMENTS:
    I. Bob is in second place in the Boston Marathon.
    II. Gregory is winning the Boston Marathon.
    III. There are four miles to go in the race, and Bob is gaining on Gregory at the rate of 100 yards every minute.
    IV. There are 1760 yards in a mile and Gregory's usual pace during the Boston Marathon is one mile every six minutes.

    CONCLUSION: Bob wins the Boston Marathon.
    A. The conclusion is proved by statements I-IV;
    B. The conclusion is disproved by statements I-IV.
    C. The facts are not sufficient to prove or disprove the conclusion.

22. FACTUAL STATEMENTS:
    I. Four brothers are named Earl, John, Gary, and Pete.
    II. Earl and Pete are unmarried.
    III. John is shorter than the youngest of the four.
    IV. The oldest brother is married, and is also the tallest.

    CONCLUSION: Gary is the oldest brother.
    A. The conclusion is proved by statements I-IV;
    B. The conclusion is disproved by statements I-IV.
    C. The facts are not sufficient to prove or disprove the conclusion.

23. FACTUAL STATEMENTS:
    I. Brigade X is ten miles from the demilitarized zone.
    II. If General Woundwort gives the order, Brigade X will advance to the demilitarized zone, but not quickly enough to reach the zone before the conflict begins.
    III. Brigade Y, five miles behind Brigade X, will not advance unless General Woundwort gives the order.
    IV. Brigade Y advances.

CONCLUSION: Brigade X reaches the demilitarized zone before the conflict begins.
    A. The conclusion is proved by statements I-IV;
    B. The conclusion is disproved by statements I-IV.
    C. The facts are not sufficient to prove or disprove the conclusion.

24. FACTUAL STATEMENTS:
    I. Jerry has decided to take a cab from Fullerton to Elverton.
    II. Chubby Cab charges $5 plus $3 a mile.
    III. Orange Cab charges $7.50 but gives free mileage for the first 5 miles.
    IV. After the first 5 miles, Orange Cab charges $2.50 a mile.

CONCLUSION: Orange Cab is the cheaper fare from Fullerton to Elverton.
    A. The conclusion is proved by statements I-IV;
    B. The conclusion is disproved by statements I-IV.
    C. The facts are not sufficient to prove or disprove the conclusion.

25. FACTUAL STATEMENTS:
    I. Dan is never in class when his friend Lucy is absent.
    II. Lucy is never absent unless her mother is sick.
    III. If Lucy is in class, Sergio is in class also.
    IV. Sergio is never in class when Dalton is absent.

CONCLUSION: If Lucy is absent, Dalton may be in class.
    A. The conclusion is proved by statements I-IV;
    B. The conclusion is disproved by statements I-IV.
    C. The facts are not sufficient to prove or disprove the conclusion.

KEY (CORRECT ANSWERS)

1.	C	11.	E
2.	B	12.	B
3.	B	13.	D
4.	C	14.	E
5.	A	15.	A
6.	A	16.	E
7.	B	17.	C
8.	C	18.	B
9.	C	19.	A
10.	B	20.	C

21.	C
22.	A
23.	B
24.	A
25.	B

SOLUTIONS TO PROBLEMS

1. CORRECT ANSWER: C
   Statement 1 only tells us that some employees who work in the Testing Department are statisticians. This means that we need to allow the possibility that at least one person in this department is not a statistician. Thus, if a person works in the Testing Department, we cannot conclude whether or not this individual is a statistician.

2. CORRECT ANSWER: B
   If Hank had six coins, then the total of Gail's collection and Lawrence's collection would be four. Thus, if Gail gave all her coins to Lawrence, Lawrence would only have four coins. Thus, it would be impossible for Lawrence to have more coins than Hank.

3. CORRECT ANSWER: B
   Statement 1 tells us that nobody loves everybody. If everybody loved Janet, then Statement 3 would imply that Ken loves everybody. This would contradict statement 1. The conclusion is disproved.

4. CORRECT ANSWER: C
   Although most of the Torres family lives in East Los Angeles, we can assume that some members of this family do not live in East Los Angeles. Thus, we cannot prove or disprove that Joe, who is a member of the Torres family, lives in East Los Angeles.

5. CORRECT ANSWER: A
   Since Dr. Johnson is on the 4th floor, either (a) Dr. Kane is on the 5th floor and Dr. Conlon is on the 3rd floor, or (b) Dr. Kane is on the 3rd floor and Dr. Conlon is on the 5th floor. If option (b) were correct, then since Dr. Assad would be on the 1st floor, it would be impossible for Dr. Steen's office to be between Dr. Conlon and Dr. Assad's office. Therefore, Dr. Kane's office must be on the 5th floor. The order of the doctors' offices, from 5th floor down to the 1st floor is: Dr. Kane, Dr. Johnson, Dr. Conlon, Dr. Steen, Dr. Assad.

6. CORRECT ANSWER: A
   Ray does not satisfy the requirement of holding his breath for two minutes under water, since he can only hold is breath for one minute in that setting. But if he tunnels through a snowbank with just a T-shirt and shorts, he will satisfy the eligibility requirement. Note that the eligibility requirement contains the key word "or." So only one of the two clauses separated by "or" need to be fulfilled.

7. CORRECT ANSWER: B
   Statement 2 says that four sharps is equivalent to one tinplot. This means that a tinplot is worth more than a sharp. The conclusion is disproved. We note that the order of these items, from most valuable to least valuable are: tinplot, sharp, mark, plunk.

8. CORRECT ANSWER: C
   We can only conclude that gibbons and lemurs are fed lettuce and bananas. We can neither prove nor disprove that these animals are types of monkeys.

9. CORRECT ANSWER: C
We know that all Salishan Indians live east of the Continental Divide. But some non-members of this tribe of Indians may also live east of the Continental Divide. Since none of the members of the Blackfoot tribe belong to the Salishan Indian tribe, we cannot draw any conclusion about the location of the Blackfoot tribe with respect to the Continental Divide.

18. CORRECT ANSWER: B
Since the pepper is second from the left and the nutmeg is between the sage and the pepper, the positions 2, 3, and 4 (from the left) are pepper, nutmeg, sage. By statement II, the basil must be in position 5, which implies that the parsley is in position 1. Therefore, the basil, not the sage, is farthest to the right. The conclusion disproved.

19. CORRECT ANSWER: A
Statement II assures us that if switch C is ON, then Gear X is rotating in a counterclockwise direction. The conclusion is proved.

20. CORRECT ANSWER: C
Based on Statement IV, followed by Statement II, we conclude that Ganz and Rourke will file their reports on time. Statement III reveals that if Terence and Jackson attend the security meeting, they will fail to file their reports on time. We have no further information if Terence and Jackson attended the security meeting, so we are not able to either confirm or deny that their reports were filed on time. This implies that we cannot know for certain that Lane will leave for his meeting in Toronto.

21. CORRECT ANSWER: C
Although Bob is in second place behind Gregory, we cannot deduce how far behind Gregory he is running. At Gregory's current pace, he will cover four miles in 24 minutes. If Bob were only 100 yards behind Gregory, he would catch up to Gregory in one minute. But if Bob were very far behind Gregory, for example 5 miles, this is the equivalent of (5)(1760) = 8800 yards. Then Bob would need 8800/100 = 88 minutes to catch up to Gregory. Thus, the given facts are not sufficient to draw a conclusion.

22. CORRECT ANSWER: A
Statement II tells us that neither Earl nor Pete could be the oldest; also, either John or Gary is married. Statement IV reveals that the oldest brother is both married and the tallest. By Statement III, John cannot be the tallest. Since John is not the tallest, he is not the oldest. Thus, the oldest brother must be Gary. The conclusion is proved.

23. CORRECT ANSWER: B
By Statements III and IV, General Woundwort must have given the order to advance. Statement II then tells us that Brigade X will advance to the demilitarized zone, but not soon enough before the conflict begins. Thus, the conclusion is disproved.

11 (#2)

24. CORRECT ANSWER: A
If the distance is 5 miles or less, then the cost for the Orange Cab is only $7.50, whereas the cost for the Chubby Cab is $5 + 3x, where x represents the number of miles traveled. For 1 to 5 miles, the cost of the Chubby Cab is between $8 and $20. This means that for a distance of 5 miles, the Orange Cab costs $7.50, whereas the Chubby Cab costs $20. After 5 miles, the cost per mile of the Chubby Cab exceeds the cost per mile of the Orange Cab. Thus, regardless of the actual distance between Fullerton and Elverton, the cost for the Orange Cab will be cheaper than that of the Chubby Cab.

25. CORRECT ANSWER: B
It looks like "Dalton" should be replaced by "Dan" in the conclusion. Then by statement I, if Lucy is absent, Dan is never in class. Thus, the conclusion is disproved.

LOGICAL REASONING
EVALUATING CONCLUSIONS IN LIGHT OF KNOWN FACTS
EXAMINATION SECTION
TEST 1

COMMENTARY

This section is designed to provide practice questions in evaluating conclusions when you are given specific data to work with.

We suggest you do the questions three at a time, consulting the answer key and then the solution section for any questions you may have missed. It's a good idea to try the questions again a week before the exam.

In the validity of conclusion type of question, you are first given a reading passage which describes a particular situation. The passage may be on any topic, as it is not your knowledge of the topic that is being tested, but your reasoning abilities. The passage is likely to detail several proposed courses of action and factors affecting these proposals. The reading passage is followed by a conclusion based on the facts in the passage, or a description of a decision taken regarding the situation. The conclusion is followed by a number of statements which have a possible connection to the conclusion. For each statement, you are to determine whether:

A. The statement proves the conclusion.
B. The statement supports the conclusion but does not prove it.
C. The statement disproves the conclusion.
D. The statement weakens the conclusion but does not disprove it.
E. The statement has no relevance to the conclusion.

Remember that the conclusion after the passage is to be accepted as the outcome of what actually happened, and that you are being asked to evaluate the impact each statement would have had on the conclusion.

Questions 1-8.

DIRECTIONS: Questions 1 through 8 are based on the following paragraph.

In May of 2018, Mr. Bryan inherited a clothing store on Main Street in a small New England town. The store has specialized in selling quality men's and women's clothing since 1920. Business has been stable throughout the years, neither increasing nor decreasing. He has an opportunity to buy two adjacent stores which would enable him to add a wider range and style of clothing. In order to do this, he would have to borrow a substantial amount of money. He also risks losing the goodwill of his present clientele.

CONCLUSION: On November 7, 2018, Mr. Bryan tells the owner of the two adjacent stores that he has decided not to purchase them. He feels that it would be best to simply maintain his present marketing position, as there would not be enough new business to support an expansion.

A. The statement proves the conclusion.
B. The statement supports the conclusion but does not prove it.
C. The statement disproves the conclusion.
D. The statement weakens the conclusion.
E. The statement is irrelevant to the conclusion.

1. A large new branch of the county's community college holds its first classes in September. 1.____

2. The town's largest factory shuts down with no indication that it will reopen. 2.____

3. The United States Census showed that the number of children per household dropped from 2.4 to 2.1 since the last census. 3.____

4. Mr. Bryan's brother tells him of a new clothing boutique specializing in casual women's clothing which is opening soon. 4.____

5. Mr. Bryan's sister buys her baby several items for Christmas at Mr. Bryan's store. 5.____

6. Mrs. McIntyre, the President of the Town Council, brings Mr. Bryan a home-baked pumpkin pie in honor of his store's 100th anniversary. They discuss the changes that have taken place in the town, and she comments on how his store has maintained the same look and feel over the years. 6.____

7. In October, Mr. Bryan's aunt lends him $50,000. 7.____

8. The Town Council has just announced that the town is eligible for funding from a federal project designed to encourage the location of new businesses in the central districts of cities and towns. 8.____

Questions 9-18.

DIRECTIONS: Questions 9 through 18 are based on the following paragraph.

A proposal was put before the legislative body of a country to require air bags in all automobiles manufactured for domestic use in that country after 2019. The air bag, made of nylon or plastic, is designed to inflate automatically within a car at the impact of a collision, thus protecting front-seat occupants from being thrown forward. There has been much support of the measure from consumer groups, the insurance industry, key legislators, and the general public. The country's automobile manufacturers, who contend the new crash equipment would add up to $1,000 to car prices and provide no more protection than existing seat belts, are against the proposed legislation

CONCLUSION: On April 21, 2014, the legislation requiring air bags in all automobiles manufactured for domestic use in that country after 2019.

A. The statement proves the conclusion.
B. The statement supports the conclusion but does not prove it.
C. The statement disproves the conclusion.
D. The statement weakens the conclusion.
E. The statement is irrelevant to the conclusion.

9. A study has shown that 59% of car occupants do not use seat belts. 9._____

10. The country's Department of Transportation has estimated that the crash protection equipment would save up to 5,900 lives each year. 10._____

11. On April 27, 2013, Augusta Raneoni was named head of an advisory committee to gather and analyze data on the costs, benefits, and feasibility of the proposed legislation on air bags in automobiles. 11._____

12. Consumer groups and the insurance industry accuse the legislature of rejecting passage of the regulation for political reasons. 12._____

13. A study by the Committee on Imports and Exports projected that the sales of imported cars would rise dramatically in 2019 because imported cars do not have to include air bags, and can be sold more cheaply. 13._____

14. Research has shown that air bags, if produced on a large scale, would cost about $200 apiece, and would provide more reliable protection than any other type of seat belt. 14._____

15. Auto sales in 2011 increased 3% over the previous year. 15._____

16. A Department of Transportation report in July of 2020 credits a drop in automobile deaths of 4,100 to the use of air bags. 16._____

17. In June of 2014, the lobbyist of the largest insurance company receives a bonus for her work on the passage of the air bag legislation. 17._____

18. In 2020, the stock in crash protection equipment has risen three-fold over the previous year. 18._____

Questions 19-25.

DIRECTIONS: Questions 19 through 25 are based on the following paragraph.

On a national television talk show, Joan Rivera, a famous comedienne, has recently insulted the physical appearances of a famous actress and the dead wife of an ex-President. There has been a flurry of controversy over her comments, and much discussion of the incident has appeared in the press. Most of the comments have been negative. It appears that this tie she might have gone too far. There have been cancellations of two of her five scheduled performances in the two weeks since the show was televised, and Joan's been receiving a lot of negative mail. Because of the controversy, she has an interview with a national news magazine at the end of the week, and her press agent is strongly urging her to apologize publicly. She feels strongly that her comments were no worse than any other she has ever made, and that the whole incident will *blow over* soon. She respects her press agent's judgment, however, as his assessment of public sentiment tends to be very accurate.

CONCLUSION: Joan does not apologize publicly, and during the interview she challenges the actress to a weight-losing contest. For every pound the actress loses, Joan says she will donate $1 to the Cellulite Prevention League.

A. The statement proves the conclusion.
   B. The statement supports the conclusion but does not prove it.
   C. The statement disproves the conclusion.
   D. The statement weakens the conclusion.
   E. The statement is irrelevant to the conclusion.

19. Joan's mother, who she is very fond of, is very upset with Joan's comments. 19._____

20. Six months after the interview, Joan's income has doubled. 20._____

21. Joan's agent is pleased with the way Joan handles the interview. 21._____

22. Joan's sister has been appointed Treasurer of the Cellulite Prevention League In her report, she states that Joan's $12 contribution is the only amount that has been donated to the League in its first six months. 22._____

23. The magazine receives many letters commending Joan for the courage it took for her to apologize publicly in the interview. 23._____

24. Immediately after the interview appears, another one of Joan's performances is cancelled. 24._____

25. Due to a printers' strike, the article was not published until the following week. 25._____

Questions 26-30.

DIRECTIONS: Questions 25 through 30 are based on the following paragraph.

The law-making body of Country X must decide what to do about the issue of recording television shows for home use. There is currently no law against recording shows directly from the TV as long as the DVDs are not used for commercial purposes. The increasing popularity of pay TV and satellite systems, combined with the increasing number of homes that own recording equipment, has caused a great deal of concern in some segments of the entertainment industry. Companies that own the rights to films, popular television shows, and sporting events feel that their copyright privileges are being violated, and they are seeking compensation or the banning of TV recording. Legislation has been introduced to make it illegal to record television programs for home use. Separate proposed legislation is also pending that would continue to allow recording of TV shows for home use, but would place a tax of 10% on each DVD that is purchased for home use. The income from that tax would then be proportionately distributed as royalties to those owning the rights to programs being aired. A weighted point system coupled with the averaging of several national viewing rating systems would be used to determine the royalties. There is a great deal of lobbying being done for both bills, as the manufacturers of DVDs and recording equipment are against the passage of the bills.

CONCLUSION: The legislature of Country X rejects both bills by a wide margin.

- A. The statement proves the conclusion.
    - B. The statement supports the conclusion but does not prove it.
    - C. The statement disproves the conclusion.
    - D. The statement weakens the conclusion.
    - E. The statement is irrelevant to the conclusion.

26. Country X's Department of Taxation hires 500 new employees to handle the increased paperwork created by the new tax on DVDs. 26.____

27. A study conducted by the country's most prestigious accounting firm shows that the cost of implementing the proposed new DVD tax would be greater than the income expected from it. 27.____

28. It is estimated that 80% of all those working in the entertainment industry, excluding performers, own DVD recorders. 28.____

29. The head of Country X's law enforcement agency states that legislation banning the home recording of TV shows would be unenforceable. 29.____

30. Financial experts predict that unless a tax is placed on DVDs, several large companies in the entertainment industry will have to file for bankruptcy. 30.____

Questions 31-38.

DIRECTIONS: Questions 31 through 38 are variations on the type of question you just had. It is important that you read the question very carefully to determine exactly what is required.

31. In this question, select the choice that is MOST relevant to the conclusion. 31.____
    I. The Buffalo Bills football team is in second place in its division.
    II. The New England Patriots are in first place in the same division.
    III. There are two games left to play in the season, and the Bills will not play the Patriots again.
    IV. The New England Patriots won ten games and lost four games, and the Buffalo Bills have won eight games and lost six games.
    CONCLUSION: The Buffalo Bills win their division.
    A. The conclusion is proved by sentences I-IV.
    B. The conclusion is disproved by sentences I-IV.
    C. The facts are not sufficient to prove or disprove the conclusion.

32. In this question, select the choice that is MOST relevant to the conclusion.
    I. On the planet of Zeinon there are only two different eye colors and only two different hair colors.
    II. Half of those beings with purple hair have golden eyes.
    III. There are more inhabitants with purple hair than there are inhabitants with silver hair.
    IV. One-third of those with silver hair have green eyes.
    CONCLUSION: There are more golden-eyed beings on Zeinon than green-eyed ones.
    A. The conclusion is proved by sentences I-IV.
    B. The conclusion is disproved by sentences I-IV.
    C. The facts are not sufficient to prove or disprove the conclusion.

33. In this question, select the choice that is MOST relevant to the conclusion.
    John and Kevin are leaving Amaranth to go to school in Bethany. They've decided to rent a small truck to move their possessions. Joe's Truck Rental charges $100 plus 30¢ a mile. National Movers charges $50 more but gives free mileage for the first 100 miles. After the first 100 miles, they charge 25¢ a mile.
    CONCLUSION: John and Kevin rent their truck from National Movers because it is cheaper.
    A. The conclusion is proved by the facts in the above paragraph.
    B. The conclusion is disproved by the facts in the above paragraph.
    C. The facts are not sufficient to prove or disprove the conclusion.

34. For this question, select the choice that supports the information given in the passage.
    Municipalities in Country X are divided into villages, towns, and cities. A village has a population of 5,000 or less. The population of a town ranges from 5,001 to 15,000. In order to be incorporated as a city, the municipality must have a population over 15,000. If, after a village becomes a town, or a town becomes a city, the population drops below the minimum required (for example, the population of a city goes below 15,000), and stays below the minimum for more than ten years, it loses its current status, and drops to the next category. As soon as a municipality rises in population to the next category (village to town, for example), however, it is immediately reclassified to the next category.
    In the 2000 census, Plainfield had a population of 12,000. Between 2000 and 2010, Plainfield grew 10%, and between 2010 and 2020 Plainfield grew another 20%. The population of Springdale doubled from 2000 to 2010, and increased 25% from 2010 to 2020. The city of Smallville's population, 20,283, has not changed significantly in recent years. Granton had a population of 25,000 people in 1990, and has decreased 25% in each ten year period since then. Ellenville had a population of 4,283 in 1990, and grew 5% in each ten year period since 1990.

In 2020,
- A. Plainfield, Smallville, and Granton are cities.
- B. Smallville is a city, Granton is a town, and Ellenville is a village.
- C. Springdale, Granton, and Ellenville are towns.
- D. Plainfield and Smallville are cities, and Ellenville is a town.

35. For this question, select the choice that is MOST relevant to the conclusion.

    A study was done for a major food-distributing firm to determine if there is any difference in the kind of caffeine containing products used by people of different ages. A sample of one thousand people between the ages of twenty and fifty were drawn from selected areas in the country. They were divided equally into three groups.

    Those individuals who were 20-29 were designated Group A, those 30-39 were Group B, and those 40-50 were placed in Group C.

    It was found that on the average, Group A drank 1.8 cups of coffee, Group B 3.1, and Group C 2.5 cups of coffee daily. Group A drank 2.1 cups of tea, Group B drank 1.2, and Group C drank 2.6 cups of tea daily. Group A drank 3 1.8 ounces glasses of cola, Group B drank 1.9, and Group C drank 1.5 glasses of cola daily.

    CONCLUSION: According to the study, the average person in the 20-29 age group drinks less tea daily than the average person in the 40-50 age group, but drinks more coffee daily than the average person in the 30-39 age group drinks cola.
    - A. The conclusion is proved by the facts in the above paragraph.
    - B. The conclusion is disproved by the facts in the above paragraph.
    - C. The facts are not sufficient to prove or disprove the conclusion.

35.____

36. For this question, select the choice that is MOST relevant to the conclusion
    I. Mary is taller than Jane but shorter than Dale.
    II. Fred is taller than Mary but shorter than Steven.
    III. Dale is shorter than Steven but taller than Elizabeth.
    IV. Elizabeth is taller than Mary but not as tall as Fred.
    CONCLUSION: Dale is taller than Fred.
    - A. The conclusion is proved by sentences I-IV.
    - B. The conclusion is disproved by sentences I-IV.
    - C. The facts are not sufficient to prove or disprove the conclusion.

36.____

37. For this question, select the choice that is MOST relevant to the conclusion.
    I. Main Street is between Spring Street and Glenn Blvd.
    II. Hawley Avenue is one block south of Spring Street and three blocks north of Main Street.
    III. Glenn Street is five blocks south of Elm and four blocks south of Main.
    IV. All the streets mentioned are parallel to one another.
    CONCLUSION: Elm Street is between Hawley Avenue and Glenn Blvd.
    - A. The conclusion is proved by the facts in sentences I-IV.
    - B. The conclusion is disproved by the facts in sentences I-IV.
    - C. The facts are not sufficient to prove or disprove the conclusion.

37.____

38. For this question, select the choice that is MOST relevant to the conclusion. 38.____
    I. Train A leaves the town of Hampshire every day at 5:50 A.M. and arrives in New London at 6:42 A.M.
    II. Train A leaves New London at 7:00 A.M. and arrives in Kellogsville at 8:42 A.M.
    III. Train B leaves Kellogsville at 8:00 A.M. and arrives in Hampshire at 10:45 A.M.
    IV. Due to the need for repairs, there is just one railroad track between New London and Hampshire.
    CONCLUSION: It is impossible for Train A and Train B to follow these schedules without colliding.
    A. The conclusion is proved by the facts in sentences I-IV.
    B. The conclusion is disproved by the facts in sentences I-IV.
    C. The facts are not sufficient to prove or disprove the conclusion.

KEY (CORRECT ANSWERS)

1.	D	11.	C	21.	D	31.	C
2.	B	12.	C	22.	A	32.	A
3.	E	13.	D	23.	C	33.	C
4.	B	14.	B	24.	B	34.	B
5.	C	15.	E	25.	E	35.	B
6.	A	16.	B	26.	C	36.	C
7.	D	17.	A	27.	B	37.	A
8.	B	18.	B	28.	E	38.	B
9.	B	19.	D	29.	B		
10.	B	20.	E	30.	D		

SOLUTIONS TO QUESTIONS

1. The answer is D. This statement weakens the conclusion, but does not disprove it. If a new branch of the community college opened in September, it could possibly bring in new business for Mr. Bryant. Since it states in the conclusion that Mr. Bryant felt there would not be enough new business to support the additional stores, this would tend to disprove the conclusion. Choice C would not be correct because it's possible that he felt that the students would not have enough additional money to support his new venture, or would not be interested in his clothing styles. It's also possible that the majority of the students already live in the area, so that they wouldn't really be a new customer population. This type of question is tricky, and can initially be very confusing, so don't feel badly if you missed it. Most people need to practice with a few of these types of questions before they feel comfortable recognizing exactly what they're being asked to do.

2. The answer is B. It supports the conclusion because the closing of the factory would probably take money and customers out of the town, causing Mr. Bryant to lose some of his present business. It doesn't prove the conclusion, however, because we don't know how large the factory was. It's possible that only a small percentage of the population was employed there, or that they found other jobs.

3. The answer is E. The fact that the number of children per household dropped slightly nationwide in the decade is irrelevant. Statistics showing a drop nationwide doesn't mean that there was a drop in the number of children per household in Mr. Bryant's hometown. This is a tricky question, as choice B, supporting the conclusion but not proving it, may seem reasonable. If the number of children per household declined nationwide, then it may not seem unreasonable to feel that this would support Mr. Bryant's decision not to expand his business. However, we're preparing you for promotional exams, not "real life." One of the difficult things about taking exams is that sometimes you're forced to make a choice between two statements that both seem like they could be the possible answer. What you need to do in that case is choose the best choice. Becoming annoyed or frustrated with the question won't really help much. If there's a review of the exam, you can certainly appeal the question. There have been many cases where, after an appeal, two possible choices have been allowed as correct answers. We've included this question, however, to help you see what to do should you get a question like this. It's most important not to get rattled, and to select the BEST choice. In this case, the connection between the statistical information and Mr. Bryant's decision is pretty remote. If the question had said that the number of children in Mr. Bryant's <u>town</u> had decreased, then choice B would have been a more reasonable choice. It could also help in this situation to visualize the situation. Picture Mr. Bryant in his armchair reading that, nationwide, the average number of children per household has declined slightly. How likely would this be to influence his decision, especially since he sells men's and women's clothing? It would take a while for this decline in population to show up, and we're not even sure if it applies to Mr. Bryant's hometown. Don't feel badly if you missed this; it was tricky. The more of these you do, the more comfortable you'll feel.

4. The answer is B. If a new clothing boutique specializing in casual women's clothing were to open soon, this would lend support to Mr. Bryant's decision not to expand, but would not prove that he had actually made the decision to expand. A new women's clothing boutique would most likely be in competition with his existing business, thus making any possible expansion a riskier venture. We can't be sure from this, however, that he didn't go ahead and expand his business despite the increased competition. Choice A, proves the conclusion, would only be the answer if we could be absolutely sure from the statement that Mr. Bryant had actually not expanded his business.

5. The answer is C. This statement disproves the conclusion. In order for his sister to buy several items for her baby at Mr. Bryant's store, he would have to have changed his business to include children's clothing.

6. The answer is A. It definitely proves the conclusion. The passage states that Mr. Bryan's store had been in business since 1920. A pie baked in honor of his store's 100th anniversary would have to be presented sometime in 2020. The conclusion states that he made his decision not to expand on November 7, 2018. If, more than a year later Mrs. MacIntyre comments that his store has maintained the same look and feel over the years, it could not have been expanded, or otherwise significantly changed.

7. The answer is D. If Mr. Bryant's aunt lent him $50,000 in October, this would tend to weaken the conclusion, which took place in November. Because it was stated that Mr. Bryant would need to borrow money in order to expand his business, it would be logical to assume that if he borrowed money he had decided to expand his business, weakening the conclusion. The reason C, disproves the conclusion, is not the correct answer is because we can't be sure Mr. Bryant didn't borrow the money for another reason.

8. The answer is B. If Mr. Bryant's town is eligible for federal funds to encourage the location of new businesses in the central district, this would tend to support his decision not to expand his business. Funds to encourage new business would increase the likelihood of there being additional competition for Mr. Bryant's store to contend with. Since we can't say for sure that there would be direct competition from a new business, however, choice A would be incorrect. Note that this is also a tricky question. You might have thought that the new funds weakened the conclusion because it would mean that Mr. Bryant could easily get the money he needed. Mr. Bryant is expanding his present business, not creating a new business. Therefore, he is not eligible for the funding.

9. The answer is B. This is a very tricky question. It's stated that 59% of car occupants don't use seat belts. The legislature is considering the use of air bags because of safety issues. The advantage of air bags over seat belts is that they inflate upon impact, and don't require car occupants to do anything with them ahead of time. Since the population has strongly resisted using seat belts, the air bags could become even more important in saving lives. Since saving lives is the purpose of the proposed legislation, the information that a small percentage of people use seat belts could be helpful to the passage of the legislation. We can't be sure that this is reason enough for the legislature to vote for the legislation, however, so choice A in incorrect.

10. The answer is B, as the information that 5,900 lives could be saved would tend to support the conclusion. Saving that many lives through the use of air bags could be a very persuasive reason to vote for the legislation. Since we don't know for sure that it's enough of a compelling reason for the legislature to vote for the legislation, however, choice A could not be the answer.

11. The answer is C, disproves the conclusion. If the legislation had been passed as stated in the conclusion, there would be no reason to appoint someone head of an advisory committee six days later to analyze the "feasibility of the proposed legislation." The key word here is "proposed." If it has been proposed, it means it hasn't been passed. This contradicts the conclusion and, therefore, disproves it.

12. The answer is C, disproves the conclusion. If the legislation had passed, there would be no reason for supporters of the legislation to accuse the legislature of rejecting the legislation for political reasons. This question may have seemed so obvious that you might have thought there was a trick to it. Exams usually have a few obvious questions, which will trip you up if you begin reading too much into them.

13. The answer is D, as this would tend to disprove the conclusion. A projected dramatic rise in imported cars could be very harmful to the country's economy and could be a very good reason for some legislators to vote against the proposed legislation. It would be assuming too much to choose C, however, because we don't know if they actually did vote against it.

14. The answer is B. This information would tend to support the passage of the legislation. The estimate of the cost of the air bags is $800 less than the cost estimated by opponents, and it's stated that the protection would be more reliable than any other type of seat belt. Both of these would be good arguments in favor of passing the legislation. Since we don't know for sure, however, how persuasive they actually were, choice A would not be the correct choice.

15. The answer is E, as this is irrelevant information. It really doesn't matter whether auto sales in 2001 have increased slightly over the previous year. If the air bag legislation were to go into effect in 2004, that might make the information somehow more relevant. But the air bag legislation would not take effect until 2009, so the information is irrelevant, since it tells us nothing about the state of the auto industry then.

16. The answer is B, supports the conclusion. This is a tricky question. While at first it might seem to prove the conclusion, we can't be sure that the air bag legislation is responsible for the drop in automobile deaths. It's possible air bags came into popular use without the legislation, or with different legislation. There's no way we can be sure that it was the proposed legislation mandating the use of air bags that was responsible.

17. The answer is A. If, in June of 2009, the lobbyist received a bonus "for her work on the air bag legislation," we can be sure that the legislation passed. This proves the conclusion.

18. The answer is B. This is another tricky question. A three-fold stock increase would strongly suggest that the legislation had been passed, but it's possible that factors other than the air bag legislation caused the increase. Note that the stock is in "crash protection

equipment." Nowhere in the statement does it say air bags. Seat belts, motorcycle helmets, and collapsible bumpers are all crash protection equipment and could have contributed to the increase. This is just another reminder to read carefully because the questions are often designed to mislead you.

19. The answer is D. This would tend to weaken the conclusion because Joan is very fond of her mother and she would not want to upset her unnecessarily. It does not prove it, however, because if Joan strongly feels she is right, she probably wouldn't let her mother's opinion sway her. Choice E would also not be correct, because we cannot assume that Joan's mother's opinion is of so little importance to her as to be considered irrelevant.

20. The answer is E. The statement is irrelevant. We are told that Joan's income has doubled but we are not old why. The phrase "six months after the interview" can be misleading in that it leads us to assume that the increase and the interview are related. Her income could have doubled because she regained her popularity but it could also have come from stocks or some other business venture. Because we are not given any reason for her income doubling, it would be impossible to say whether or not this statement proves or disproves the conclusion. Choice E is the best choice of the five possible choices. One of the problems with promotional exams is that sometimes you need to select a choice you're not crazy about. In this case, "not having enough information to made a determination" would be the best choice. However, that's not an option, so you're forced to work with what you've got. On these exams it's sometimes like voting for President; you have to pick the "lesser of the two evils" or the least awful choice. In this case, the information is more irrelevant to the conclusion than it is anything else.

21. The answer is D, weakens the conclusion. We've been told that Joan's agent feels that she should apologize. If he is pleased with her interview, then it would tend to weaken the conclusion but not disprove it. We can't be sure that he hasn't had a change of heart, or that there weren't other parts of the interview he liked so much that they outweighed her unwillingness to apologize.

22. The answer is A. The conclusion states that Joan will donate $1 to the Cellulite Prevention League for every pound the actress loses. Joan's sister's financial report on the League's activities directly supports and proves the conclusion.

23. The answer is C, disproves the conclusion. If the magazine receives many letters commending Joan for her courage in apologizing, this directly contradicts the conclusion, which states that Joan didn't apologize.

24. The answer is B. It was stated in the passage that two of Joan's performances were cancelled after the controversy first occurred. The cancellation of another performance immediately after her interview was published would tend to support the conclusion that she refused to apologize. Because we can't be sure, however, that her performance wasn't cancelled for another reason, choice A would be incorrect.

25. The answer is E, as this information is irrelevant. Postponing the article an extra week does not affect Joan's decision or the public's reaction to it.

26. The answer is C. If 500 new employees are hired to handle the "increased paperwork created by the new tax on DVDs," this would directly contradict the conclusion, which states that the legislature defeated both bills. (They should all be this easy.)

27. The answer is B. The results of the study would support the conclusion. If implementing the legislation was going to be so costly, it is likely that the legislature would vote against it. Choice A is not the answer, however, because we can't be sure that the legislature didn't pass it anyway.

28. The answer is E. It's irrelevant to the conclusion that 80% of all those working in the entertainment industry own DVD recorders. Sometimes if you're not sure about these, it can help a lot to try and visualize the situation. Why would someone voting on this legislation care about this fact? It doesn't seem to be the kind of information that would make any difference or impact upon the conclusion.

29. The answer is B. The head of the law enforcement agency's statement that the legislation would be unenforceable would support the conclusion. It's possible that many legislators would question why they should bother to pass legislation that would be impossible to enforce. Choice A would be incorrect, however, because we can't be sure that the legislation wasn't passed in spite of his statement.

30. The answer is D. This would tend to weaken the conclusion because the prospect of several large companies going bankrupt would seem to be a good argument in favor of the legislation. The possible loss of jobs and businesses would be a good reason for some people to vote for the legislation. We can't be sure, however, that this would be a competing enough reason to ensure passage of the legislation so choice C is incorrect.

This concludes our section on the "Validity of Conclusion" type of questions. We hope these weren't too horrible for you. It's important to keep in mind exactly what you've been given and exactly what they want you to do with it. It's also necessary to remember that you may have to choose between two possible answers. In that case, you must choose the one that seems the best. Sometimes you may think there is no good answer. You will probably be right, but you can't let that upset you. Just choose the one you dislike the least.

We want to repeat that it is unlikely that this exact format will appear on the exam. The skills required to answer these questions, however, are the same as those you'll need for the exam so we suggest that you review this section before taking the actual exam.

31. The answer is C. This next set of questions requires you to "switch gears" slightly, and get used to different formats. In this type of question, you have to decide whether the conclusion is proved by the facts give, disproved by the facts given, or neither because note enough information has been provided. Fortunately, unlike the previous questions, you don't have to decide whether particular facts support or don't support the conclusion. This type of question is more straight forward, but the reasoning behind it is the same. We are told that the Bills have won two games less than the Patriots, and that the Patriots are in first place and the Bills are in second place. We are also told that there are two games left to play, and that they won't play each other again. The conclusion states that the Bills won the division. Is there anything in the four statements that would prove this? We have

no idea what the outcome of the last two games of the season was. The Bills and Patriots could have ended up tied at the end of the season, or the Bills could have lost both or one of their last games while the Patriots did the same. There might even be another team tied for first or second place with the Bills or Patriots. Since we don't know for sure, Choice A is incorrect. Choice B is trickier. It might seem at first glance that the best the Bills could do would be to tie the Patriots if the Patriots lost their last two games and the Bills won their last two games. But it would be too much to assume that there is no procedure for a tiebreaker that wouldn't give the Bills the division championship. Since we don't know what the rules are in the event of a tie (for example, what if a tie was decided on the results of what happened when the two teams had played each other, or on the best record in the division, or on most points scored?), we can't say for sure that it would be impossible for the Bills to win their division. For this reason, choice C is the answer, as we don't have enough information to prove or disprove the conclusion. This question looked more difficult than it actually was. It's important to disregard any factors outside of the actual question, and to focus only on what you've been given. In this case, as on all of these types of questions, what you know or don't know about a subject is actually irrelevant. It's best to concentrate only on the actual facts given.

32. The answer is A. The conclusion is proved by the facts given.

In this type of problem, it is usually best to pull as many facts as possible from the sentences and then put them into a simpler form. The phrasing and the order of exam questions are designed to be confusing so you need to restate things as clearly as possible by eliminating the extras.

Sentence I tells us that there are only two possible colors for eyes and two for hair. Looking at the other sentences we learn that eyes are either green or gold and that hair is either silver or purple. If half the beings with purple hair have golden eyes, then the other half must have green eyes since it is the only other eye color. Likewise, if one-third of those with silver hair have green eyes, the other two-thirds must have golden eyes.

This information makes it clear that there are more golden-eyed beings on Zeinon than green-eyed ones. It doesn't matter that we don't know exactly how many are actually living on the planet. The number of those with gold eyes (1/2 plus 2/3) will always be greater than the number of those with green eyes (1/2 plus 1/3), no matter what the actual figures might be. Sentence III is totally irrelevant because even if there were more silver-haired inhabitants it would not affect the conclusion.

33. The answer is C. The conclusion is neither proved nor disproved by the facts because we don't know how many miles Bethany is from Amoranth.

With this type of question, if you're not sure how to approach it, you can always substitute in a range of "real numbers" to see what the result would be. If they were 200 miles apart, Joe's Truck Rental would be cheaper because they would charge a total of $160 while National Movers would charge $175.

Joe's - $100 plus .30 x 200 (or $60) = $160
National - $150 plus .25 x 100 (or $25) = $175

If the towns were 600 miles apart, however, National Movers would be cheaper. The cost of renting from National would be $275 compared to the $280 charged by Joe's Trucking.

Joe's - $100 plus .30 x 600 (or $180) = $280
National - $150 plus .25 x 500 (or $125) = $275

15 (#1)

34. The answer is B. We've varied the format once more, but the reasoning is similar. This is a tedious question that is more like a math question, but we wanted to give you some practice with this type, just in case. You won't be able to do this question if you've forgotten how to do percents. Many exams require this knowledge, so if you feel you need a review we suggest you read Booklets 1, 2 or 3 in this series.

The only way to attack this problem is to go through each choice until you find the one that is correct. Choice A states that Plainfield, Smallville, and Granton are cities. Let's begin with Plainfield. The passage states that in 1990 Plainfield had a population of 12,000, and that it grew 10% between 1990 and 2000, and another 20% between 2000 and 2010. Ten percent of 12,000 is 1200 (12,000 x .10 = 1200). Therefore, the population grew from 12,000 in 1990 to 12,000 + 1200 between 1990 and 2000. At the time of the 2000 Census, Plainfield's population was 13,200. It then grew another 20% between 2000 and 2010, so, 13,200 x .20 = 2640. 13,200 plus the additional increase of 2640 would make the population of Plainfield 15,840. This would qualify it as a city, since its population is over 15,000. Since a change upward in the population of a municipality is re-classified immediately, Plainfield would have become a city right away. So far, statement A is true. The passage states that Smallville's population has not changed significantly in the last twenty years. Since Smallville's population was 20,283, Smallville would still be a city. Granton had a population of 25,000 (what a coincidence that so any of these places have such nice, even numbers) in 1980. The population has decreased 25% in each ten year period since that time. So from 1980 to 1990, the population decreased 25%. 25,000 x .25 = 6,250. 25,000 minus 6,250 = 18,750. So the population of Granton in 1990 would have been 18,750. (Or, you could have saved a step and multiplied 25,000 by .75 to get 18,750.) The population from 1990 to 2000 decreased an additional 25%. So: 18,750 x .25 = 4,687.50. 18,750 minus 4,687.50 = 14,062.50. Or: 18,750 x .75 = 14,062.50. (Don't let the fact that a half of a person is involved confuse you; these are exam questions, not real life.) From 2000 to 2010 the population decreased an additional 25%. This would mean that Granton's population was below 15,000 for more than ten years, so it's status as a city would have changed to that of a town, which would make choice A incorrect.

Choice B states that Smallville is a city and Granton is a town, which we know to be true from the information above. Choice B is correct so far. We next need to determine if Ellenville is a village. Ellenville had a population of 4,283 in 1980, and increased 5% in each ten year period since 1980. 4,283 x .05 = 214.15. 4,283 plus 214.15 = 4,497.15, so Ellenville's population from 1980 to 1990 increased to 4,497.15. (Or: 4,283 x 1.05 – 4,497.15.) From 1990 to 2000 Ellenville's population increased another 5%: 4,497.15 x .05 = 224.86. 4,497.15 plus 224.86 = 4,772.01 (or: 4,497.15 x 1.05 = 4,722.01.) From 2000 to 2010, Ellenville's population increased another 5%: 4,722.01 x .05 = 236.10. 4,722.01 plus 236.10 = 4,958.11. (Or: 4,722.01 x 1.05 = 4,958.11.).
Ellenville's population is still under 5,000 in 2010, so it would continue to be classified as a village. Since all three statements in choice B are true, choice B must be the answer. However, we'll go through the other choices. Choice C states that Springdale is a town. The passage tells us that the population of Springdale doubled from 1990 to 2000, and increased 25% from 2000 to 2010. It doesn't give us any actual population figures, however, so it's impossible to know what the population of Springdale is, making choice C incorrect. Choice C also states that Granton is a town, which is true, and that Ellenville is

a town, which is false (from choice B we know it's a village). Choice D states that Plainfield and Smallville are cities, which is information we already know is true, and that Ellenville is a town. Since Ellenville is a village, choice D is also incorrect.

This was a lot of work for just one question and we doubt you'll get one like this on this section of the exam, but we included it just in case. On an exam, you can always put a check mark next to a question like this and come back to it later, if you feel you're pressed for time and cold spend your time more productively on other, less time-consuming problems.

35. The answer is B. This question requires very careful reading. It's best to break the conclusion down into smaller parts in order to solve the problem. The first half of the conclusion states that the average person in the 20-29 age group (Group A) drinks less tea daily than the average person in the 40-50 age group (Group C). The average person in Group A drinks 2.1 cups of tea daily, while the average person in Group C drinks 2.6 cups of tea daily. Since 2.1 is less than 2.6, the conclusion is correct so far. The second half of the conclusion states that the average person in Group A drinks more coffee daily than the average person in the 30-39 age group (Group B) drinks cola. The average person in Group A drinks 1.8 cups of coffee daily, while the average person in Group B drinks 1.9 glasses of cola. This disproves the conclusion, which states that the average person in Group A drinks more coffee daily than the average person in Group B drinks cola.

36. The answer is C. The easiest way to approach a problem that deals with the relationship between a number of different people or things is to set up a diagram. This type of problem is usually too confusing to do in your head. For this particular problem, the "diagram" could be a line, one end of which would be labeled tall and the other end labeled short. Then, taking one sentence at a time, place the people on the line to see where they fall in relation to one another.

The diagram of the first sentence would look like this:

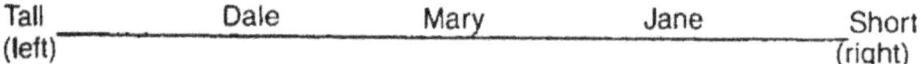

Mary is taller than Jane but shorter than Dale, so she would fall somewhere between the two of them. We have placed tall on the left and labeled it left just to make the explanation easier. You could just as easily have reversed the position.

The second sentence places Fred somewhere to the left of Mary because he is taller than she is. Steven would be to the left of Fred for the same reason. At this point we don't know whether Steven and Fred are taller or shorter than Dale. The new diagram would look like this:

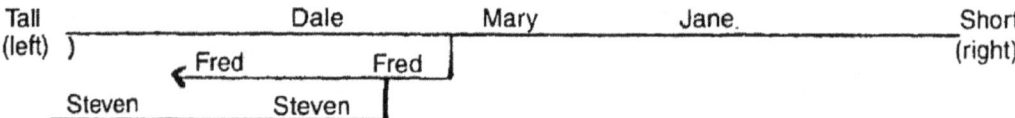

The third sentence introduces Elizabeth, presenting a new problem. Elizabeth can be anywhere to the right of Dale. Don't make the mistake of assuming she falls between Dale and Mary. At this point we don't know where she fits in relation to Mary, Jane, or even Fred.

We do get information about Steven, however. He is taller than Dale so he would be to the left of Dale. Since he is also taller than Fred (see sentence II), we know that Steven is the tallest person thus far. The diagram would now look like this:

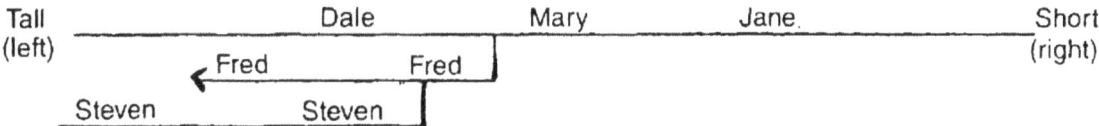

Fred's height is somewhere between Steven and Mary, Elizabeth's anywhere between Dale and the end of the line.

The fourth sentence tells us where Elizabeth stands, in relation to Fred and the others in the problem. The fact that she is taller than Mary means she is also taller than Jane. The final diagram would look like this:

| Tall | Steven | Dale | Elizabeth | Mary | Jane | Short |
| (left) | | Fred | | | | (right) |

We still don't know whether Dale or Fred is taller, however. Therefore, the conclusion that Dale is taller than Fred can't be proved. It also can't be disproved because we don't know for sure that he isn't. The answer has to be choice C, as the conclusion can't be proved or disproved.

37. The answer is A. This is another problem that is easiest for most people if they make a diagram. Sentence I states that Main Street is between Spring Street and Glenn Blvd. At this point we don't know if they are next to each other or if they are separated by a number of streets. Therefore, you should leave space between streets as you plot your first diagram.

The order of the streets could go either:

    Spring St.   or   Glenn Blvd.
    Main St.   Main St.
    Glenn Blvd.   Spring St.

Sentence II states that Hawley Street is one block south of Spring Street and 3 blocks north of Main Street. Because most people think in terms of north as above and south as below and because it was stated that Hawley is one block south of Spring Street and three blocks north of Main Street, the next diagram could look like this:

18 (#1)

<u>Spring</u>
<u>Hawley</u>

———

<u>Main</u>
<u>Glenn</u>

The third sentence states that Glenn Street is five blocks south of Elm and four blocks south of Main. It could look like this:

<u>Spring</u>
<u>Hawley</u>

<u>Elm</u>
<u>Main</u>

———
———
———

<u>Glenn</u>

The conclusion states that Elm Street is between Hawley Avenue and Glenn Blvd. From the above diagram, we can see that this is the case.

38. The answer is B. For most people, the best way to do this problem is to draw a diagram, plotting the course of both trains. Sentence I states that Train A leaves Hampshire at 5:50 A.M. and reaches New London at 6:42. Your first diagram might look like this:

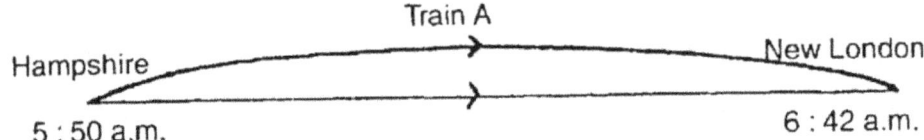

Sentence II states that the train leaves New London at 7:00 a.m. and arrives in Kellogsville at 8:42 a.m. The diagram might now look like this:

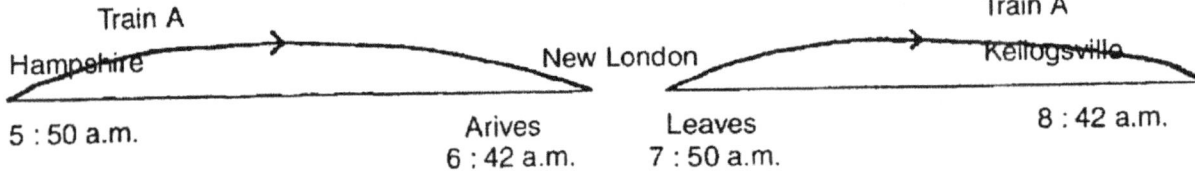

Sentence III gives us the rest of the information that must be included in the diagram. It introduces Train B, which moves in the opposite direction, leaving Kellogsville at 8:00 a.m. and arriving at Hampshire at 10:42 a.m. The final diagram might look like this:

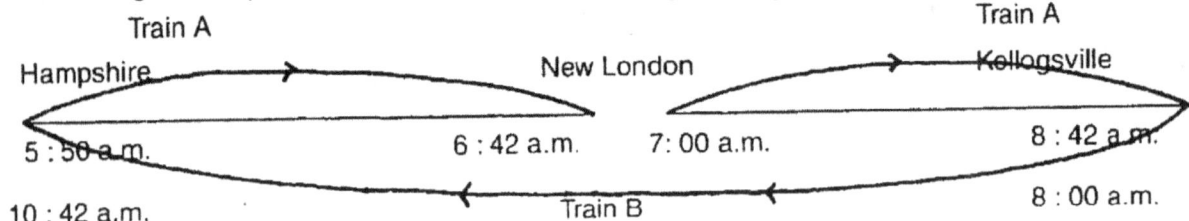

19 (#1)

As you can see from the diagram, the routes of the two trains will overlap somewhere between Kellogsville and New London. If you read sentence IV quickly and assumed that that was the section with only one track, you probably would have assumed that there would have had to be a collision. Sentence IV states, however, that there is only one railroad track between New London and Hampshire. That is the only section, then, where the two trains could collide. By the time Train B gets to that section, however, Train A will have passed it. The two trains will pass each other somewhere between New London and Kellogsville, not New London and Hampshire.

COMMUNICATION

EXAMINATION SECTION
TEST 1

DIRECTIONS: Each question or incomplete statement is followed by several suggested answers or completions. Select the one that BEST answers the question or completes the statement. *PRINT THE LETTER OF THE CORRECT ANSWER IN THE SPACE AT THE RIGHT.*

1. In some agencies the counsel to the agency head is given the right to bypass the chain of command and issue orders directly to the staff concerning matters that involve certain specific processes and practices.
   This situation MOST nearly illustrates the principle of _____ authority.
   A. the acceptance theory of
   B. multiple-linear
   C. splintered
   D. functional

2. It is commonly understood that communication is an important part of the administrative process.
   Which of the following is NOT a valid principle of the communication process in administration?
   A. The channels of communication should be spontaneous.
   B. The lines of communication should be as direct and as short as possible.
   C. Communications should be authenticated.
   D. The persons serving in communications centers should be competent.

3. Of the following, the one factor which is generally considered LEAST essential to successful committee operations is
   A. stating a clear definition of the authority and scope of the committee
   B. selecting the committee chairman carefully
   C. limiting the size of the committee to four persons
   D. limiting the subject matter to that which can be handled in group discussion

4. Of the following, the failure by line managers to accept and appreciate the benefits and limitations of a new program or system VERY FREQUENTLY can be traced to the
   A. budgetary problems involved
   B. resultant need to reduce staff
   C. lack of controls it engenders
   D. failure of top management to support its implementation

5. If a manager were thinking about using a committee of subordinates to solve an operating problem, which of the following would generally NOT be an advantage of such use of the committee approach?
   A. Improved coordination
   B. Low cost
   C. Increased motivation
   D. Integrated judgment

6. Every supervisor has many occasions to lead a conference or participate in a conference of some sort.
Of the following statements that pertain to conferences and conference leadership, which is generally considered to be MOST valid?
   A. Since World War II, the trend has been toward fewer shared decisions and more conferences.
   B. The most important part of a conference leader's job is to direct discussion.
   C. In providing opportunities for group interaction, management should avoid consideration of its past management philosophy.
   D. A good administrator cannot lead a good conference if he is a poor public speaker.

7. Of the following, it is usually LEAST desirable for a conference leader to
   A. call the name of a person after asking a question
   B. summarize proceedings periodically
   C. make a practice of repeating questions
   D. ask a question without indicating who is to reply

8. Assume that, in a certain organization, a situation has developed in which there is little difference in status or authority between individuals.
Which of the following would be the MOST likely result with regard to communication in this organization?
   A. Both the accuracy and flow of communication will be improved.
   B. Both the accuracy and flow of communication will substantially decrease.
   C. Employees will seek more formal lines of communication.
   D. Neither the flow nor the accuracy of communication will be improved over the former hierarchical structure.

9. The main function of many agency administrative officers is "information management." Information that is received by an administrative officer may be classified as active or passive, depending upon whether or not it requires the recipient to take some action.
Of the following, the item received which is clearly the MOST active information is
   A. an appointment of a new staff member
   B. a payment voucher for a new desk
   C. a press release concerning a past event
   D. the minutes of a staff meeting

10. Of the following, the one LEAST considered to be a communication barrier is
    A. group feedback   B. charged words
    C. selective perception   D. symbolic meanings

3 (#1)

11. Management studies support the hypothesis that, in spite of the tendency of employees to censor the information communicated to their supervisor, subordinates are more likely to communicate problem-oriented information UPWARD when they have a
    A. long period of service in the organization
    B. high degree of trust in the supervisor
    C. high educational level
    D. low status on the organizational ladder

11.____

12. Electronic data processing equipment can produce more information faster than can be generated by any other means.
    In view of this, the MOST important problem faced by management at present is to
    A. keep computers fully occupied
    B. find enough computer personnel
    C. assimilate and properly evaluate the information
    D. obtain funds to establish appropriate information systems

12.____

13. A well-designed management information system essentially provides each executive and manager the information he needs for
    A. determining computer time requirements
    B. planning and measuring results
    C. drawing a new organization chart
    D. developing a new office layout

13.____

14. It is generally agreed that management policies should be periodically reappraised and restated in accordance with current conditions.
    Of the following, the approach which would be MOST effective in determining whether a policy should be revised is to
    A. conduct interviews with staff members at all levels in order to ascertain the relationship between the policy and actual practice
    B. make proposed revisions in the policy and apply it to current problems
    C. make up hypothetical situations using both the old policy and a revised version in order to make comparisons
    D. call a meeting of top level staff in order to discuss ways of revising the policy

14.____

15. Your superior has asked you to notify division employees of an important change in one of the operating procedures described in the division manual. Every employee presently has a copy of this manual.
    Which of the following is normally the MOST practical way to get the employees to understand such a change?
    A. Notify each employee individually of the change and answer any questions he might have
    B. Send a written notice to key personnel, directing them to inform the people under them

15.____

C. Call a general meeting, distribute a corrected page for the manual, and discuss the change
D. Send a memo to employees describing the change in general terms and asking them to make the necessary corrections in their copies of the manual

16. Assume that the work in your department involves the use of any technical terms.
In such a situation, when you are answering inquiries from the general public, it would usually be BEST to
    A. use simple language and avoid the technical terms
    B. employ the technical terms whenever possible
    C. bandy technical terms freely, but explain each term in parentheses
    D. apologize if you are forced to use a technical term

17. Suppose that you receive a telephone call from someone identifying himself as an employee in another city department who asks to be given information which your own department regards as confidential.
Which of the following is the BEST way of handling such a request?
    A. Give the information requested, since your caller as official standing
    B. Grant the request, provided the caller gives you a signed receipt
    C. Refuse the request, because you have no way of knowing whether the caller is really who he claims to be
    D. Explain that the information is confidential and inform the caller of the channels he must go through to have the information released to him

18. Studies show that office employees place high importance on the social and human aspects of the organization. What office employees like best about their jobs is the kind of people with whom they work. So strive hard to group people who are most likely to get along well together.
Based on this information, it is MOST reasonable to assume that office workers are most pleased to work in a group which
    A. is congenial   B. has high productivity
    C. allows individual creativity   D. is unlike other groups

19. A certain supervisor does not compliment members of his staff when they come up with good ideas. He feels that coming up with good ideas is part of the job and does not merit special attention.
This supervisor's practice is
    A. *poor*, because recognition for good ideas is a good motivator
    B. *poor*, because the staff will suspect that the supervisor has no good ideas of his own
    C. *good*, because it is reasonable to assume that employees will tell their supervisor of ways to improve office practice
    D. *good*, because the other members of the staff are not made to seem inferior by comparison

20. Some employees of a department have sent an anonymous letter containing many complaints to the department head.
Of the following, what is this MOST likely to show about the department?
    A. It is probably a good place to work.
    B. Communications are probably poor.
    C. The complaints are probably unjustified.
    D. These employees are probably untrustworthy.

21. Which of the following actions would usually be MOST appropriate for a supervisor to take after receiving an instruction sheet from his superior explaining a new procedure which is to be followed?
    A. Put the instruction sheet aside temporarily until he determines what is wrong with the old procedure.
    B. Call his superior and ask whether the procedure is one he must implement immediately.
    C. Write a memorandum to the superior asking for more details.
    D. Try the new procedure and advise the superior of any problems or possible improvements.

22. Of the following, which one is considered the PRIMARY advantage of using a committee to resolved a problem in an organization?
    A. No one person will be held accountable for the decision since a group of people was involved.
    B. People with different backgrounds give attention to the problem.
    C. The decision will take considerable time so there is unlikely to be a decision that will later be regretted.
    D. One person cannot dominate the decision-making process.

23. Employees in a certain office come to their supervisor with all their complaints about the office and the work. Almost every employee has had at least one minor complaint at some time.
The situation with respect to complaints in this office may BEST be described as probably
    A. *good*; employees who complain care about their jobs and work hard
    B. *good*; grievances brought out into the open can be corrected
    C. *bad*; only serious complaints should be discussed
    D. *bad*; it indicates the staff does not have confidence in the administration

24. The administrator who allows his staff to suggest ways to do their work will usually find that
    A. this practice contributes to high productivity
    B. the administrator's ideas produce greater output
    C. clerical employees suggest inefficient work methods
    D. subordinate employees resent performing a management function

25. The MAIN purpose for a supervisor's questioning the employees at a conference he is holding is to
    A. stress those areas of information covered but not understood by the participants
    B. encourage participants to think through the problem under discussion
    C. catch those subordinates who are not paying attention
    D. permit the more knowledgeable participants to display their grasp of the problems being discussed

KEY (CORRECT ANSWERS)

1.	D		11.	B
2.	A		12.	C
3.	C		13.	B
4.	D		14.	A
5.	B		15.	C
6.	B		16.	A
7.	C		17.	D
8.	D		18.	A
9.	A		19.	A
10.	A		20.	B

21.	D
22.	B
23.	B
24.	A
25.	B

TEST 2

DIRECTIONS: Each question or incomplete statement is followed by several suggested answers or completions. Select the one that BEST answers the question or completes the statement. *PRINT THE LETTER OF THE CORRECT ANSWER IN THE SPACE AT THE RIGHT.*

1. For a superior to use *consultative supervision* with his subordinates effectively, it is ESSENTIAL that he
   A. accept the fact that his formal authority will be weakened by the procedure
   B. admit that he does not know more than all his men together and that his ideas are not always best
   C. utilize a committee system so that the procedure is orderly
   D. make sure that all subordinates are consulted so that no one feels left out

   1.____

2. The *grapevine* is an informal means of communication in an organization. The attitude of a supervisor with respect to the grapevine should be to
   A. ignore it since it deals mainly with rumors and sensational information
   B. regard it as a serious danger which should be eliminated
   C. accept it as a real line of communication which should be listened to
   D. utilize it for most purposes instead of the official line of communication

   2.____

3. The supervisor of an office that must deal with the public should realize that planning in this type of work situation
   A. is useless because he does not know how many people will request service or what service they will request
   B. must be done at a higher level but that he should be ready to implement the results of such planning
   C. is useful primarily for those activities that are not concerned with public contact
   D. is useful for all the activities of the office, including those that relate to public contact

   3.____

4. Assume that it is your job to receive incoming telephone calls. Those calls which you cannot handle yourself have to be transferred to the appropriate office.
   If you receive an outside call for an extension line which is busy, the one of the following which you should do FIRST is to
   A. interrupt the person speaking on the extension and tell him a call is waiting
   B. tell the caller the line is busy and let him know every thirty seconds whether or not it is free
   C. leave the caller on "hold" until the extension is free
   D. tell the caller the line is busy and ask him if he wishes to wait

   4.____

5. Your superior has subscribed to several publications directly related to your division's work, and he has asked you to see to it that the publications are circulated among the supervisory personnel in the division. There are eight supervisors involved.
The BEST method of insuring that all eight see these publications is to
   A. place the publication in the division's general reference library as soon as it arrives
   B. inform each supervisor whenever a publication arrives and remind all of them that they are responsible for reading it
   C. prepare a standard slip that can be stapled to each publication, listing the eight supervisors and saying, "Please read, initial your name, and pass along"
   D. send a memo to the eight supervisors saying that they may wish to purchase individual subscriptions in their own names if they are interested in seeing each issue

5.____

6. Your superior has telephoned a number of key officials in your agency to ask whether they can meet at a certain time next month. He has found that they can all make it, and he has asked you to confirm the meeting.
Which of the following is the BEST way to confirm such a meeting?
   A. Note the meeting on your superior's calendar.
   B. Post a notice of the meeting on the agency bulletin board.
   C. Call the officials on the day of the meeting to remind them of the meeting.
   D. Write a memo to each official involved, repeating the time and place of the meeting.

6.____

7. Assume that a new city regulation requires that certain kinds of private organizations file information forms with your department. You have been asked to write the short explanatory message that will be printed on the front cover of the pamphlet containing the forms and instructions.
Which of the following would be the MOST appropriate way of beginning this message?
   A. Get the readers' attention by emphasizing immediately that there are legal penalties for organizations that fail to file before a certain date.
   B. Briefly state the nature of the enclosed forms and the types of organizations that must file.
   C. Say that your department is very sorry to have to put organizations to such an inconvenience.
   D. Quote the entire regulation adopted by the city, even if it is quite long and is expressed din complicated legal language.

7.____

8. Suppose that you have been told to make up the vacation schedule for the 18 employees in a particular unit. In order for the unit to operate effectively, only a few employees can be on vacation at the same time.
Which of the following is the MOST advisable approach in making up the schedule?
   A. Draw up a schedule assigning vacations in alphabetical order
   B. Find out when the supervisors want to take their vacations, and randomly assign whatever periods are left to the non-supervisory personnel

8.____

C. Assign the most desirable times to employees of longest standing and the least desirable times to the newest employees
D. Have all employees state their own preference, and then work out any conflicts in consultation with the people involved

9. Assume that you have been asked to prepare job descriptions for various positions in your department.
Which of the following are the basic points that should be covered in a *job description*?
   A. General duties and responsibilities of the position, with examples of day-to-day tasks
   B. Comments on the performances of present employees
   C. Estimates of the number of openings that may be available in each category during the coming year
   D. Instructions for carrying out the specific tasks assigned to your department

9.____

10. Of the following, the biggest DISADVANTAGE in allowing a free flow of communications in an agency is that such a free flow
    A. decreases creativity
    B. increases the use of the *grapevine*
    C. lengthens the chain of command
    D. reduces the executive's power to direct the flow of information

10.____

11. A downward flow of authority in an organization is one example of _____ communication.
    A. horizontal   B. informal   C. circular   D. vertical

11.____

12. Of the following, the one that would MOST likely block effective communication is
    A. concentration only on the issues at hand
    B. lack of interest or commitment
    C. use of written reports
    D. use of charts and graphs

12.____

13. An ADVANTAGE of the *lecture* as a teaching tool is that it
    A. enables a person to present his ideas to a large number of people
    B. allows the audience to retain a maximum of the information given
    C. holds the attention of the audience for the longest time
    D. enables the audience member to easily recall the main points

13.____

14. An ADVANTAGE of the *small-group* discussion as a teaching tool is that
    A. it always focuses attention on one person as the leader
    B. it places collective responsibility on the group as a whole
    C. its members gain experience by summarizing the ideas of others
    D. each member of the group acts as a member of a team

14.____

15. The one of the following that is an ADVANTAGE of a *large-group* discussion, when compared to a small-group discussion, is that the large-group discussion
    A. moves along more quickly than a small-group discussion
    B. allows its participants to feel more at ease, and speak out more freely
    C. gives the whole group a chance to exchange ideas on a certain subject at the same occasion
    D. allows its members to feel a greater sense of personal responsibility

15.____

KEY (CORRECT ANSWERS)

1.	D	6.	D	11.	D
2.	C	7.	B	12.	B
3.	D	8.	D	13.	A
4.	D	9.	A	14.	D
5.	C	10.	D	15.	C

EXAMINATION SECTION
TEST 1

DIRECTIONS: Each question or incomplete statement is followed by several suggested answers or completions. Select the one that BEST answers the question or completes the statement. *PRINT THE LETTER OF THE CORRECT ANSWER IN THE SPACE AT THE RIGHT.*

1. In public agencies, communications should be based PRIMARILY on a
   A. two-way flow from the top down and from the bottom up, most of which should be given in writing to avoid ambiguity
   B. multi-direction flow among all levels and with outside persons
   C. rapid, internal one-way flow from the top down
   D. two-way flow of information, most of which should be given orally for purposes of clarity

    1.____

2. In some organizations, changes in policy or procedures are often communicated by word of mouth from supervisors to employees with no prior discussion or exchange of viewpoints with employees.
   This procedure often produces employee dissatisfaction CHIEFLY because
   A. information is mostly unusable since a considerable amount of time is required to transmit information
   B. lower-level supervisors tend to be excessively concerned with minor details
   C. management has failed to seek employees' advice before making changes
   D. valuable staff time is lost between decision-making and the implementation of decisions

    2.____

3. For good letter writing, you should try to visualize the person to whom you are writing, especially if you know him.
   Of the following rules, it is LEAST helpful in such visualization to think of
   A. the person's likes and dislikes, his concerns, and his needs
   B. what you would be likely to say if speaking in person
   C. what you would expect to be asked if speaking in person
   D. your official position in order to be certain that your words are proper

    3.____

4. One approach to good informal letter writing is to make letters and conversational.
   All of the following practices will usually help to do this EXCEPT:
   A. If possible, use a style which is similar to the style used when speaking
   B. Substitute phrases for single words (e.g., *at the present time* for *now*)
   C. Use contractions of words (e.g., *you're* for *you are*)
   D. Use ordinary vocabulary when possible

    4.____

5. All of the following rules will aid in producing clarity in report-writing EXCEPT: 5.____
   A. Give specific details or examples, if possible
   B. Keep related words close together in each sentence
   C. Present information in sequential order
   D. Put several thoughts or ideas in each paragraph

6. The one of the following statements about public relations which is MOST accurate is that 6.____
   A. in the long run, appearance gains better results than performance
   B. objectivity is decreased if outside public relations consultants are employed
   C. public relations is the responsibility of every employee
   D. public relations should be based on a formal publicity program

7. The form of communication which is usually considered to be MOST personally directed to the intended recipient is the 7.____
   A. brochure   B. film   C. letter   D. radio

8. In general, a document that presents an organization's views or opinions on a particular topic is MOST accurately known as a 8.____
   A. tear sheet   B. position paper
   C. flyer   D. journal

9. Assume that you have been asked to speak before an organization of persons who oppose a newly announced program in which you are involved. You feel tense about talking to this group. 9.____
   Which of the following rules generally would be MOST useful in gaining rapport when speaking before the audience?
   A. Impress them with your experience
   B. Stress all areas of disagreement
   C. Talk to the group as to one person
   D. Use formal grammar and language

10. An organization must have an effective public relations program since, at its best, public relations is a bridge to change. 10.____
    All of the following statements about communication and human behavior have validity EXCEPT:
    A. People are more likely to talk about controversial matters with like-minded people than with those holding other views
    B. The earlier an experience, the more powerful its effect since it influences how later experiences will be interpreted
    C. In periods of social tension, official sources gain increased believability
    D. Those who are already interested in a topic are the ones who are most open to receive new communications about it

11. An employee should be encouraged to talk easily and frankly when he is dealing with his supervisor.
    In order to encourage such free communication, it would be MOST appropriate for a supervisor to behave in a(n)
    A. sincere manner; assure the employee that you will deal with him honestly and openly
    B. official manner; you are a supervisor and must always act formally with subordinates
    C. investigative manner; you must probe and question to get to a basis of trust
    D. unemotional manner; the employee's emotions and background should play no part in your dealings with him

11.____

12. Research findings show that an increase in free communication within an agency GENERALLY results in which one of the following?
    A. Improved morale and productivity
    B. Increased promotional opportunities
    C. An increase in authority
    D. A spirit of honesty

12.____

13. Assume that you are a supervisor and your superiors have given you a new-type procedure to be followed.
    Before passing this information on to your subordinates, the one of the following actions that you should take FIRST is to
    A. ask your superiors to send out a memorandum to the entire staff
    B. clarify the procedure in your own mind
    C. set up a training course to provide instruction on the new procedure
    D. write a memorandum to your subordinates

13.____

14. Communication is necessary for an organization to be effective.
    The one of the following which is LEAST important for most communication systems is that
    A. messages are sent quickly and directly to the person who needs them to operate
    B. information should be conveyed understandably and accurately
    C. the method used to transmit information should be kept secret so that security can be maintained
    D. senders of messages must know how their messages are received and acted upon

14.____

15. Which one of the following is the CHIEF advantage of listening willingly to subordinates and encouraging them to talk freely and honestly?
    It
    A. reveals to supervisors the degree to which ideas that are passed down are accepted by subordinates
    B. reduces the participation of subordinates in the operation of the department
    C. encourages subordinates to try for promotion
    D. enables supervisors to learn more readily what the *grapevine* is saying

15.____

16. A supervisor may be informed through either oral or written reports. 16._____
Which one of the following is an ADVANTAGE of using oral reports?
    A. There is no need for a formal record of the report.
    B. An exact duplicate of the report is not easily transmitted to others.
    C. A good oral report requires little time for preparation.
    D. An oral report involves two-way communication between a subordinate and his supervisor.

17. Of the following, the MOST important reason why supervisors should 17._____
communicate effectively with the public is to
    A. improve the public's understanding of information that is important for them to know
    B. establish a friendly relationship
    C. obtain information about the kinds of people who come to the agency
    D. convince the public that services are adequate

18. Supervisors should generally NOT use phrases like *too hard, too easy,* and 18._____
a lot PRINCIPALLY because such phrases
    A. may be offensive to some minority groups
    B. are too informal
    C. mean different things to different people
    D. are difficult to remember

19. The ability to communicate clearly and concisely is an important element in 19._____
effective leadership.
Which of the following statements about oral and written communication is GENERALLY true?
    A. Oral communication is more time-consuming.
    B. Written communication is more likely to be misinterpreted.
    C. Oral communication is useful only in emergencies.
    D. Written communication is useful mainly when giving information to fewer than twenty people.

20. Rumors can often have harmful and disruptive effects on an organization. 20._____
Which one of the following is the BEST way to prevent rumors from becoming a problem?
    A. Refuse to act on rumors, thereby making them less believable.
    B. Increase the amount of information passed along by the *grapevine*.
    C. Distribute as much factual information as possible.
    D. Provide training in report writing.

21. Suppose that a subordinate asks you about a rumor he has heard. The rumor 21._____
deals with a subject which your superiors consider *confidential*.
Which of the following BEST describes how you should answer the subordinate? Tell

A. the subordinate that you don't make the rules and that he should speak to higher ranking officials
B. the subordinate that you will ask your superior for information
C. him only that you cannot comment on the matter
D. him the rumor is not true

22. Supervisors often find it difficult to *get their message across* when instructing newly appointed employees in their various duties.
The MAIN reason for this is generally that the
    A. duties of the employees have increased
    B. supervisor is often so expert in his area that he fails to see it from the learner's point of view
    C. supervisor adapts his instruction to the slowest learner in the group
    D. new employees are younger, less concerned with job security and more interested in fringe benefits

22.____

23. Assume that you are discussing a job problem with an employee under your supervision. During the discussion, you see that the man's eyes are turning away from you and that he is not paying attention.
In order to get the man's attention, you should FIRST
    A. ask him to look you in the eye
    B. talk to him about sports
    C. tell him he is being very rude
    D. change your tone of voice

23.____

24. As a supervisor, you may find it necessary to conduct meetings with your subordinates.
Of the following, which would be MOST helpful in assuring that a meeting accomplishes the purpose for which it was called?
    A. Give notice of the conclusions you would like to reach at the start of the meeting.
    B. Delay the start of the meeting until everyone is present.
    C. Write down points to be discussed in proper sequence.
    D. Make sure everyone is clear on whatever conclusions have been reached and on what must be done after the meeting.

24.____

25. Every supervisor will occasionally be called upon to deliver a reprimand to a subordinate. If done properly, this can greatly help an employee improve his performance.
Which one of the following is NOT a good practice to follow when giving a reprimand?
    A. Maintain your composure and temper
    B. Reprimand a subordinate in the presence of other employees so they can learn the same lesson
    C. Try to understand why the employee was not able to perform satisfactorily
    D. Let your knowledge of the man involved determine the exact nature of the reprimand

25.____

KEY (CORRECT ANSWERS)

1.	C		11.	A
2.	B		12.	A
3.	D		13.	B
4.	B		14.	C
5.	D		15.	A
6.	C		16.	D
7.	C		17.	A
8.	B		18.	C
9.	C		19.	B
10.	C		20.	C

21.	B
22.	B
23.	D
24.	D
25.	B

TEST 2

DIRECTIONS: Each question or incomplete statement is followed by several suggested answers or completions. Select the one that BEST answers the question or completes the statement. *PRINT THE LETTER OF THE CORRECT ANSWER IN THE SPACE AT THE RIGHT.*

1. Usually one thinks of communication as a single step, essentially that of transmitting an idea.
   Actually, however, this is only part of a total process, the FIRST step of which should be
   A. the prompt dissemination of the idea to those who may be affected by it
   B. motivating those affected to take the required action
   C. clarifying the idea in one's own mind
   D. deciding to whom the idea is to be communicated

   1.____

2. Research studies on patterns of informal communication have concluded that most individuals in a group tend to be passive recipients of news, while a few make it their business to spread it around in an organization.
   With this conclusion in mind, it would be MOST correct for the supervisor to attempt to identify these few individuals and
   A. give them the complete facts on important matters in advance of others
   B. inform the other subordinates of the identity of these few individuals so that their influence may be minimized
   C. keep them straight on the facts on important matters
   D. warn them to cease passing along any information to others

   2.____

3. The one of the following which is the PRINCIPAL advantage of making an oral report is that it
   A. affords an immediate opportunity for two-way communication between the subordinate and superior
   B. is an easy method for the superior to use in transmitting information to others of equal rank
   C. saves the time of all concerned
   D. permits more precise pinpointing of praise or blame by means of follow-up questions by the superior

   3.____

4. An agency may sometimes undertake a public relations program of a defensive nature.
   With reference to the use of defensive public relations, it would be MOST correct to state that it
   A. is bound to be ineffective since defensive statements, even though supported by factual data, can never hope to even partly overcome the effects of prior unfavorable attacks
   B. proves that the agency has failed to establish good relationships with newspapers, radio stations, or other means of publicity

   4.____

C. shows that the upper echelons of the agency have failed to develop sound public relations procedures and techniques
D. is sometimes required to aid morale by protecting the agency from unjustified criticism and misunderstanding of policies or procedures

5. Of the following factors which contribute to possible undesirable public attitudes towards an agency, the one which is MOST susceptible to being changed by the efforts of the individual employee in an organization is that
    A. enforcement of unpopular regulations as offended many individuals
    B. the organization itself has an unsatisfactory reputation
    C. the public is not interested in agency matters
    D. there are many errors in judgment committed by individual subordinates

6. It is not enough for an agency's services to be of a high quality; attention must also be given to the acceptability of these services to the general public.
This statement is GENERALLY
    A. *false*; a superior quality of service automatically wins public support
    B. *true*; the agency cannot generally progress beyond the understanding and support of the public
    C. *false*; the acceptance by the public of agency services determines their quality
    D. *true*; the agency is generally unable to engage in any effective enforcement activity without public support

7. Sustained agency participation in a program sponsored by a community organization is MOST justified when
    A. the achievement of agency objectives in some area depends partly on the activity of this organization
    B. the community organization is attempting to widen the base of participation in all community affairs
    C. the agency is uncertain as to what the community wants
    D. the agency is uncertain as to what the community wants

8. Of the following, the LEAST likely way in which a records system may serve a supervisor is in
    A. developing a sympathetic and cooperative public attitude toward the agency
    B. improving the quality of supervision by permitting a check on the accomplishment of subordinates
    C. permit a precise prediction of the exact incidences in specific categories for the following year
    D. helping to take the guesswork out of the distribution of the agency

9. Assuming that the *grapevine* in any organization is virtually indestructible, the one of the following which it is MOST important for management to understand is:
   A. What is being spread by means of the *grapevine* and the reason for spreading it
   B. What is being spread by means of the *grapevine* and how it is being spread
   C. Who is involved in spreading the information that is on the *grapevine*
   D. Why those who are involved in spreading the information are doing so

10. When the supervisor writes a report concerning an investigation to which he has been assigned, it should be LEAST intended to provide
    A. a permanent official record of relevant information gathered
    B. a summary of case findings limited to facts which tend to indicate the guilt of a suspect
    C. a statement of the facts on which higher authorities may base a corrective or disciplinary action
    D. other investigators with information so that they may continue with other phases of the investigation

11. In survey work, questionnaires rather than interviews are sometimes used. The one of the following which is a DISADVANTAGE of the questionnaire method as compared with the interview is the
    A. difficulty of accurately interpreting the results
    B. problem of maintaining anonymity of the participant
    C. fact that it is relatively uneconomical
    D. requirement of special training for the distribution of questionnaires

12. in his contacts with the public, an employee should attempt to create a good climate of support for his agency.
    This statement is GENERALLY
    A. *false*; such attempts are clearly beyond the scope of his responsibility
    B. *true*; employees of an agency who come in contact with the public have the opportunity to affect public relations
    C. *false*; such activity should be restricted to supervisors trained in public relations techniques
    D. *true*; the future expansion of the agency depends to a great extent on continued public support of the agency

13. The repeated use by a supervisor of a call for volunteers to get a job done is objectionable MAINLY because it
    A. may create a feeling of animosity between the volunteers and the non-volunteers
    B. may indicate that the supervisor is avoiding responsibility for making assignments which will be most productive
    C. is an indication that the supervisor is not familiar with the individual capabilities of his men
    D. is unfair to men who, for valid reasons, do not, or cannot volunteer

14. Of the following statements concerning subordinates' expressions to a supervisor of their opinions and feelings concerning work situations, the one which is MOST correct is that
    A. by listening and responding to such expressions the supervisor encourages the development of complaints
    B. the lack of such expressions should indicate to the supervisor that there is a high level of job satisfaction
    C. the more the supervisor listens to and responds to such expressions, the more he demonstrates lack of supervisory ability
    D. by listening and responding to such expressions, the supervisor will enable many subordinates to understand and solve their own problems on the job

15. In attempting to motivate employees, rewards are considered preferable to punishment PRIMARILY because
    A. punishment seldom has any effect on human behavior
    B. punishment usually results in decreased production
    C. supervisors find it difficult to punish
    D. rewards are more likely to result in willing cooperation

16. In an attempt to combat the low morale in his organization, a high level supervisor publicized an *open-door policy* to allow employees who wished to do so to come to him with their complaints.
    Which of the following is LEAST likely to account for the fact that no employee came in with a complaint?
    A. Employees are generally reluctant to go over the heads of their immediate supervisor.
    B. The employees did not feel that management would help them.
    C. The low morale was not due to complaints associated with the job.
    D. The employees felt that they had more to lose than to gain.

17. It is MOST desirable to use written instructions rather than oral instructions for a particular job when
    A. a mistake on the job will not be serious
    B. the job can be completed in a short time
    C. there is no need to explain the job minutely
    D. the job involves many details

18. If you receive a telephone call regarding a matter which your office does not handle, you should FIRST
    A. give the caller the telephone number of the proper office so that he can dial again
    B. offer to transfer the caller to the proper office
    C. suggest that the caller re-dial since he probably dialed incorrectly
    D. tell the caller he has reached the wrong office and then hang up

19. When you answer the telephone, the MOST important reason for identifying yourself and your organization is to
    A. give the caller time to collect his or her thoughts
    B. impress the caller with your courtesy
    C. inform the caller that he or she has reached the right number
    D. set a business-like tone at the beginning of the conversation

20. As soon as you pick up the phone, a very angry caller begins immediately to complain about city agencies and *red tape*. He says that he has been shifted to two or three different offices. It turs out that he is seeking information which is not immediately available to you. You believe, you know, however, where it can be found.
    Which of the following actions is the BEST one for you to take?
    A. To eliminate all confusion, suggest that the caller write the agency stating explicitly what he wants.
    B. Apologize by telling the caller how busy city agencies now are, but also tell him directly that you do not have the information he needs.
    C. Ask for the caller's telephone number and assure him you will call back after you have checked further.
    D. Give the caller the name and telephone number of the person who might be able to help, but explain that you are not positive he will get results/

21. Which of the following approaches usually provides the BEST communication in the objectives and values of a new program which is to be introduced?
    A. A general written description of the program by the program manager for review by those who share responsibility
    B. An effective verbal presentation by the program manager to those affected
    C. Development of the plan and operational approach in carrying out the program by the program manager assisted by his key subordinates
    D. Development of the plan by the program manager's supervisor

22. What is the BEST approach for introducing change?
    A
    A. combination of written and also verbal communication to all personnel affected by the change
    B. general bulletin to all personnel
    C. meeting pointing out all the values of the new approach
    D. written directive to key personnel

23. Of the following, committees are BEST used for
    A. advising the head of the organization
    B. improving functional work
    C. making executive decisions
    D. making specific planning decisions

24. An effective discussion leader is one who
    A. announces the problem and his preconceived solution at the start of the discussion
    B. guides and directs the discussion according to pre-arranged outline
    C. interrupts or corrects confused participants to save time
    D. permits anyone to say anything at any time

25. The human relations movement in management theory is basically concerned with
    A. counteracting employee unrest
    B. eliminating the *time and motion* man
    C. interrelationships among individuals in organizations
    D. the psychology of the worker

KEY (CORRECT ANSWERS)

1.	C	11.	A
2.	C	12.	B
3.	A	13.	B
4.	D	14.	D
5.	D	15.	D
6.	B	16.	C
7.	A	17.	D
8.	C	18.	B
9.	A	19.	C
10.	B	20.	C

21.	C
22.	A
23.	A
24.	B
25.	C

EDUCATING AND INTERACTING WITH THE PUBLIC

These questions test for knowledge of techniques used to interact effectively with individual citizens and/or community groups, to educate or inform them about topics of concern, to publicize or clarify agency programs or policies, to negotiate conflicts or resolve complaints, and to represent one's agency or program in a manner in keeping with good public relations practices. Questions may also cover interacting with others in cooperative efforts of public outreach or service. There will be 15 questions in this subject area on the written test.

TEST TASK:
You will be presented with a variety of situations in which you must apply knowledge of how best to interact with other people.

SAMPLE QUESTION:
A person approaches you expressing anger about a recent action by your department. Which one of the following should be your first response to this person?

A. Interrupt to say you cannot discuss the situation until he calms down.
B. Say you are sorry that he has been negatively affected by your department's action.
C. Listen and express understanding that he has been upset by your department's action.
D. Give him an explanation of the reasons for your department's action.

The correct answer to this sample question is choice C

C. SOLUTION:

Choice A is not correct. It would be inappropriate to interrupt. In addition, saying that you cannot discuss the situation until the person calms down will likely aggravate him further.

Choice B is not correct. Apologizing for your department's action implies that the action was improper.

Choice C is the correct answer to this question. By listening and expressing understanding that your department's action has upset him, you demonstrate that you have heard and understand his feelings and point of view.

Choice D is not correct. While an explanation of the reasons for the action may be appropriate at a later time, at this moment the person is angry and would not be receptive to such an explanation.

EXAMINATION SECTION
TEST 1

DIRECTIONS: Each question or incomplete statement is followed by several suggested answers or completions. Select the one that BEST answers the question or completes the statement. *PRINT THE LETTER OF THE CORRECT ANSWER IN THE SPACE AT THE RIGHT.*

1. When conducting a needs assessment for the purpose of education planning, an agency's FIRST step is to identify or provide
   A. a profile of population characteristics
   B. barriers to participation
   C. existing resources
   D. profiles of competing resources

   1.____

2. Research has demonstrated that of the following, the MOST effective medium for communicating with external publics is(are)
   A. video news releases   B. television
   C. radio   D. newspapers

   2.____

3. Basic ideas behind the effort to influence the attitudes and behaviors of a constituency include each of the following EXCEPT the idea that
   A. words, rather than actions or events, are most likely to motivate
   B. demands for action are a usual response
   C. self-interest usually figures heavily into public involvement
   D. the reliability of change programs is difficult to assess

   3.____

4. An agency representative is trying to craft a pithy message to constituents in order to encourage the use of agency program resources.
   Choosing an audience for such messages is easiest when the message
   A. is project- or behavior-based   B. is combined with other messages
   C. is abstract   D. has a broad appeal

   4.____

5. Of the following factors, the MOST important to the success of an agency's external education or communication programs is the
   A. amount of resources used to implement them
   B. public's prior experiences with the agency
   C. real value of the program to the public
   D. commitment of the internal audience

   5.____

6. A representative for a state agency is being interviewed by a reporter from a local news network. The representative is being asked to defend a program that is extremely unpopular in certain parts of the municipality.
   When a constituency is known to be opposed to a position, the MOST useful communication strategy is to present

   6.____

A. only the arguments that are consistent with constituents' views
B. only the agency's side of the issue
C. both sides of the argument as clearly as possible
D. both sides of the argument, omitting key information about the opposing position

7. The MOST significant barriers to effective agency community relations include
   I. widespread distrust of communication strategies
   II. the media's "watchdog" stance
   III. public apathy
   IV. statutory opposition

   The CORRECT answer is:
   A. I only   B. I and II   C. II and III   D. III and IV

8. In conducting an education program, many agencies use workshops and seminars in a classroom setting.
   Advantages of classroom-style teaching over other means of educating the public include each of the following, EXCEPT
   A. enabling an instructor to verify learning through testing and interaction with the target audience
   B. enabling hands-on practice and other participatory learning techniques
   C. ability to reach an unlimited number of participants in a given length of time
   D. ability to convey the latest, most up-to-date information

9. The _____ model of community relations is characterized by an attempt to persuade the public to adopt the agency's point of view.
   A. two-way symmetric   B. two-way asymmetric
   C. public information   D. press agency/publicity

10. Important elements of an internal situation analysis include the
    I. list of agency opponents   II. communication audit
    III. updated organizational almanac   IV. stakeholder analysis

    The CORRECT answer is:
    A. I and II   B. I, II, and III   C. II and III   D. I, II, III and IV

11. Government agency information efforts typically involve each of the following objectives, EXCEPT to
    A. implement changes in the policies of government agencies to align with public opinion
    B. communicate the work of agencies
    C. explain agency techniques in a way that invites input from citizens
    D. provide citizen feedback to government administrators

12. Factors that are likely to influence the effectiveness of an educational campaign include the
    I. level of homogeneity among intended participants
    II. number and types of media used
    III. receptivity of the intended participants
    IV. level of specificity in the message or behavior to be taught

    The CORRECT answer is:
    A. I and II   B. I, II, and III   C. II and III   D. I, II, III, and IV

13. An agency representative is writing instructional objectives that will later help to measure the effectiveness of an educational program.
    Which of the following verbs, included in an objective, would be MOST helpful for the purpose of measuring effectiveness?
    A. Know   B. Identify   C. Learn   D. Comprehend

14. A state education agency wants to encourage participation in a program that has just received a boost through new federal legislation. The program is intended to include participants from a wide variety of socioeconomic and other demographic characteristics. The agency wants to launch a broad-based program that will inform virtually every interested party in the state about the program's new circumstances.
    In attempting to deliver this message to such a wide-ranging constituency, the agency's BEST practice would be to
    A. broadcast the same message through as many different media channels as possible
    B. focus on one discrete segment of the public at a time
    C. craft a message whose appeal is as broad as the public itself
    D. let the program's achievements speak for themselves and rely on word-of-mouth

15. Advantages associated with using the World Wide Web as an educational tool include
    I. an appeal to younger generations of the public
    II. visually-oriented, interactive learning
    III. learning that is not confined by space, time, or institutional association
    IV. a variety of methods for verifying use and learning

    The CORRECT answer is:
    A. I only   B. I and II   C. I, II, and III   D. I, II, II, and IV

16. In agencies involved in health care, community relations is a critical function because it
    A. serves as an intermediary between the agency and consumers
    B. generates a clear mission statement for agency goals and priorities
    C. ensures patient privacy while satisfying the media's right to information
    D. helps marketing professionals determine the wants and needs of agency constituents

17. After an extensive campaign to promote its newest program to constituents, an agency learns that most of the audience did not understand the intended message.
MOST likely, the agency has
    A. chosen words that were intended to inform, rather than persuade
    B. not accurately interpreted what the audience really needed to know
    C. overestimated the ability of the audience to receive and process the message
    D. compensated for noise that may have interrupted the message

17.____

18. The necessary elements that lead to conviction and motivation in the minds of participants in an educational or information program include each of the following, EXCEPT the _____ of the message.
    A. acceptability   B. intensity
    C. single-channel appeal   D. pervasiveness

18.____

19. Printed materials are often at the core of educational programs provided by public agencies.
The PRIMARY disadvantage associated with print is that it
    A. does not enable comprehensive treatment of a topic
    B. is generally unreliable in term of assessing results
    C. is often the most expensive medium available
    D. is constrained by time

19.____

20. Traditional thinking on public opinion holds that there is about _____ percent of the public who are pivotal to shifting the balance and momentum of opinion—they are concerned about an issue, but not fanatical, and interested enough to pay attention to a reasoned discussion.
    A. 2   B. 10   C. 33   D. 51

20.____

21. One of the most useful guidelines for influencing attitude change among people is to
    A. invite the target audience to come to you, rather than approaching them
    B. use moral appeals as the primary approach
    C. use concrete images to enable people to see the results of behaviors or indifference
    D. offer tangible rewards to people for changes in behavior

21.____

22. An agency is attempting to evaluate the effectiveness of its educational program. For this purpose, it wants to observe several focus groups discussing the same program.
Which of the following would NOT be a guideline for the use of focus groups?
    A. Focus groups should only include those who have participated in the program.
    B. Be sure to accurately record the discussion.
    C. The same questions should be asked at each focus group meeting.
    D. It is often helpful to have a neutral, non-agency employee facilitate discussions.

22.____

23. Research consistently shows that _____ is the determinant most likely to make a newspaper editor run a news release.
    A. novelty   B. prominence   C. proximity   D. conflict

24. Which of the following is NOT one of the major variables to take into account when considering a population-needs assessment?
    A. State of program development   B. Resources available
    C. Demographics   D. Community attitudes

25. The FIRST step in any communications audit is to
    A. develop a research instrument
    B. determine how the organization currently communicates
    C. hire a contractor
    D. determine which audience to assess

KEY (CORRECT ANSWERS)

1. A
2. D
3. A
4. A
5. D

6. C
7. D
8. C
9. B
10. C

11. A
12. D
13. B
14. B
15. C

16. A
17. B
18. C
19. B
20. B

21. C
22. A
23. C
24. C
25. D

TEST 2

DIRECTIONS: Each question or incomplete statement is followed by several suggested answers or completions. Select the one that BEST answers the question or completes the statement. *PRINT THE LETTER OF THE CORRECT ANSWER IN THE SPACE AT THE RIGHT.*

1. A public relations practitioner at an agency has just composed a press release highlighting a program's recent accomplishments and success stories.
   In pitching such releases to print outlets, the practitioner should
   I. e-mail, mail, or send them by messenger
   II. address them to "editor" or "news director"
   III. have an assistant call all media contacts by telephone
   IV. ask reporters or editors how they prefer to receive them

   The CORRECT answer is:
   A. I and II   B. I and IV   C. II, III, and IV   D. III only   1.____

2. The "output goals" of an educational program are MOST likely to include   2.____
   A. specified ratings of services by participants on a standardized scale
   B. observable effects on a given community or clientele
   C. the number of instructional hours provided
   D. the number of participants served

3. An agency wants to evaluate satisfaction levels among program participants, and mails out questionnaires to everyone who has been enrolled in the last year.   3.____
   The PRIMARY problem associated with this method of evaluative research is that it
   A. poses a significant inconvenience for respondents
   B. is inordinately expensive
   C. does not allow for follow-up or clarification questions
   D. usually involves a low response rate

4. A communications audit is an important tool for measuring   4.____
   A. the depth of penetration of a particular message or program
   B. the cost of the organization's information campaigns
   C. how key audiences perceive an organization
   D. the commitment of internal stakeholders

5. The "ABCs" of written learning objectives include each of the following, EXCEPT   5.____
   A. Audience   B. Behavior   C. Conditions   D. Delineation

6. When attempting to change the behaviors of constituents, it is important to keep in mind that
   I. most people are skeptical of communications that try to get them to change their behaviors
   II. in most cases, a person selects the media to which he exposes himself
   III. people tend to react defensively to messages or programs that rely on fear as a motivating factor
   IV. programs should aim for the broadest appeal possible in order to include as many participants as possible

   The CORRECT answer is:
   A. I and II   B. I, II and III   C. II and III   D. I, II, III, and IV

   6.____

7. The "laws" of public opinion include the idea that it is
   A. useful for anticipating emergencies
   B. not sensitive to important events
   C. basically determined by self-interest
   D. sustainable through persistent appeals

   7.____

8. Which of the following types of evaluations is used to measure public attitudes before and after an information/educational program?
   A. Retrieval study   B. Copy test
   C. Quota sampling   D. Benchmark study

   8.____

9. The PRIMARY source for internal communications is(are) usually
   A. flow charts   B. meetings
   C. voice mail   D. printed publications

   9.____

10. An agency representative is putting together informational materials—brochures and a newsletter—outlining changes in one of the state's biggest benefits programs.
    In assembling print materials as a medium for delivering information to the public, the representative should keep in mind each of the following trends:
    I. For various reasons, the reading capabilities of the public are in general decline
    II. Without tables and graphs to help illustrate the changes, it is unlikely that the message will be delivered effectively
    III. Professionals and career-oriented people are highly receptive to information written in the form of a journal article or empirical study
    IV. People tend to be put off by print materials that use itemized and bulleted (●) lists

    The CORRECT answer is:
    A. I and II   B. I, II and III   C. II and III   D. I, II, III, and IV

    10.____

11. Which of the following steps in a problem-oriented information campaign would typically be implemented FIRST?
    A. Deciding on tactics
    B. Determining a communications strategy
    C. Evaluating the problem's impact
    D. Developing an organizational strategy

12. A common pitfall in conducting an educational program is to
    A. aim it at the wrong target audience
    B. overfund it
    C. leave it in the hands of people who are in the business of education, rather than those with expertise in the business of the organization
    D. ignore the possibility that some other organization is meeting the same educational need for the target audience

13. The key factors that affect the credibility of an agency's educational program include
    A. organization
    B. scope
    C. sophistication
    D. penetration

14. Research on public opinion consistently demonstrates that it is
    A. easy to move people toward a strong opinion on anything, as long as they are approached directly through their emotions
    B. easier to move people away from an opinion they currently hold than to have them form an opinion about something they have not previously cared about
    C. easy to move people toward a strong opinion on anything, as long as the message appeals to their reason and intellect
    D. difficult to move people toward a strong opinion on anything, no matter what the approach

15. In conducting an education program, many agencies use meetings and conferences to educate an audience about the organization and its programs. Advantages associated with this approach include
    I. a captive audience that is known to be interested in the topic
    II. ample opportunities for verifying learning
    III. cost-efficient meeting space
    IV. the ability to provide information on a wider variety of subjects

    The CORRECT answer is:
    A. I and II   B. I, III and IV   C. II and III   D. I, II, III and IV

16. An agency is attempting to evaluate the effectiveness of its educational programs. For this purpose, it wants to observe several focus groups discussing particular programs.
    For this purpose, a focus group should never number more than _____ participants.
    A. 5   B. 10   C. 15   D. 20

17. A _____ speech is written so that several agency members can deliver it to different audiences with only minor variations. 17.____
    A. basic   B. printed   C. quota   D. pattern

18. Which of the following statements about public opinion is generally considered to be FALSE? 18.____
    A. Opinion is primarily reactive rather than proactive.
    B. People have more opinions about goals than about the means by which to achieve them.
    C. Facts tend to shift opinion in the accepted direction when opinion is not solidly structured.
    D. Public opinion is based more on information than desire.

19. An agency is trying to promote its educational program. 19.____
    As a general rule, the agency should NOT assume that
    A. people will only participate if they perceive an individual benefit
    B. promotions need to be aimed at small, discrete groups
    C. if the program is good, the audience will find out about it
    D. a variety of methods, including advertising, special events, and direct mail, should be considered

20. In planning a successful educational program, probably the first and most important question for an agency to ask is: 20.____
    A. What will be the content of the program?
    B. Who will be served by the program?
    C. When is the best time to schedule the program?
    D. Why is the program necessary?

21. Media kits are LEAST likely to contain 21.____
    A. fact sheets   B. memoranda
    C. photographs with captions   D. news releases

22. The use of pamphlets and booklets as media for communication with the public often involves the disadvantage that 22.____
    A. the messages contained within them are frequently nonspecific
    B. it is difficult to measure their effectiveness in delivering the message
    C. there are few opportunities for people to refer to them
    D. color reproduction is poor

23. The MOST important prerequisite of a good educational program is an 23.____
    A. abundance of resources to implement it
    B. individual staff unit formed for the purpose of program delivery
    C. accurate needs assessment
    D. uneducated constituency

24. After an education program has been delivered, an agency conducts a program evaluation to determine whether its objectives have been met.
General rules about how to conduct such an education program valuation include each of the following, EXCEPT that it
   A. must be done immediately after the program has been implemented
   B. should be simple and easy to use
   C. should be designed so that tabulation of responses can take place quickly and inexpensively
   D. should solicit mostly subjective, open-ended responses if the audience was large

25. Using electronic media such as television as means of educating the public is typically recommended ONLY for agencies that
   I. have a fairly simple message to begin with
   II. want to reach the masses, rather than a targeted audience
   III. have substantial financial resources
   IV. accept that they will not be able to measure the results of the campaign with much precision

   The CORRECT answer is:
   A. I and II   B. I, II and III   C. II and IV   D. I, II, III and IV

KEY (CORRECT ANSWERS)

1.	B		11.	C
2.	C		12.	D
3.	D		13.	A
4.	C		14.	D
5.	D		15.	B
6.	B		16.	B
7.	C		17.	D
8.	D		18.	D
9.	D		19.	C
10.	A		20.	D

21.	B
22.	B
23.	C
24.	D
25.	D

EXAMINATION SECTION
TEST 1

DIRECTIONS: Each question or incomplete statement is followed by several suggested answers or completions. Select the one that BEST answers the question or completes the statement. *PRINT THE LETTER OF THE CORRECT ANSWER IN THE SPACE AT THE RIGHT.*

1. When a supervisor in a large office introduces a change in the regular office procedure, it is USUAL to expect
    A. immediate acceptance by office staff, unless the change is unnecessary
    B. an immediate production increase, since new procedures are more stimulating than old ones
    C. a temporary production loss, even if the change is really an overall improvement
    D. resistance to the change only if it has been put into writing

    1.____

2. A supervisor evaluates the performance of subordinates and then applies measures, where needed, which result in bringing performance up to desired standards.
   Which of the following functions of management might he BEST be described as performing?
    A. Organizing   B. Controlling   C. Directing   D. Planning

    2.____

3. Assume that, as a supervisor, you have been assigned responsibility for a new and complex project which entails collection and analysis of data. You have prepared general written instructions which explain the project and procedures to be followed by several statisticians.
   Which of the following procedures would be MOST advisable for you, as the supervisor, to follow?
    A. Distribute the instructions to your subordinates to come to you with any important questions
    B. Distribute the instructions and advise subordinates to come to you with any important questions
    C. Meet with subordinates as a group and explain the project using the written instructions as a handout
    D. Delegate responsibility for further explanation of the project to an immediate qualified subordinate to free you for concentration on research design

    3.____

4. Supervisors have an obligation to make careful and thorough appraisals and reports of probationary employees.
   Of the following, the MOST important justification for this statement is that the probationary period
    A. should be used for positive development of the employee's understanding of the organization
    B. is the most effective period for changing a new employee's knowledges, skills, and attitudes

    4.____

C. insures that the employee will meet work standard requirements on future assignments
D. should be considered as the final step in the selection process

5. Many studies of management indicate that a principal reason for failure of supervisors lies in their ability to delegate duties effectively.
Which one of the following practices by a supervisor would NOT be a block to successful delegation?
A. Instructing the delegate to follow a set procedure in carrying out the assignment
B. Maintaining point-by-point control over the process delegated
C. Transferring ultimate responsibility for the duties assigned to the delegate
D. Requiring the delegate to keep the delegator informed of his progress

5.____

6. Crosswise communication occurs between personnel at lower or middle levels of different organizational units. It often speeds information and improves understanding, but has certain dangers.
Of the following proposed policies, which would NOT be important as a safeguard in crosswise communication?
A. Supervisors should agree as to how crosswise communication should occur.
B. Crosswise relationships must exist only between employees of equal status.
C. Subordinates must keep their superiors informed about their interdepartmental communications.
D. Subordinates must refrain from making commitments beyond their authority.

6.____

7. Systems theory has given us certain principles which are as applicable to organizational and social activities as they are to those of science.
With regard to the training of employees in an organization, which of the following is likely to be MOST consistent with the modern systems approach?
Training can be effective ONLY when it is
A. related to the individual abilities of the employees
B. done on all levels of the organizational hierarchy
C. evaluated on the basis of experimental and control groups
D. provided on the job by the immediate supervisor

7.____

8. The management of a large agency, before making a decision as to whether or not to computerize its operations, should have a feasibility study made.
Of the following, the one which is LEAST important to include in such a study is
A. the current abilities of management and staff to use a computer
B. projected workloads and changes in objectives of functional units in the agency
C. the contributions expected of each organizational unit towards achievement of agency objectives
D. the decision-making activity and informational needs of each management function

8.____

9. Managing information covers the creation, collection, processing, storage, and transmission of information that appears in a variety of forms. A supervisor responsible for a statistical unit can be considered, in many respects, an information manager.
Of the following, which would be considered the LEAST important aspect of the information manager's job?
   A. Establishing better information standards and forms
   B. Reducing the amount of unnecessary paperwork performed
   C. Producing progressively greater numbers of informational reports
   D. Developing a greater appreciation for information among management members

10. Because of the need for improvement in information systems throughout industry and government, various techniques for improving these systems have been developed.
Of these, *systems simulation* is a technique for improving systems which
   A. creates new ideas and concepts through the use of a computer
   B. deals with time controlling of interrelated systems which make up an overall project
   C. permits experimentation with various ideas to see what results might be obtained
   D. does not rely on assumptions which condition the value of the results

11. The one of the following which it is NOT advisable for a supervisor to do when dealing with individual employees is to
   A. recognize a person's outstanding service as well as his mistakes
   B. help an employee satisfy his need to excel
   C. encourage an efficient employee to seek better opportunities even if this action may cause the supervisor to lose a good worker
   D. take public notice of an employee's mistakes so that fewer errors will be made in the future

12. Suppose that you are in a department where you are given the responsibility for teaching seven new assistants a number of routine procedures that all assistants should know.
Of the following, the BEST method for you to follow in teaching these procedures is to
   A. separate the slower learners from the faster learners and adapt your presentation to their level of ability
   B. instruct all the new employees in a group without attempting to assess differences in learning rates
   C. restrict your approach to giving them detailed written instructions in order to save time
   D. avoid giving the employees written instructions in order to force them to memorize job procedures quickly

13. Suppose that you are a supervisor to whom several assistants must hand in work for review. You notice that one of the assistants gets very upset whenever you discover an error in his work, although all the assistants make mistakes from time to time.
Of the following, it would be BEST for you to
    A. arrange discreetly for the employee's work to be reviewed by another supervisor
    B. ignore his reaction since giving attention to such behavior increases its intensity
    C. suggest that the employee seek medical help since he has such great difficulty in accepting normal criticism
    D. try to build the employee's self-confidence by emphasizing those parts of his work that are done well

14. Suppose you are a supervisor responsible for supervising a number of assistants in an agency where each assistant receives a manual of policies and procedures when he first reports for work. You have been asked to teach your subordinates a new procedure which requires knowledge of several items of policy and procedure found in the manual.
The one of the following techniques which it would be BEST for you to employ is to
    A. give verbal instructions which include a review of the appropriate standard procedures as well as an explanation of new tasks
    B. give individual instruction restricted to the new procedure to each assistant as the need arises
    C. provide written instructions for new procedural elements and refer employees to their manuals for explanation of standard procedures
    D. ask employees to review appropriate sections of their manual and then explain those aspects of the new procedure which the manual did not cover

15. Supposes that you are a supervisor in charge of a unit in which changes in work procedures are about to be instituted.
The one of the following which you, as the supervisor, should anticipate as being MOST likely to occur during the changeover is
    A. a temporary rise in production because of interest in the new procedures
    B. uniform acceptance of these procedures on the part of your staff
    C. varying interpretations of the new procedures by your staff
    D. general agreement among staff members that the new procedures are advantageous

16. Suppose that a supervisor and one of the assistants under his supervision are known to be friends who play golf together on weekends.
The maintenance of such a friendship on the part of the supervisor is GENERALLY
    A. *acceptable* as long as this assistant continues to perform his duties satisfactorily
    B. *unacceptable* since the supervisor will find it difficult to treat the assistant as a subordinate

C. *acceptable* if the supervisor does not favor this assistant above other employees
D. *unacceptable* because the other assistants will resent the friendship regardless of the supervisor's behavior on the job

17. Suppose that you are a supervisor assigned to review the financial records of an agency which has recently undergone a major reorganization.
Which of the following would it be BEST for you to do FIRST?
    A. Interview the individual in charge of agency financial operations to determine whether the organizational changes affect the system of financial review
    B. Discuss the nature of the reorganization with your own supervisor to anticipate and plan a new financial review procedure
    C. Carry out the financial review as usual, and adjust your methods to any problems arising from the reorganization
    D. Request a written report from the agency head explaining the nature of the reorganization and recommending changes in the system of financial review

17.____

18. Suppose that a newly assigned supervisor finds that he must delegate some of his duties to subordinates in order to get the work done.
Which one of the following would NOT be a block to his delegating these duties effectively?
    A. Inability to give proper directions as to what he wants done
    B. Reluctance to take calculated risks
    C. Lack of trust in his subordinates
    D. Retaining ultimate responsibility for the delegated work

18.____

19. A supervisor sometimes performs the staff function of preparing and circulating reports among bureau chiefs.
Which of the following is LEAST important as an objective in designing and writing such reports?
    A. Providing relevant information on past, present, and future actions
    B. Modifying his language in order to insure goodwill among the bureau chiefs
    C. Helping the readers of the report to make appropriate decisions
    D. Summarizing important information to help readers see trends or outstanding points

19.____

20. Suppose you are a supervisor assigned to prepare a report to be read by all bureau chiefs in your agency.
The MOST important reason for avoiding highly technical accounting terminology in writing this report is to
    A. ensure the accuracy and relevancy of the text
    B. insure winning the readers' cooperation
    C. make the report more interesting to the readers
    D. make it easier for the readers to understand

20.____

21. Which of the following conditions is MOST likely to cause low morale in an office?
   A. Different standards of performance for individuals in the same title
   B. A requirement that employees perform at full capacity
   C. Standards of performance that vary with titles of employees
   D. Careful attention to the image of the division or department

22. A wise supervisor or representative of management realizes that, in the relationship between supervisor and subordinates, all power is not on the side of management, and that subordinates do sometimes react to restrictive authority in such a manner as to seriously retard management's objectives. A wise supervisor does not stimulate such reactions.
In the subordinate's attempt to retaliate against an unusually authoritative management style, which of the following actions would generally be LEAST successful for the subordinate? He
   A. joins with other employees in organizations to deal with management
   B. obviously delays in carrying out instructions which are given in an arrogant or incisive manner
   C. performs assignments exactly as instructed even when he recognizes errors in instructions
   D. holds back the flow of feedback information to superiors

23. Which of the following is the MOST likely and costly effect of vague and indefinite instructions given to subordinates by a supervisor?
   A. Misunderstanding and ineffective work on the part of the subordinates
   B. A necessity for the supervisor to report identical instructions with each assignment
   C. A failure of the supervisor to adequately keep the attention of subordinates
   D. Inability of subordinates to assist each other in the absence of the supervisor

24. At the professional level, there is a kind of informal authority which exercises itself even though no delegation of authority has taken place from higher management. It occurs within the context of knowledge required and professional competence in a special area.
An example of the kind of authority described in this statement is MOST clearly exemplified in the situation where a senior supervisor influences associates and subordinates by virtue of the
   A. salary level fixed for his particular set of duties
   B. amount of college training he possesses
   C. technical position he has gained and holds on the work team
   D. initiative and judgment he has demonstrated to his supervisor

25. An assistant under your supervision attempts to conceal the fact that he has made an error.
Under this circumstance, it would be BEST for you, as the supervisor, to proceed on the assumption that

A. this evasion indicates something wrong in the fundamental relationship between you and the assistant
B. this evasion is not deliberate, if the error is subsequently corrected by the assistant
C. this evasion should be overlooked if the error is not significant
D. detection and correction of errors will come about as an automatic consequence of internal control procedures

KEY (CORRECT ANSWERS)

1.	C	11.	D
2.	B	12.	B
3.	C	13.	D
4.	D	14.	A
5.	D	15.	C
6.	B	16.	C
7.	B	17.	A
8.	A	18.	D
9.	C	19.	B
10.	C	20.	D

21. A
22. B
23. A
24. C
25. A

TEST 2

DIRECTIONS: Each question or incomplete statement is followed by several suggested answers or completions. Select the one that BEST answers the question or completes the statement. *PRINT THE LETTER OF THE CORRECT ANSWER IN THE SPACE AT THE RIGHT.*

1. The unit which you supervise has a number of attorneys, accountants, examiners, statisticians, and clerks who prepare some of the routine papers required to be filed. In order to be certain that nothing goes out of your office that is improper, you have instituted a system that requires that you review and initial all moving papers, memoranda of law and briefs that are prepared. As a result, you put in a great deal of overtime and even must take work home with you frequently.
A situation such as this is
    A. inevitable if you are to keep proper controls over the quality of the office work product
    B. indicative of the fact that the agency must provide an additional position within your office for an assistant supervisor who would do all the reviewing, leaving you free for other pressing administrative work and to handle the most difficult work in your unit
    C. the logical result of an ever-increasing caseload
    D. symptomatic of poor supervision and management

2. Your unit has been assigned a new employee who has never worked for the city.
To orient him to his job in your unit, of the following, the BEST procedure is first to
    A. assign him to another employee to whatever work that employee gives him so that he can become familiar with your work and at the same time be productive
    B. give him copies of the charter and code provisions affecting your operations plus any in-office memoranda or instructions that are available and have him read them
    C. assign him to work on a relatively simple problem and then, after he has finished it, tell him politely what he did wrong
    D. explain to him the duties of his position and the functions of the office

3. A bureau chief who supervises other supervisors makes it a practice to assign them more cases than they can possibly handle.
This approach is
    A. *right*, because it results in getting more work done than would otherwise be the case
    B. *right*, because it relieves the bureau chief making the assignments of the responsibility of getting the work done
    C. *wrong*, because it builds resistance on the part of those called upon to handle the caseload
    D. *wrong*, because superiors lose track of cases

4. Assume you are a supervisor and are expected to exercise *authority* over subordinates.
   Which of the following BEST defines *authority*? The
   A. ability to control the nature of the contribution a subordinate is desirous of making
   B. innate inability to get others to do for you what you want to get done irrespective of their own wishes
   C. legal right conferred by the agency to control the actions of others
   D. power to determine a subordinate's attitude toward his agency and his superiors

5. Paternalistic leadership stresses a paternal or fatherly influence in the relationships between the leader and the group and is manifest in a watchful care for the comfort and welfare of the followers.
   Which one of the following statements regarding paternalistic leadership is MOST accurate?
   A. Employees who work well under paternalistic leadership come to expect such leadership even when the paternal leader has left the organization.
   B. Most disputes arising out of supervisor-subordinate relationships develop because group leaders do not understand the principles of paternalistic leadership.
   C. Paternalistic leadership frequently destroys office relationships because most employees are turned into non-thinking dependent robots.
   D. Paternalistic leadership is rarely, if ever, successful because employees resent paternalistic leadership which they equate with weakness.

6. Employees who have extensive dealings with members of the public should have, as much as possible, *real acceptance* of all people and a willingness to serve everyone impartially and objectively.
   Assuming that this statement is correct, the one of the following which would be the BEST demonstration of *real acceptance* is
   A. condoning antisocial behavior
   B. giving the appearance of agreeing with everyone encountered
   C. refusing to give opinions on anyone's behavior
   D. understanding the feelings expressed through a person's behavior

7. Assume that the agency chief has requested you to help plan a public relations program because of recent complaints from citizens about the unbecoming conduct and language of various groups of city employees who have dealings with the public.
   In carrying out this assignment, the one of the following steps which should be undertaken FIRST is to
   A. study the characteristics of the public clientele dealt with by employees in your agency
   B. arrange to have employees attend several seminars on human relations
   C. develop several procedures for dealing with the public and allow the staff to choose the one which is best
   D. find out whether the employees in your agency may oppose any plan proposed by you

8. The one of the following statements which BEST expresses the relationship between the morale of government employees and the public relations aspects of their work is:
   A. There is little relationship between employee morale and public relations, chiefly because public opinion is shaped primarily by response to departmental policy formulation.
   B. Employee morale is closely related to public relations, chiefly because the employee's morale will largely determine the manner in which he deals with the public.
   C. There is little relationship between employee morale and public relations, chiefly because public relations is primarily a function of the agency's public relations department.
   D. Employee morale is closely related to public relations, chiefly because employee morale indicates the attitude of the agency's top officials toward the public.

9. As a supervisor, you are required to deal extensively with the public. The agency chief has indicated that he is considering holding a special in-service training course for employees in communications skills
   Holding this training course would be
   A. *advisable*, chiefly because government employees should receive formal training in public relations skills
   B. *inadvisable*, chiefly because the public regards such training as a *waste of the taxpayers money*
   C. *advisable*, chiefly because such training will enable the employee to aid in drafting departmental press releases
   D. *inadvisable*, chiefly because of the great difficulty involved in developing skills through formal instruction

10. Assume that you have extensive contact with the public. In dealing with the public, sensitivity to an individual's attitudes is important because these attitudes can be used to predict behavior.
    However, the MAIN reason that attitudes CANNOT successfully predict all behavior is that
    A. attitudes are highly resistant to change
    B. an individual acquires attitudes as a function of growing up in a particular cultural environment
    C. attitudes are only one of many factors which determine a person's behavior
    D. an individual's behavior is not always observable

11. Rotation of employees from assignment to assignment is sometimes advocated by management experts.
    Of the following, the MOST probable advantage to the organization of this practice is that it leads to
    A. higher specialization of duties so that excessive identification with the overall organization is reduced
    B. increased loyalty of employees to their immediate supervisors

C. greater training and development of employees
D. intensified desire of employees to obtain additional, outside formal education

12. Usually, a supervisor should attempt to standardize the work for which he is responsible.
The one of the following which is a BASIC reason for doing this is to
A. eliminate the need to establish priorities
B. permit the granting of exceptions to rules and special circumstances
C. facilitate the taking of action based on applicable standards
D. learn the identity of outstanding employees

12.____

13. The differences between line and staff authority are often quite ambiguous. Of the following, the ESSENTIAL difference is that
A. *line authority* is exercised by first-level supervisors; *staff authority* is exercised by higher-level supervisors and managerial staff
B. *staff authority* is the right to issue directives; *line authority* is entirely consultative
C. *line authority* is the power to make decisions regarding intra-agency matters; *staff authority* involves decisions regarding inter-agency matters
D. *staff authority* is largely advisory; *line authority* is the right to command

13.____

14. Modern management theory stresses work-centered motivation as one way of increasing the productivity of employees.
The one of the following which is PARTICULARLY characteristic of such motivation is that it
A. emphasizes the crucial role of routinization of procedures
B. stresses the satisfaction to be found in performing work
C. features the value of wages and fringe benefits
D. uses a firm but fair method of discipline

14.____

15. The agency's informal communications network is called the *grapevine.*
If employees are learning about important organizational developments primarily through the grapevine, this is MOST likely an indication that
A. official channels of communication are not functioning so efficiently as they should
B. supervisory personnel are making effective use of the grapevine to communicate with subordinates
C. employees already have a clear understanding of the agency's policies and procedures
D. upward formal channels of communication within the agency are informing management of employee grievances

15.____

16. Of the following, a flow chart is BEST described as a chart which shows
A. the places through which work moves in the course of the job process
B. which employees perform specific functions leading to the completion of a job

16.____

C. the schedules for production and how they eliminate waiting time between jobs
D. how work units are affected by the actions of related work units

17. Evaluation of the results of training is necessary in order to assess its value. Of the following, the BEST technique for the supervisor to use in determining whether the training under consideration actually resulted in the desired modification of the behavior of the employee concerned is through
    A. inference   B. job analysis   C. observation   D. simulation

17.____

18. The usual distinction between line and staff authority is that staff authority is mainly advisory, whereas line authority is the right to command. However, a third category has been suggested-prescriptive-to distinguish those personnel whose functions may be formally defined as staff but in practice exercise considerable authority regarding decisions relating to their specialties.
    The one of the following which indicates the MAJOR purpose of creating this third category is to
    A. develop the ability of each employee to perform a greater number of tasks
    B. reduce line-staff conflict
    C. prevent over-specialization of functions
    D. encourage decision-making by line personnel

18.____

19. It is sometimes considered desirable to train employees to a standard of proficiency higher than that deemed necessary for actual job performance.
    The MOST likely reason for such overtraining would be to
    A. eliminate the need for standards
    B. increase the value of refresher training
    C. compensate for previous lack of training
    D. reduce forgetting or loss of skill

19.____

20. Assume that you have been directed to immediately institute various new procedures in the handling of records.
    Of the following, the BEST method for you to use to insure that your subordinates know exactly what to do is to
    A. circulate a memorandum explaining the new procedure have your subordinates initial it
    B. explain the new procedures to one or two subordinates and ask them to tell the others
    C. have a meeting with your subordinates to give them copies of the procedures and discuss it with them
    D. post the new procedures where they can be referred to by all those concerned

20.____

21. A supervisor decided to hold a problem-solving conference with his entire staff and distributed an announcement and agenda one week before the meeting.
Of the following, the BEST reason for providing each participant with an agenda is that
    A. participants will feel that something will be accomplished
    B. participants may prepare for the conference
    C. controversy will be reduced
    D. the top man should state the expected conclusions

21.____

22. In attempting to motivate employees, rewards are considered preferable to punishment PRIMARILY because
    A. punishment seldom has any effect on human behavior
    B. punishment usually results in decreased production
    C. supervisors find it difficult to punish
    D. rewards are more likely to result in willing cooperation

22.____

23. In an attempt to combat the low morale in his organization, a high-level supervisor publicized an *open-door* policy to allow employees who wished to do so to come to him with their complaints.
Which of the following is LEAST likely to account for the fact that no employee came in with a complaint?
    A. Employees are generally reluctant to go over the heads of their immediate supervisors.
    B. The employees did not feel that management would help them.
    C. The low morale was not due to complaints association with the job
    D. The employees felt that they had more to lose than to gain.

23.____

24. It is MOST desirable to use written instructions rather than oral instructions for a particular job when
    A. a mistake on the job will not be serious
    B. the job can be completed in a short time
    C. there is no need to explain the job minutely
    D. the job involves many details

24.____

25. You have been asked to prepare for public distribution a statement dealing with a controversial matter.
Of the following approaches, the one which would usually be MOST effective is to present your department's point of view
    A. as tersely as possible with no reference to any other matters
    B. developed from ideas and facts well known to most readers
    C. and show all the statistical data and techniques which were used in arriving at it
    D. in such a way that the controversial parts are omitted

25.____

KEY (CORRECT ANSWERS)

1.	D	11.	C
2.	D	12.	C
3.	C	13.	D
4.	C	14.	B
5.	A	15.	A
6.	D	16.	A
7.	A	17.	C
8.	B	18.	B
9.	A	19.	D
10.	C	20.	C

21. B
22. D
23. C
24. D
25. B

TEST 3

DIRECTIONS: Each question or incomplete statement is followed by several suggested answers or completions. Select the one that BEST answers the question or completes the statement. *PRINT THE LETTER OF THE CORRECT ANSWER IN THE SPACE AT THE RIGHT.*

1. An administrator who supervises other supervisors makes it a practice to set deadline dates for completion of assignments.
   A NATURAL consequence of setting deadline dates is that
   A. supervisors will usually wait until the deadline date before they give projects their wholehearted attention
   B. projects are completed sooner than if no deadline dates are set
   C. such dates are ignored even though they are conspicuously posted
   D. the frequency of errors sharply increases resulting in an inability to meet deadlines

   1.____

2. Assume that you are chairing a meeting of the members of your staff. You throw out a question to the group. No one answers your question immediately, so that you find yourself faced with silence.
   In the circumstances, it would probably be BEST for you to
   A. ask the member of the group who appears to be least attentive to repeat the question
   B. change the topic quickly
   C. repeat the question carefully, pronouncing each word, and if there is still no response, repeat the question an additional time
   D. wait for an answer since someone will usually say something to break the tension

   2.____

3. Assume that you are holding a meeting with the members of your staff. John, a member of the unit, keeps sidetracking the subject of the discussion by bringing up extraneous matters. You deal with the situation by saying to him after he has raised an immaterial point, *"That's an interesting point John, but can you show me how it ties in with what we're talking about?"*
   Your approach in this situation would GENERALLY be considered
   A. *bad*; you have prevented the group from discussing not only extraneous matters but pertinent material as well
   B. *bad*; you have seriously humiliated John in front of the entire group
   C. *good*; you have pointed out how the discussion is straying from the main topic
   D. *good*; you have prevented John from presenting extraneous matters at future meetings

   3.____

4. Assume that a senior supervisor is asked to supervise a group of staff personnel. The work of one of these staff men meets minimum standards of acceptability. However, this staff man constantly looks for something at which to take offense. In any conversation with either a fellow staff man or with a superior, he views the slightest criticism as a grave insult.

   4.____

123

In this case, the senior supervisor should
- A. advise the staff man that the next time he refuses to accept criticism, he will be severely reprimanded
- B. ask member of the group for advice on how to deal with this staff man
- C. make it a practice to speak calmly, slowly, and deliberately to this staff man and question him frequently to make sure that there is no breakdown in communications
- D. recognize that professional help may be required and that this problem may not be conducive to a solution by a supervisor

5. Assume that you discover that one of the staff in preparing certain papers has made a serious mistake which has become obvious.
In dealing with this situation, it would be BEST for you to begin by
   - A. asking the employee how the mistake happened
   - B. asking the employee to read through the papers to see whether he can correct the mistake
   - C. pointing out to the employee that, while an occasional error is permissible, frequent errors can prove a source of embarrassment to all concerned
   - D. pointing to the mistake and asking the employee whether he realizes the consequences of the mistake

5._____

6. You desire to develop teamwork among the members of your staff. You are assigned a case which will require that two of the staff work together if the papers are to be prepared in time. You decided to assign two employees, whom you know to be close friends, to work on these papers.
Your action in this regard would GENERALLY be considered
   - A. *bad*; friends working together tend to do as little as they can get away with
   - B. *bad*; people who are friends socially often find that the bonds of friendship disintegrate in work situations
   - C. *good*; friends who are permitted to work together show their appreciation by utilizing every opportunity to reinforce the group leader's position of authority
   - D. *good*; the evidence suggests that more work can be done in this way

6._____

7. You notice that all of the employees, without exception, take lunch hours which in your view are excessively long. You call each of them to your desk and point out that unless this practice is brought to a stop, appropriate action will be taken.
The way in which you handled this problem would GENERALLY be considered
   - A. *proper*, primarily because a civil servant, no matter what his professional status, owes the public a full day's work for a full day's pay
   - B. *proper*, primarily because employees need to have a clear picture of the rewards and penalties that go with public employment
   - C. *improper*, primarily because group problems require group discussion which need not be formal in character
   - D. *improper*, primarily because professional personnel resent having such matters as lunch hours brought to their attention

7._____

8. In communicating with superiors or subordinates, it is well to bear in mind a phenomenon known as the *halo effect*. An example of this *halo effect* occurs when we
   A. employ informal language in a formal setting as a means of attracting attention
   B. ignore the advice of someone we distrust without evaluating the advice
   C. ask people to speak up who have a tendency to speak softly or occasionally indistinctly
   D. react to a piece of good work by inquiring into the motivations of those who did the work

8.____

9. Which of the following dangers is MOST likely to arise when a work group becomes too tightly knit? The
   A. group may appoint an informal leader who gradually sets policies and standards for the group to the detriment of the agency
   B. group may be reluctant to accept new employees as members
   C. quantity and quality of work produced may tend to diminish sharply despite the group's best efforts
   D. group may focus too strongly on employee benefits at inappropriate times

9.____

10. The overall managerial problem has become more complex because each group of management specialists will tend to view the interests of the enterprise in terms which are compatible with the survival or the increase of its special function. That is, each group will have a trained capacity for its own function and a *trained incapacity* to see its relation to the whole.
    The *trained incapacity* to which the foregoing passage refers PROBABLY results from
    A. an imbalance in the number of specialists as compared with the number of generalists
    B. development by each specialized group of a certain dominant value or goal that shapes its entire way of doing things
    C. low morale accompanied by lackadaisical behavior by large segments of the managerial staff
    D. supervisory failure to inculcate pride in workmanship

10.____

11. Of the following, the MOST important responsibility of a supervisor in charge of a section is to
    A establish close personal relationships with each of his subordinates in the section
    B. insure that each subordinate in the section knows the full range of his duties and responsibilities
    C. maintain friendly relations with his immediate supervisor
    D. protect his subordinates from criticism from any source

11.____

12. The BEST way to get a good work output from employees is to
    A. hold over them the threat of disciplinary action or removal
    B. maintain a steady, unrelenting pressure on them
    C. show them that you can do anything they can do faster and better
    D win their respect and liking so they want to work for you

12.____

13. Supervisors should GENERALLY
    A. lean more toward management than toward their subordinates
    B. lean neither toward subordinates nor management
    C. lean more toward their subordinates than toward their management
    D. maintain a proper balance between management and subordinates

14. For a supervisor in charge of a section to ask occasionally the opinion of a subordinate concerning a problem is
    A. *desirable*; but it would be even better if the subordinate were consulted routinely on every problem
    B. *desirable*; subordinates may make good suggestions and will be pleased by being consulted
    C. *undesirable*; subordinates may be resentful if their advice is not followed
    D. *undesirable*; the supervisor should not attempt to shift his responsibilities to subordinates

15. The PRIMARY responsibility of a supervisor is to
    A. gain the confidence and make friends of all his subordinates
    B. get the work done properly
    C. satisfy his superior and gain his respect
    D. train the men in new methods for doing the work

16. In starting a work simplification study, the one of the following steps that should be taken FIRST is to
    A. break the work down into its elements
    B. draw up a chart of operations
    C. enlist the interest and cooperation of the personnel
    D. suggest alternative procedures

17. Of the following, the MOST important value of a manual of procedures is that it usually
    A. eliminates the need for on-the-job training
    B. decreases the span of control which can be exercised by individual supervisory personnel
    C. outlines methods of operation for ready reference
    D. provides concrete examples of work previously performed by employees

18. Reprimanding a subordinate when he has done something wrong should be done PRIMARILY in order to
    A. deter others from similar acts
    B. improve the subordinate in future performance
    C. maintain discipline
    D. uphold departmental rules

19. Most of the training of new employees in a public agency is USUALLY accomplished by
    A. formal classes
    B. general orientation
    C. internship
    D. on-the-job activities

20. You find that delivery of a certain item cannot possibly be made to a using agency by the date the using agency requested.
    Of the following, the MOST advisable course of action for you to take FIRST is to
    A. cancel the order and inform the using agency
    B. discuss the problem with the using agency
    C. notify the using agency to obtain the item through direct purchase
    D. schedule the delivery for the earliest possible date

21. Assume that one of your subordinates has gotten into the habit of regularly and routinely referring every small problem which arises in his work to you.
    In order to help him overcome this habit, it is generally MOST advisable for you to
    A. advise him that you do not have time to discuss each problem with him and that he should do whatever he wants
    B. ask your subordinate for his solution and approve any satisfactory approach that he suggests
    C. refuse to discuss such routine problems with him
    D. tell him that he should consider looking for another position if he does not feel competent to solve such routine problems

22. The BEST of the following reasons for developing understudies to supervisory staff is that this practice
    A. assures that capable staff will not leave their jobs since they are certain to be promoted
    B. helps to assure continued efficiency when persons in important positions leave their jobs
    C. improves morale by demonstrating to employees the opportunities for advancement
    D. provides an opportunity for giving on-the-job training

23. When a supervisor delegates some of his work to a subordinate, the
    A. supervisor retains final responsibility for the work
    B. supervisor should not check on the work until it has been completed
    C. subordinate assumes full responsibility for the successful completion of the work
    D. subordinate is likely to lose interest and get less satisfaction from the work

24. Sometimes it is necessary to give out written orders or to post written or typed information on a bulletin board rather than to merely give spoken orders. The supervisor must decide how he will do it.
    In which of the following situations would it be BETTER for him to give written rather than spoken orders?
    A. He is going to reassign a man from one unit to another under his supervision.
    B. His staff must be informed of a permanent change in a complicated operating procedure.

C. A man must be transferred from a clerical unit to an operating unit.
D. He must order a group of staff men to do a difficult and tedious inventory job to which most of them are likely to object.

25. Of the following symbolic patterns, which one is NOT representative of a normal direction in which formal organizational communications flow?

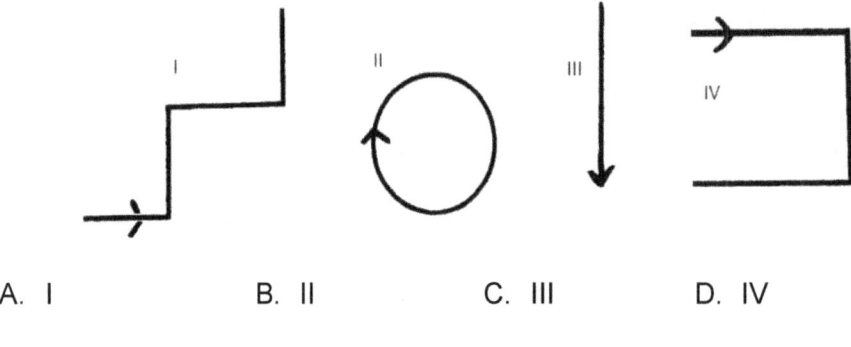

A. I B. II C. III D. IV

KEY (CORRECT ANSWERS)

1. B
2. D
3. C
4. D
5. A

6. D
7. C
8. B
9. B
10. B

11. B
12. D
13. D
14. B
15. B

16. C
17. C
18. B
19. D
20. B

21. B
22. B
23. A
24. B
25. B

EXAMINATION SECTION
TEST 1

DIRECTIONS: Each question or incomplete statement is followed by several suggested answers or completions. Select the one that BEST answers the question or completes the statement. *PRINT THE LETTER OF THE CORRECT ANSWER IN THE SPACE AT THE RIGHT.*

1. Professional staff members in large organizations are sometimes frustrated by a lack of vital work-related information because of the failure of some middle-management supervisors to pass along unrestricted information from top management.
   All of the following are considered to be reasons for such failure to pass along information EXCEPT the supervisors'
   A. belief that information affecting procedures will be ignored unless they are present to supervise their subordinates
   B. fear that specific information will require explanation or justification
   C. inclination to regard the possession of information as a symbol of higher status
   D. tendency to treat information a private property

   1.____

2. Increasingly in government, employees' records are being handled by automated data processing systems. However, employees frequently doubt a computer's ability to handle their records properly.
   Which of the following is the BEST way for management to overcome such doubts?
   A. Conduct a public relations campaign to explain the savings certain to result from the use of computers
   B. Use automated data processing equipment made by the firm which has the best repair facilities in the industry
   C. Maintain a clerical force to spot check on the accuracy of the computer's recordkeeping
   D. Establish automated data processing systems that are objective, impartial, and take into account individual factors as far as possible

   2.____

3. Some management experts question the usefulness of offering cash to individual employees for their suggestions.
   Which of the following reasons for opposing cash awards is MOST valid?
   A. Emphasis on individual gain deters cooperative effort.
   B. Money spent on evaluating suggestions may outweigh the value of the suggestions.
   C. Awards encourage employees to think about unusual methods of doing work.
   D. Suggestions too technical for ordinary evaluation are usually presented.

   3.____

4. The use of outside consultants, rather than regular staff, in studying and recommending improvements in the operations of public agencies has been criticized.
   Of the following, the BEST argument in favor of using regular staff is that such staff can better perform the work because they
   A. are more knowledgeable about operations and problems
   B. can more easily be organized into teams consisting of technical specialists
   C. may wish to gain additional professional experience
   D. will provide reports which will be more interesting to the public since they are more experienced

5. One approach to organizational problem-solving is to have all problem-solving authority centralized at the top of the organization.
   However, from the viewpoint of providing maximum service to the public, this practice is UNWISE chiefly because it
   A. reduces the responsibility of the decision-makers
   B. produces delays
   C. reduces internal communications
   D. requires specialists

6. Research has shown that problem-solving efficiency is optimal when the motivation of the problem-solver is at a moderate rather than an extreme level.
   Of the following, probably the CHIEF reason for this is that the problem-solver
   A. will cause confusion among his subordinates when his motivation is too high
   B. must avoid alternate solutions that tend to lead him up blind alleys
   C. can devote his attention to both the immediate problem as well as to other relevant problems in the general area
   D. must feel the need to solve the problem but not so urgently as to direct all his attention to the need and none to the means of solution

7. Don't be afraid to make mistakes. Many organizations are paralyzed from the fear of making mistakes. As a result, they don't do the things they should; they don't try new and different ideas.
   For the effective supervisor, the MOST valid implication of this statement is that
   A. mistakes should not be encouraged, but there are some unavoidable risks in decision-making
   B. mistakes which stem from trying new and different ideas are usually not serious
   C. the possibility of doing things wrong is limited by one's organizational position
   D. the fear of making mistakes will prevent future errors

8. The duties of an employee under your supervision may be either routine, problem-solving, innovative, or creative.
   Which of the following BEST describes duties which are both innovative and creative?

A. Checking to make sure that work is done properly
B. Applying principles in a practical matter
C. Developing new and better methods of meeting goals
D. Working at two or more jobs at the same time

9. According to modern management theory, a supervisor who uses as little authority as possible and as much as is necessary would be considered to be using a mode that is
   A. autocratic
   B. inappropriate
   C. participative
   D. directive

9.____

10. Delegation involves establishing and maintaining effective working arrangements between a supervisor and the persons who report to him.
    Delegation is MOST likely to have taken place when the
    A. entire staff openly discusses common problems in order to reach solutions satisfactory to the supervisor
    B. performance of specified work is entrusted to a capable person, and the expected results are mutually understood
    C. persons assigned to properly accomplish work are carefully evaluated and given a chance to explain shortcomings
    D. supervisor provides specific written instructions in order to prevent anxiety on the part of inexperienced persons

10.____

11. Supervisors often not aware of the effect that their behavior has on their subordinates.
    The one of the following training methods which would be BEST for changing such supervisory behavior is _____ training.
    A. essential skills
    B. off-the-job
    C. sensitivity
    D. developmental

11.____

12. A supervisor, in his role as a trainer, may have to decide on the length and frequency of training sessions.
    When the material to be taught is new, difficult, and lengthy, the trainer should be guided by the principle that for BEST results in such circumstances, sessions should be
    A. longer, relatively fewer in number, and held on successive days
    B. shorter, relatively greater in number, and spaced at intervals of several days
    C. of average length, relatively fewer in number, and held at intermittent intervals
    D. of random length and frequency, but spaced at fixed intervals

12.____

13. Employee training which is based on realistic simulation, sometimes known as *game play* or *role play*, is sometimes preferable to learning from actual experience on the job.
    Which of the following is NOT a correct statement concerning the value of simulation to trainees?

13.____

A. Simulation allows for practice in decision-making without any need for subsequent discussion.
B. Simulation is intrinsically motivating because it offers a variety of challenges.
C. Compared to other, more traditional training techniques, simulation is dynamic.
D. The simulation environment is nonpunitive as compared to real life.

14. Programmed instruction as a method of training has all of the following advantages EXCEPT:
    A. Learning is accomplished in an optimum sequence of distinct steps.
    B. Trainees have wide latitude in deciding what is to be learned within each program.
    C. The trainee takes an active part in the learning process.
    D. The trainee receives immediate knowledge of the results of his response.

15. In a work-study program, trainees were required to submit weekly written performance reports in order to insure that work assignments fulfilled the program objectives.
    Such reports would also assist the administrator of the work-study program PRIMARILY to
    A. eliminate personal counseling for the trainees
    B. identify problems requiring prompt resolution
    C. reduce the amount of clerical work for all concerned
    D. estimate the rate at which budgeted funds are being expended

16. Which of the following would be MOST useful in order to avoid misunderstanding when preparing correspondence or reports?
    A. Use vocabulary which is at an elementary level
    B. Present each sentence as an individual paragraph
    C. Have someone other than the writer read the material for clarity
    D. Use general words which are open to interpretation

17. Which of the following supervisory methods would be MOST likely to train subordinates to give a prompt response to memoranda in an organizational setting where most transactions are informal?
    A. Issue a written directive setting forth a schedule of strict deadlines
    B. Let it be known, informally, that those who respond promptly will be rewarded
    C. Follow up each memorandum by a personal inquiry regarding the receiver's reaction to it
    D. Direct subordinates to furnish a precise explanation for ignoring memos

18. Conferences may fail for a number of reasons. Still, a conference that is an apparent failure may have some benefit.
    Which of the following would LEAST likely be such a benefit?
    It may
    A. increase for most participants their possessiveness about information they have

B. produce a climate of good will and trust among many of the participants
C. provide most participants with an opportunity to learn things about the others
D. serve as a unifying force to keep most of the individuals functioning as a group

19. Assume that you have been assigned to study and suggest improvements in an operating unit of a delegate agency whose staff has become overwhelmed with problems, has had inadequate resources, and has become accustomed to things getting worse. The staff is indifferent to cooperating with you because they see no hope of improvement.
Which of the following steps would be LEAST useful in carrying out your assignment?
    A. Encourage the entire staff to make suggestions to you for change
    B. Inform the staff that management is somewhat dissatisfied with their performance
    C. Let staff know that you are fully aware of their problems and stresses
    D. Look for those problem area where changes can be made quickly

19.____

20. Which of the following statements about employer-employee relations is NOT considered to be correct by leading managerial experts?
    A. An important factor in good employer-employee relations is treating workers respectfully.
    B. Employer-employee relations are profoundly influenced by the fundamentals of human nature.
    C. Good employer-employee relations must stem from top management and reach downward.
    D. Employee unions are usually a major obstacle to establishing good employer-employee relations.

20.____

21. In connection with labor relations, the term *management rights* GENERALLY refers to
    A. a managerial review system in a grievance system
    B. statutory prohibitions that bar monetary negotiations
    C. the impact of collective bargaining on government
    D. those subjects which management considers to be non-negotiable

21.____

22. Barriers may exist to the utilization of women in higher level positions. Some of these barriers are attitudinal in nature.
Which of the following is MOST clearly attitudinal in nature?
    A. Advancement opportunities which are vertical in nature and thus require seniority
    B. Experience which is inadequate or irrelevant to the needs of a dynamic and progressive organization
    C. Inadequate means of early identification of employees with talent and potential for advancement
    D. Lack of self-confidence on the part of some women concerning their ability to handle a higher position

22.____

23. Because a reader reacts to the meaning he associates with a word, we can neve be sure what emotional impact a word may carry or how it may affect our readers.
    The MOST logical implication of this statement for employees who correspond with members of the public is that
    A. a writer should try to select a neutral word that will not bias his writing by its hidden emotional meaning
    B. simple language should be used in writing letters denying requests so that readers are not upset by the denial
    C. every writer should adopt a writing style which he finds natural and easy
    D. whenever there is doubt as to how a word is defined, the dictionary should be consulted

23.____

24. A public information program should be based on clear information about the nature of actual public knowledge and opinion. One way of learning about the views of the public is through the use of questionnaires.
    Which of the following is of LEAST importance in designing a questionnaire?
    A. A respondent should be asked for his name and address.
    B. A respondent should be asked to choose from among several statements the one which expresses his views.
    C. Questions should ask for responses in a form suitable for processing.
    D. Questions should be stated in familiar language.

24.____

25. Assume that you have accepted an invitation to speak before an interested group about a problem. You have brought with you for distribution a number of booklets and other informational material.
    Of the following, which would be the BEST way to use this material?
    A. Distribute it before you begin talking so that the audience may read it at their leisure.
    B. Distribute it during your talk to increase the likelihood that it will be read.
    C. Hold it until the end of your talk, then announce that those who wish may take or examine the material.
    D. Before starting the talk, leave it on a table in the back of the room so that people may pick it up as they enter.

25.____

KEY (CORRECT ANSWERS)

1.	A		11.	C
2.	D		12.	B
3.	A		13.	A
4.	A		14.	B
5.	B		15.	B
6.	D		16.	C
7.	A		17.	C
8.	C		18.	A
9.	C		19.	B
10.	B		20.	D

21. D
22. D
23. A
24. A
25. C

TEST 2

DIRECTIONS: Each question or incomplete statement is followed by several suggested answers or completions. Select the one that BEST answers the question or completes the statement. *PRINT THE LETTER OF THE CORRECT ANSWER IN THE SPACE AT THE RIGHT.*

1. Of the following, the FIRST step in planning an operation is to   1.____
   A. obtain relevant information
   B. identify the goal to be achieved
   C. consider possible alternatives
   D. make necessary assignments

2. A supervisor who is extremely busy performing routine tasks is MOST likely making INCORRECT use of what basic principle of supervision?   2.____
   A. Homogeneous Assignment
   B. Span of Control
   C. Work Distribution
   D. Delegation of Authority

3. Controls help supervisors to obtain information from which they can determine whether their staffs are achieving planned goals.
   Which one of the following would be LEAST useful as a control device?   3.____
   A. Employee diaries
   B. Organization charts
   C. Periodic inspections
   D. Progress charts

4. A certain employee has difficulty in effectively performing a particular portion of his routine assignments, but his overall productivity is average.
   As the direct supervisor of his individual, your BEST course of action would be to   4.____
   A. attempt to develop the man's capacity to execute the problematic facets of his assignments
   B. diversify the employee's work assignments in order to build up his confidence
   C. reassign the man to less difficult tasks
   D. request in a private conversation that the employee improve his work output

5. A supervisor who uses persuasion as a means of supervising a unit would GENERALLY also use which of the following practices to supervise his unit?   5.____
   A. Supervise and control the staff with an authoritative attitude to indicate that he is a *take-charge* individual
   B. Make significant changes in the organizational operations so as to improve job efficiency
   C. Remove major communication barriers between himself, subordinates, and management
   D. Supervise everyday operations while being mindful of the problems of his subordinates

6. Whenever a supervisor in charge of a unit delegate a routine task to a capable subordinate, he tells him exactly how to do it.   6.____

This practice is GENERALLY
- A. *desirable*, chiefly because good supervisors should be aware of the traits of their subordinates and delegate responsibilities to them accordingly
- B. *undesirable*, chiefly because only non-routine tasks should be delegated
- C. *desirable*, chiefly because a supervisor should frequently test the willingness of his subordinates to perform ordinary tasks
- D. *undesirable*, chiefly because a capable subordinate should usually be allowed to exercise his own discretion in doing a routine job

7. The one of the following activities through which a supervisor BEST demonstrates leadership ability is by
    - A. arranging periodic staff meetings in order to keep his subordinates informed about professional developments in the field
    - B. frequently issuing definite orders and directives which will lessen the need for subordinates to make decisions in handling any tasks assigned to them
    - C. devoting the major part of his time to supervising subordinates so as to simulate continuous improvement
    - D. setting aside time for self-development and research so as to improve the skills, techniques, and procedures of his unit

8. The following three statements relate to the supervision of employees:
    - I. The assignment of difficult tasks that offer a challenge is more conducive to good morale than the assignment of easy tasks.
    - II. The same general principles of supervision that apply to men are equally applicable to women.
    - III. The best retraining program should cover all phases of an employee's work in a general manner.

    Which of the following choices list ALL of the above statements that are generally correct?
    A. II, III   B. I   C. I, II   D. I, II, III

9. Which of the following examples BEST illustrates the application of the *exception principle* as a supervisory technique?
    - A. A complex job is divided among several employees who work simultaneously to complete the whole job in a shorter time.
    - B. An employee is required to complete any task delegated to him to such an extent that nothing is left for the superior who delegated the task except to approve it.
    - C. A superior delegates responsibility to a subordinate but retains authority to make the final decisions.
    - D. A superior delegates all work possible to his subordinates and retains that which requires his personal attention or performance

10. Assume that you are a supervisor. Your immediate superior frequently gives orders to your subordinates without your knowledge.
    Of the following, the MOST direct and effective way for you to handle this problem is to

A. tell our subordinates to take orders only from you
B. submit a report to higher authority in which you cite specific instances
C. discuss it with your immediate superior
D. find out to what extent your authority and prestige as a supervisor have been affected

11. In an agency which has as its primary purpose the protection of the public against fraudulent business practices, which of the following would GENERALLY be considered an *auxiliary* or *staff* rather than a *line* function? 11.____
    A. Interviewing victims of frauds and advising them about their legal remedies
    B. Daily activities directed toward prevention of fraudulent business practices
    C. Keeping records and statistics about business violations reported and corrected
    D. Follow-up inspections by investigators after corrective action has been taken

12. A supervisor can MOST effectively reduce the spread of false rumors through the *grapevine* by 12.____
    A. identifying and disciplining any subordinate responsible for initiating such rumors
    B. keeping his subordinates informed as much as possible about matters affecting them
    C. denying false rumors which might tend to lower staff morale and productivity
    D. making sure confidential matters are kept secure from access by unauthorized employees

13. A supervisor has tried to learn about the background, education, and family relationships of his subordinates through observation, personal contact, and inspection of their personnel records. 13.____
    These supervisor actions are GENERALLY
    A. *inadvisable*, chiefly because they may lead to charges of favoritism
    B. *advisable*, chiefly because they may make him more popular with his subordinates
    C. *inadvisable*, chiefly because his efforts may be regarded as an invasion of privacy
    D. *advisable*, chiefly because the information may enable him to develop better understanding of each of his subordinates

14. In an emergency situation, when action must be taken immediately, it is BEST for the supervisor to give orders in the form of 14.____
    A. direct commands which are brief and precise
    B. requests, so that his subordinates will not become alarmed
    C. suggestions which offer alternative courses of action
    D. implied directives, so that his subordinates may use their judgment in carrying them out

15. When demonstrating a new and complex procedure to a group of subordinates, it is ESSENTIAL that a supervisor
    A. go slowly and repeat the steps involved at least once
    B. show the employees common errors and the consequences of such errors
    C. go through the process at the usual speed so that the employees can see the rate at which they should work
    D. distribute summaries of the procedure during the demonstration and instruct his subordinates to refer to them afterwards

16. After a procedures manual has been written and distributed,
    A. continuous maintenance work is necessary to keep the manual current
    B. it is best to issue new manuals rather than make changes in the original manual
    C. no changes should be necessary
    D. only major changes should be considered

17. Of the following, the MOST important criterion of effective report writing is
    A. eloquence of writing style
    B. the use of technical language
    C. to be brief and to the point
    D. to cover all details

18. The use of electronic data processing
    A. has proven unsuccessful in most organizations
    B. has unquestionable advantages for all organizations
    C. is unnecessary in most organizations
    D. should be decided upon only after careful feasibility studies by individual organizations

19. The PRIMARY purpose of work measurement is to
    A. design and install a wage incentive program
    B. determine who should be promoted
    C. establish a yardstick to determine extent of progress
    D. set up a spirit of competition among employee

20. The action which is MOST effective in gaining acceptance of a study by the agency which is being studied is
    A. a directive from the agency head to install a study based on recommendations included in a report
    B. a lecture-type presentation following approval of the procedure
    C. a written procedure in narrative form covering the proposed system with visual presentations and discussions
    D. procedural charts showing the *before* situation, forms, steps, etc., to the employees affected

21. Which organization principle is MOST closely related to procedural analysis and improvement?
    A. Duplication, overlapping, and conflict should be eliminated.
    B. Managerial authority should be clearly defined.
    C. The objectives of the organization should be clearly defined.
    D. Top management should be freed of burdensome detail.

22. Which one of the following is the MAJOR objective of operational audits?
    A. Detecting fraud
    B. Determining organization problems
    C. Determining the number of personnel needed
    D. Recommending opportunities for improving operating and management practices

23. Of the following, the formalization of organization structure is BEST achieved by
    A. a narrative description of the plan of organization
    B. functional charts
    C. job descriptions together with organization charts
    D. multi-flow charts

24. Budget planning is MOST useful when it achieves
    A. cost control
    B. forecast of receipts
    C. performance review
    D. personnel reduction

25. GENERALLY, in applying the principle of delegation in dealing with subordinates, a supervisor
    A. allows his subordinates to set up work goals and to fix the limits within which they can work
    B. allows his subordinates to set up work goals and then gives detailed orders as to how they are to be achieved
    C. makes relatively few decisions by himself and frames his orders in broad, general terms
    D. provides externalized motivation for his subordinate

KEY (CORRECT ANSWERS)

1. B
2. D
3. B
4. A
5. D

6. D
7. C
8. C
9. D
10. C

11. C
12. B
13. D
14. A
15. A

16. A
17. C
18. D
19. C
20. C

21. A
22. D
23. C
24. A
25. C

SUPERVISION, ADMINISTRATION, MANAGEMENT, AND ORGANIZATION

EXAMINATION SECTION

TEST 1

DIRECTIONS: Each question or incomplete statement is followed by several suggested answers or completions. Select the one that BEST answers the question or completes the statement. *PRINT THE LETTER OF THE CORRECT ANSWER IN THE SPACE AT THE RIGHT.*

1. In coaching a subordinate on the nature of decision-making, an executive would be right if he stated that the one of the following which is general the BEST definition of decision-making is:
   A. Choosing between alternatives
   B. Making diagnoses of feasible ends
   C. Making diagnoses of feasible means
   D. Comparing alternatives

2. Of the following, which one would be LEAST valid as a purpose of an organizational policy statement?
   To
   A. keep personnel from performing improper actions and functions on routine matters
   B. prevent the mishandling of non-routine matters
   C. provide management personnel with a tool that precludes the need for their use of judgment
   D. provide standard decisions and approaches in handling problems of a recurrent nature

3. Much has been written criticizing bureaucratic organizations. Current thinking on the subject is GENERALLY that
   A. bureaucracy is on the way out
   B. bureaucracy, though not perfect, is unlikely to be replaced
   C. bureaucratic organizations are most effective in dealing with constant change
   D. bureaucratic organizations are most effective when dealing with sophisticated customers or clients

4. The development of alternate plans as a major step in planning will normally result in the planner having several possible courses of action available. GENERALLY, this is
   A. *desirable*, since such development helps to determine the most suitable alternative and to provide for the unexpected
   B. *desirable*, since such development makes the use of planning premises and constraints unnecessary

C. *undesirable*, since the planners should formulate only one way of achieving given goals at a given time
D. *undesirable*, since such action restricts efforts to modify the planning to take advantage of opportunities

5. The technique of departmentation by task force includes the assigning of a team or task force to a definite project or block of work which extends from the beginning to the completing of a wanted and definite type and quantity of work.
Of the following, the MOST important actor aiding the successful use of this technique *normally* is
   A. having the task force relatively large, at least one hundred members
   B. having a definite project termination date established
   C. telling each task force member what his next assignment will be only after the current project ends
   D. utilizing it only for projects that are regularly recurring

6. With respect to communication in small group settings such as may occur in business, government, and the military, it is generally TRUE that people usually derive more satisfaction and are usually more productive under conditions which
   A. permit communication only with superiors
   B. permit the minimum intragroup communication possible
   C. are generally restricted by management
   D. allow open communication among all group members

7. If an executive were asked to list some outstanding features of decentralization, which one of the following would NOT be such a feature?
Decentralization
   A. provides decision-making experience for lower level managers
   B. promotes uniformity of policy
   C. is a relatively new concept in management
   D. is similar to the belief in encouragement of free enterprise

8. Modern management experts have emphasized the importance of the informal organization in motivating employees to increase productivity.
Of the following, the characteristic which would have the MOST direct influence on employee motivation is the tendency of members of the informal organization to
   A. resist change
   B. establish their own norms
   C. have similar outside interests
   D. set substantially higher goals than those of management

9. According to leading management experts, the decision-making process contains separate and distinct steps that must be taken in an orderly sequence.
Of the following arrangements, which one is in CORRECT order?

A. I. Search for alternatives; II. diagnosis; III. comparison; IV. choice
B. I. Diagnose; II. comparison; III. search for alternatives; IV. choice
C. I. Diagnose; II. search for alternatives; III. comparison; IV. choice
D. I. Diagnose; II. search for alternatives; III. choice; IV. comparison

10. Of the following, the growth of professionalism in large organizations can PRIMARILY be expected to result in   10.____
    A. greater equalization of power
    B. increased authoritarianism
    C. greater organizational disloyalty
    D. increased promotion opportunities

11. Assume an executive carries out his responsibilities to his staff according to what is now known about managerial leadership.   11.____
    Which of the following statements would MOST accurately reflect his assumptions about proper management?
    A. Efficiency in operations results from allowing the human element to participate in a minimal way.
    B. Efficient operation result from balancing work considerations with personnel considerations.
    C. Efficient operation results from a workforce committed to its self-interest.
    D. Efficient operation results from staff relationships that produce a friendly work climate.

12. Assume that an executive is called upon to conduct a management audit. To do this properly, he would have to take certain steps in a specific sequence.   12.____
    Of the following steps, which step should this manager take FIRST?
    A. Managerial performance must be surveyed.
    B. A method of reporting must be established.
    C. Management auditing procedures and documentation must be developed.
    D. Criteria for the audit must be considered.

13. If a manager is required to conduct a scientific investigation of an organizational problem, the FIRST step he should take is to   13.____
    A. state his assumptions about the problem
    B. carry out a search for background information
    C. choose the right approach to investigate the validity of his assumptions
    D. define and state the problem

14. An executive would be right to assert that the principle of delegation states that decisions should be made PRIMARILY   14.____
    A. by persons in an executive capacity qualified to make them
    B. by persons in a non-executive capacity
    C. at as low an organization level of authority as practicable
    D. by the next lower level of authority

15. Of the following, which one is NOT regarded by management authorities as a FUNDAMENTAL characteristic of an *ideal* bureaucracy?
    A. Division of labor and specialization
    B. An established hierarchy
    C. Decentralization of authority
    D. A set of operating rules and regulations

16. As the number of subordinates in a manager's span of control increases, the ACTUAL number of possible relationships
    A. increases disproportionately to the number of subordinates
    B. increases in equal number to the number of subordinates
    C. reaches a stable level
    D. will first increase then slowly decrease

17. An executive's approach to controlling the activities of his subordinates concentrated on ends rather than means, and was diagnostic rather than punitive.
    This manager may MOST properly be characterized as using the managerial technique of management-by-
    A. exception   B. objectives   C. crisis   D. default

18. In conducting a training session on the administrative control process, which of the following statements would be LEAST valid for an executive to make? Controlling
    A. requires checking upon assignments to see what is being done
    B. involves comparing what is being done to what ought to be done
    C. requires corrective action when what is being done does not meet expectations
    D. occurs after all the other managerial processes have been performed

19. The "brainstorming" technique for creative solutions of management problems MOST generally consists of
    A. bringing staff together in an exchange of a quantity of freewheeling ideas
    B. isolating individual staff members to encourage thought
    C. developing improved office procedures
    D. preparation of written reports on complex problems

20. Computer systems hardware MOST often operates in relation to which one of the following steps in solving a data-processing problem?
    A. Determining the problem
    B. Defining and stating the problem
    C. Implementing the programmed solution
    D. Completing the documentation of every unexplored solution

21. There is a tendency in management to upgrade objectives.
    This trend is generally regarded as
    A. *desirable*; the urge to improve is demonstrated by adopting objectives that have been adjusted to provide improved service

B. *undesirable*; the typical manager searches for problems which obstruct his objectives
C. *desirable*; it is common for a manager to find that the details of an immediate operation have occupied so much of his time that he has lost sight of the basic overall objective
D. *undesirable*; efforts are wasted when they are expended on a mass of uncertain objectives, since the primary need of most organizations is a single target or several major ones

22. Of the following, it is generally LEAST effective for an executive to delegate authority where working conditions involve
    A. rules establishing normal operating procedures
    B. consistent methods of operation
    C. rapidly changing work standards
    D. complex technology

22.____

23. If an executive was explaining the difficulty of making decisions under *risk* conditions, he would be MOST accurate if he said that such decisions would be difficult to make when the decision maker has _____ information and experience and can expect _____ outcomes for each action.
    A. limited; many
    B. much; many
    C. much; few
    D. limited; few

23.____

24. If an executive were asked to list some outstanding features of centralized organization, which one of the following would be INCORRECT?
Centralized organization
    A. lessens risks of errors by unskilled subordinates
    B. utilizes the skills of specialized experts at a central location
    C. produces uniformity of policy and non-uniformity of action
    D. enables closer control of operations than a decentralized set-up

24.____

25. It is possible for an organization's management to test whether or not the organization has a sound structure.
Of the following, which one is NOT a test of soundness in an organization's structure?
The
    A. ability to replace key personnel with minimum loss of effectiveness
    B. ability of information and decisions to flow more freely through the *grapevine* than through formal channels
    C. provision for orderly organizational growth with the ability to handle change as the need arises.

25.____

KEY (CORRECT ANSWERS)

1.	A		11.	B
2.	C		12.	D
3.	B		13.	D
4.	A		14.	C
5.	B		15.	C
6.	D		16.	A
7.	B		17.	B
8.	B		18.	D
9.	C		19.	A
10.	A		20.	C

21. A
22. C
23. A
24. C
25. B

TEST 2

DIRECTIONS: Each question or incomplete statement is followed by several suggested answers or completions. Select the one that BEST answers the question or completes the statement. *PRINT THE LETTER OF THE CORRECT ANSWER IN THE SPACE AT THE RIGHT.*

1. Management experts generally believe that computer-based management information systems (MIS) have greater potential for improving the process of management than any other development in recent decades.
   The one of the following which MOST accurately describes the objectives of MIS is to
   A. provide information for decision-making on planning, initiating, and controlling the operations of the various units of the organization
   B. establish mechanization of routine functions such as clerical records, payroll, inventory, and accounts receivable in order to promote economy and efficiency
   C. computerize decision-making on planning, initiative, organizing, and controlling the operations of an organization
   D. provide accurate facts and figures on the various programs of the organization to be used for purposes of planning and research

1.____

2. The one of the following which is the BEST application on the *management-by-exception* principle is that this principle
   A. stimulates communication and aids in management of crisis situations, thus reducing the frequency of decision-making
   B. saves time and reserves top-management decisions only for crisis situations, thus reducing the frequency of decision-making
   C. stimulates communication, saves time, and reduces the frequency of decision-making
   D. is limited to crisis-management situations

2.____

3. It is generally recognized that each organization is dependent upon availability of qualified personnel.
   Of the following, the MOST important factor affecting the availability of qualified people to each organization is
   A. innovations in technology and science
   B. the general decline in the educational levels of our population
   C. the rise of sentiment against racial discrimination
   D. pressure by organized community groups

3.____

4. A fundamental responsibility of all managers is to decide what physical facilities and equipment are needed to help attain basic goals.
   Good planning for the purchase and use of equipment is seldom easy to do and is complicated MOST by the fact that
   A. organizations rarely have stable sources of supply
   B. nearly all managers tend to be better at personnel planning than at equipment planning

4.____

C. decisions concerning physical resources are made too often on a *crash basis* rather than under carefully prepared policies
D. legal rulings relative to depreciation fluctuate very frequently

5. In attempting to reconcile managerial objectives and an individual employee's goals, it is generally LEAST desirable for management to
   A. recognize the capacity of the individual to contribute toward realization of managerial goals
   B. encourage self-development of the employee to exceed minimum job performance
   C. consider an individual employee's work separately from other employees
   D. demonstrate that an employee advances only to the extent that he contributes directly to the accomplishment of stated goals

5.____

6. As a management tool for discovering individual training needs a job analysis would generally be of LEAST assistance in determining
   A. the performance requirements of individual jobs
   B. actual employee performance on the job
   C. acceptable standards of performance
   D. training needs for individual jobs

6.____

7. One of the major concerns of organizational managers today is how the spread of automation will affect them and the status of their positions. Realistically speaking, one can say that the MOST likely effect of our newer forms of highly automated technology on managers will be to
   A. make most top-level positions superfluous or obsolete
   B. reduce the importance of managerial work in general
   C. replace the work of managers with the work of technicians
   D. increase the importance of and demand for top managerial personnel

7.____

8. Which one of the following is LEAST likely to be an area or cause of trouble in the use of staff people (e.g., assistants to the administrator)?
   A. Misunderstanding of the role the staff people are supposed to play, as a result of vagueness of definition of their duties and authority
   B. Tendency of staff personnel almost always to be older than line personnel at comparable salary levels with who they must deal
   C. Selection of staff personnel who fail to have simultaneously both competence in their specialties and skill in staff work
   D. The staff person fails to understand mixed staff and operating duties

8.____

9. The one of the following which is the BEST measure of decentralization in an agency is the
   A. amount of checking required on decisions made at lower levels in the chain of command
   B. amount of checking required on decisions made at lower levels of the chain of command and the number of functions affected thereby
   C. number of functions affected by decisions made at higher levels
   D. number of functions affected by middle echelon decision-making

9.____

10. Which of the following is generally NOT a valid statement with respect to the supervisory process?
    A. General supervision is more effective than close supervision.
    B. Employee-centered supervisors lead more effectively than do production-centered supervisors.
    C. Employee satisfaction is directly related to productivity.
    D. Low-producing supervisors use techniques that are different from high-producing supervisors.

10.____

11. The one of the following which is the MOST essential element for proper evaluation of the performance of subordinate supervisors is a
    A. careful definition of each supervisor's specific job responsibilities and of his progress in meeting mutually agreed upon work goals
    B. system of rewards and penalties based on each supervisor's progress in meeting clearly defined performance standards
    C. definition of personality traits, such as industry, initiative, dependability, and cooperativeness, required for effective job performance
    D. breakdown of each supervisor's job into separate components and a rating of his performance on each individual task

11.____

12. The one of the following which is the PRINCIPAL advantage of specialization for the operating efficiency of a public service agency is that specialization
    A. reduces the amount of red tape in coordinating the activities of mutually dependent departments
    B. simplifies the problem of developing adequate job controls
    C. provides employees with a clear understanding of the relationship of their activities to the overall objectives of the agency
    D. reduces destructive competition for power between departments

12.____

13. Of the following, the group which generally benefits MOST from supervisory training programs in public service agencies are those supervisors who have
    A. accumulated a long period of total service to the agency
    B. responsibility for a large number of subordinate personnel
    C. been in the supervisory ranks for a long period of time
    D. a high level of formalized academic training

13.____

14. A list of conditions which encourages good morale inside a work group would NOT include a
    A. high rate of agreement among group members on values and objectives
    B. tight control system to minimize the risk of individual error
    C. good possibility that joint action will accomplish goals
    D. past history of successful group accomplishment

14.____

15. Of the following, the MOST important factor to be considered in selecting a training strategy or program is the
    A. requirements of the job to be performed by the trainees
    B. educational level or prior training of the trainees
    C. size of the training group
    D. quality and competence of available training specialists

15.____

16. Of the following, the one which is considered to be LEAST characteristic of the higher ranks of management is
    A. that higher levels of management benefit from modern technology
    B. that success is measured by the extent to which objectives are achieved
    C. the number of subordinates that directly report to an executive
    D. the de-emphasis of individual and specialized performance

17. Assume that an executive is preparing a training syllabus to be used in training members of his staff.
    Which of the following would NOT be a valid principle of the learning process for this manager to keep in mind in the preparation of the training syllabus?
    A. When a person has thoroughly learned a task, it takes a lot of effort to create a little more improvement.
    B. In complicated learning situations, there is a period in which an additional period of practice produces an equal amount of improvement in learning.
    C. The less a person knows about the task, the slower the initial progress.
    D. The more the person knows about the risk, the slower the initial progress.

18. Of the following, which statement BEST illustrates when collective bargaining agreements are working well?
    A. Executives strongly support subordinate managers.
    B. The management rights clause in the contract is clear and enforced.
    C. Contract provisions are competently interpreted.
    D. The provisions of the agreement are properly interpreted, communicated, and observed.

19. An executive who wishes to encourage subordinates to communicate freely with him about a job-related problem should FIRST
    A. state his own position on the problem before listening to the subordinates' ideas
    B. invite subordinates to give their own opinions on the problem
    C. ask subordinates for their reactions to his own ideas about the problem
    D. guard the confidentiality of management information about the problem

20. The ability to deal constructively with intra-organizational conflict is an essential attribute of the successful manager.
    The one of the following types of conflict which would be LEAST difficult to handle constructively is a situation in which there is
    A. agreement on objectives, but disagreement as to the probable results of adopting the various alternatives
    B. agreement on objectives, disagreement on alternative courses of action, and relative certainty as to the outcome of one of the alternatives
    C. disagreement on objectives and on alternate courses of action, but relative certainty as to the outcome of the alternatives
    D. disagreement on objectives and on alternative course of action, but uncertainty as to the outcome of the alternatives

21. Which of the following statements is LEAST accurate in describing formal job evaluation and wage and salary classification plans?
    A. Parties that disagree on wage matters can examine an established system rather than unsupported opinions.
    B. The use of such plans tends to overlook the effect of age and seniority of employees on job values in the plan.
    C. Such plans can eliminate salary controversies in organizations designing and using them properly.
    D. These plans are not particularly useful in checking on executive compensation.

22. In carrying out disciplinary action, the MOST important procedure for all managers to follow is to
    A. sell all levels of management on the need for discipline from the organization's viewpoint
    B. follow up on a disciplinary action and not assume that the action has been effective
    C. convince all executives that proper discipline is a legitimate tool for their use
    D. convince all executives that they need to display confidence in the organization's rules

Questions 23-25.

DIRECTIONS: Questions 23 through 25 are to be answered on the basis of the following situation. Richard Ford, a top administrator, is responsible for output in his organization. Because productivity had been lagging for two periods in a row, Ford decided to establish a committee of his subordinate managers to investigate the reasons for the poor performance and to make recommendations for improvements. After two meetings, the committee came to the conclusions and made the recommendations that follow:

Output forecasts had been handed down from the top without prior consultation with middle management and first level supervision. Lines of authority and responsibility had been unclear. The planning and control process should be decentralized.

After receiving the committee's recommendations, Ford proceeded to take the following actions:

Ford decided he would retain final authority to establish quotas but would delegate to the middle managers the responsibility for meeting quotas.

After receiving Ford's decision, the middle managers proceeded to delegate to the first-line supervisors the authority to establish their own quotas. The middle managers eventually received and combined the first-line supervisors' quotas so that these conformed with Ford's.

23. Ford's decision to delegate responsibility for meeting quotas to the middle managers is INCONSISTENT with sound management principles because of which one of the following?
    A. Ford shouldn't have involved himself in the first place.
    B. Middle managers do not have the necessary skills.

C. Quotas should be established by the chief executive.
D. Responsibility should not be delegated.

24. The principle of co-extensiveness of responsibility and authority bears on Ford's decision.
    In this case, it IMPLIES that
    A. authority should exceed responsibility
    B. authority should be delegated to match the degree of responsibility
    C. both authority and responsibility should be retained and not delegated
    D. responsibility should be delegated but authority should be retained

25. The middle manager's decision to delegate to the first-line supervisors the authority to establish quotas was INCORRECTLY reasoned because
    A. delegation and control must go together
    B. first-line supervisors are in no position to establish quotas
    C. one cannot delegate authority that one does not possess
    D. the meeting of quotas should not be delegated

KEY (CORRECT ANSWERS)

1.	A	11.	A
2.	C	12.	B
3.	A	13.	D
4.	C	14.	B
5.	C	15.	A
6.	B	16.	C
7.	D	17.	D
8.	B	18.	D
9.	B	19.	B
10.	C	20.	B

21.	C
22.	B
23.	D
24.	B
25.	C

TEST 3

DIRECTIONS: Each question or incomplete statement is followed by several suggested answers or completions. Select the one that BEST answers the question or completes the statement. *PRINT THE LETTER OF THE CORRECT ANSWER IN THE SPACE AT THE RIGHT.*

1. A danger which exists in any organization as complex as that required for administration of a large public agency is that each department comes to believe that it exists for its own sake.
   The one of the following which has been attempted in some organizations as a cure for this condition is to
   A. build up the departmental esprit de corps
   B. expand the functions and jurisdictions of the various departments so that better integration is possible
   C. develop a body of specialists in the various subject matter fields which cut across departmental lines
   D. delegate authority to the lowest possible echelon
   E. systematically transfer administrative personnel from one department to another

1.____

2. At best, the organization chart is ordinarily and necessarily an idealized picture of the intent of top management, a reflection of hopes and aims rather than a photograph of the operating facts within the organization.
   The one of the following which is the basic reason for this is that the organization chart
   A. does not show the flow of work within the organization
   B. speaks in terms of positions rather than of live employees
   C. frequently contains unresolved internal ambiguities
   D. is a record of past organization or proposed future organization and never a photograph of the living organization
   E. does not label the jurisdiction assigned to each component unit

2.____

3. The drag of inadequacy is always downward. The need in administration is always for the reverse; for a department head to project his thinking to the city level, for the unit chief to try to see the problems of the department.
   The inability of a city administration to recruit administrators who can satisfy this need usually results in departments characterized by
   A. disorganization   B. poor supervision
   C. circumscribed viewpoints   D. poor public relations
   E. a lack of programs

3.____

4. When, as a result of a shift in public sentiment, the elective officers of a city are changed, is it desirable for career administrators to shift ground without performing any illegal or dishonest act in order to conform to the policies of the new elective officers?
   A. *No*; the opinions and beliefs of the career officials are the result of long experience in administration and are more reliable than those of politicians

4.____

2 (#3)

    B. *Yes*; only in this way can citizens, political officials, and career administrators alike have confidence in the performance of their respective functions
    C. *No*; a top career official who is so spineless as to change his views or procedures as a result of public opinion is of little value to the public service
    D. *Yes*; legal or illegal, it is necessary that a city employee carry out the orders of his superior officers
    E. *No*; shifting ground with every change in administration will preclude the use of a constant overall policy

5. Participation in developing plans which will affect levels in the organization in addition to his own, will contribute to an individual's understanding of the entire system. When possible, this should be encouraged.
This policy is, in general,
    A. *desirable*; the maintenance of any organization depends upon individual understanding
    B. *undesirable*; employees should participate only in these activities which affect their own level, otherwise conflicts in authority may arise
    C. *desirable*; an employee's will to contribute to the maintenance of an organization depends to a great extent on the level which he occupies
    D. *undesirable*; employees can be trained more efficiently and economically in an organized training program than by participating in plan development
    E. *desirable*; it will enable the employee to make intelligent suggestions for adjustment of the plan in the future

5.____

6. Constant study should be made of the information contained in reports to isolate those elements of experience which are static, those which are variable and repetitive, and those which are variable and due to chance.
Knowledge of those elements of experience in his organization which are static or constant will enable the operating official to
    A. fix responsibility for their supervisor at a lower level
    B. revise the procedure in order to make the elements variable
    C. arrange for follow-up and periodic adjustment
    D. bring related data together
    E. provide a frame of reference within which detailed standards for measurement can be installed

6.____

7. A chief staff officer, serving as one of the immediate advisors to the department head, has demonstrated a special capacity for achieving internal agreements and for sound judgment. As a result he has been used more and more as a source of counsel and assistance by the department head. Other staff officers and line officials as well have discovered that it is wise for them to check with this colleague in advance on all problematical matters handed up to the department head.

7.____

Developments such as this are
- A. *undesirable*; they disrupt the normal lines for flow of work in an organization
- B. *desirable*; they allow an organization to make the most of its strength wherever such strength resides
- C. *undesirable*; they tend to undermine the authority of the department head and put it in the hands of a staff officer who does not have the responsibility
- D. *desirable*; they tend to resolve internal ambiguities in organization
- E. *undesirable*; they make for bad morale by causing *cutthroat* competition

8. A common difference among executives is that some are not content unless they are out in front of everything that concerns their organization, while others prefer to run things by pulling strings, by putting others out in front and by stepping into the breach only when necessary.
Generally speaking, an advantage this latter method of operation has over the former is that it
- A. results in a higher level of morale over a sustained period of time
- B. gets results by exhortation and direct stimulus
- C. makes it unnecessary to calculate integrated moves
- D. makes the personality of the executive felt further down the line
- E. results in the executive getting the reputation for being a good fellow

9. Administrators frequently have to get facts by interviewing people. Although the interview is a legitimate fact gathering technique, it has definite limitations which should not be overlooked.
The one of the following which is an important limitation is that
- A. people who are interviewed frequently answer questions with guesses rather than admit their ignorance
- B. it is a poor way to discover the general attitude and thinking of supervisors interviewed
- C. people sometimes hesitate to give information during an interview which they will submit in written form
- D. it is a poor way to discover how well employees understand departmental policies
- E. the material obtained from the interview can usually be obtained at lower cost from existing records

10. It is desirable and advantageous to leave a maximum measure of planning responsibility to operating agencies or units, rather than to remove the responsibility to a central planning staff agency.
Adoption of the former policy (decentralized planning) would lead to
- A. *less effective planning*; operating personnel do not have the time to make long-term plans
- B. *more effective planning*; operating units are usually better equipped technically than any staff agency and consequently are in a better position to set up valid plans
- C. *less effective planning*; a central planning agency has a more objective point of view than any operating agency can achieve

D. *more effective planning*; plans are conceived in terms of the existing situation and their execution is carried out with the will to succeed
E. *less effective planning*; there is little or no opportunity to check deviation from plans in the proposed set-up

Questions 11-15.

DIRECTIONS: The following sections appeared in a report on the work production of two bureaus of a department. Base your answers to Questions 11 through 15 on this information. Throughout the report, assume that each month has 4 weeks.

Each of the two bureaus maintains a chronological file. In Bureau A, every 9 months on the average, this material fills a standard legal size cabinet sufficient for 12,000 work units. In Bureau B the same type of cabinet is filled in 18 months. Each bureau maintains three complete years of information plus a current file. When the current file cabinet is filled, the cabinet containing the oldest material is emptied, the contents disposed of, and the cabinet used for current material. The similarity of these operations makes it possible to consolidate these files with little effort.

Study of the practice of using typists as filing clerks for periods when there is no typing work showed: (1) Bureau A has for the past 6 months completed a total of 1,500 filing work units a week using on the average 100 man-hours of trained file clerk time and 20 man-hours of typist time; (2) Bureau B has in the same period completed a total of 2,000 filing work units a week using on the average 125 man-hours of trained file clerk time and 60 hours of typist time. This includes all work in chronological files. Assuming that all clerks work at the same speed and that all typists work at the same speed, this indicates that work other than filing should be found for typists or that they should be given some training in the filing procedures used. It should be noted that Bureau A has not been producing the 1,600 units of technical (not filing) work per 30-day period required by Schedule K, but is at present 200 units behind. The Bureau should be allowed 3 working days to get on schedule.

11. What percentage (approximate) of the total number of filing work units completed in both units consists of the work involved in the maintenance of the chronological files?
    A. 5%   B. 10%   C. 15%   D. 20%   E. 25%

11.____

12. If the two chronological files are consolidated, the number of months which should be allowed for filling a cabinet is
    A. 2   B. 4   C. 6   D. 8   E. 14

12.____

13. The MAXIMUM number of file cabinets which can be released for other uses as a result of the consolidation recommended is
    A. 0
    B. 1
    C. 2
    D. 3
    E. not determinable on the basis of the data given

13.____

5 (#3)

14. If all the filing work for both units is consolidated without diminution in the amount to be done and all filing work is done by trained file clerks, the number of clerks required (35-hour work week) is
    A. 4   B. 5   C. 6   D. 7   E. 8

    14._____

15. In order to comply with the recommendation with respect to Schedule K, the present work production of Bureau A must be increased by
    A. 50%
    B. 100%
    C. 150%
    D. 200%
    E. an amount which is not determinable

    15._____

16. A certain training program during World War II resulted in the training of thousands of supervisors in industry. The methods of this program were later successfully applied in various government agencies. The program was based upon the assumption that there is an irreducible minimum of three supervisory skills.
    The one of these skills among the following is
    A. to know how to perform the job at hand well
    B. to be able to deal personally with workers, especially face-to-face
    C. to be able to imbue workers with the will to perform the job well
    D. to know the kind of work that is done by one's unit and the policies and procedures of one's agency
    E. the *know-how* of administrative and supervisory processes

    16._____

17. A comment made by an employee about a training course was, "*We never have any idea how we ae getting along in that course.*"
    The fundamental error in training methods to which this criticism points is
    A. insufficient student participation
    B. failure to develop a feeling of need or active want for the material being presented
    C. the training sessions may be too long
    D. no attempt may have been made to connect the new material with what was already known
    E. no goals have been set for the students

    17._____

18. Assume that you are attending a departmental conference on efficiency ratings at which it is proposed that a man-to-man rating scale be introduced.
    You should point out that, of the following, the CHIEF weakness of the man-to-man rating scale is that
    A. it involves abstract numbers rather than concrete employee characteristics
    B. judges are unable to select their own standards for comparison
    C. the standard for comparison shifts from man-to-man for each person rated
    D. not every person rated is given the opportunity to serve as a standard for comparison
    E. standards for comparison will vary from judge to judge

    18._____

19. Assume that you are conferring with a supervisor who has assigned to his subordinates efficiency ratings which you believe to be generally too low. The supervisor argues that his ratings are generally low because his subordinates are generally inferior.
    Of the following, the evidence MOST relevant to the point at issue can be secured by comparing efficiency ratings assigned by the supervisor
    A. with ratings assigned by other supervisors in the same agency
    B. this year with ratings assigned by him in previous years
    C. to men recently transferred to his unit with ratings previously earned by these men
    D. with the general city average of ratings assigned by all supervisors to all employees
    E. with the relative order of merit of his employees as determined independently by promotion test marks

19.____

20. The one of the following which is NOT among the most common of the compensable factors used in wage evaluation studies is
    A. initiative and ingenuity required
    B. physical demand
    C. responsibility for the safety of others
    D. working conditions
    E. presence of avoidable hazards

20.____

21. If independent functions are separated, there is an immediate gain in conserving special skills. If we are to make optimum use of the abilities of our employees, these skills must be conserved.
    Assuming the correctness of this statement, it follows that
    A. if we are not making optimum use of employee abilities, independent functions have not been separated
    B. we are making optimum uses of employee abilities if we conserve special skills
    C. we are making optimum use of employee abilities if independent functions have been separated
    D. we are not making optimum use of employee abilities if we do not conserve special skills
    E. if special skills are being conserved, independent functions need not be separated

21.____

22. A reorganization of the bureau to provide for a stenographic pool instead of individual unit stenographers will result in more stenographic help being available to each unit when it is required, and consequently will result in greater productivity for each unit. An analysis of the space requirements shows that setting up a stenographic pool will require a minimum of 400 square feet of good space. In order to obtain this space, it will be necessary to reduce the space available for technical personnel, resulting in lesser productivity for each unit.

22.____

On the basis of the above discussion, it can be stated that, in order to obtain greater productivity for each unit,
- A. a stenographic pool should be set up
- B. further analysis of the space requirement should be made
- C. it is not certain as to whether or not a stenographic pool should be set up
- D. the space available for each technician should be increased in order to compensate for the absence of a stenographic pool
- E. a stenographic pool should not be set up

23. The adoption of single consolidated form will mean that most of the form will not be used in any one operation. This would create waste and confusion. This conclusion is based upon the unstated hypothesis that
    - A. if waste and confusion are to be avoided, a single consolidated form should be used
    - B. if a single consolidated form is constructed, most of it can be used in each operation
    - C. if waste and confusion are to be avoided, most of the form employed should be used
    - D. most of a single consolidation form is not used
    - E. a single consolidated form should not be used

23.____

KEY (CORRECT ANSWERS)

1.	E		11.	C
2.	B		12.	C
3.	C		13.	B
4.	B		14.	D
5.	E		15.	E
6.	A		16.	B
7.	B		17.	E
8.	A		18.	E
9.	A		19.	C
10.	D		20.	E

21. D
22. C
23. C

EXAMINATION SECTION
TEST 1

DIRECTIONS: Each question or incomplete statement is followed by several suggested answers or completions. Select the one that BEST answers the question or completes the statement. *PRINT THE LETTER OF THE CORRECT ANSWER IN THE SPACE AT THE RIGHT.*

1. Assume that a civil service list has been established for a position in an agency which had provisional appointees serving in three permanent vacancies. One of these provisionals is on the eligible list, but was discharged because permanent appointments were accepted by three eligibles who were higher on the list. The former provisional has complained to the agency head, alleging that special efforts were made to appoint these eligible. The personnel officer of the agency should advise the agency head that
    A. the court could compel them to appoint the former provisional appointee
    B. he is required by civil service law to appoint the higher ranking eligibles from the list
    C. the human rights commission could compel him to appoint the former provisional appointee
    D. he should attempt conciliation

2. Assume that two accountants working in a section under your supervision were appointed from the same eligible list. Accountant Jones received a higher score on the competitive examination than Accountant Doe; Jones was third on the eligible list and Doe was fifth. Jones was told to report to work on March 15 but Doe, who was working under a provisional appointment, was given permanent status as of March 1. For economic reasons, your agency head is considering abolishing one position of accountant and requests guidance from you before making any decision.
It would be BEST to tell him that
    A. if he decides to abolish one position of accountant, he should lay off Jones because Doe was given permanent status before Jones
    B. under the rule of *one in three*, Doe could not have been reached for appointment before Jones, so that Doe would have to be laid off first
    C. if he decides to abolish one position of accountant, he should lay off Doe because Doe's provisional appointment was in violation of the Civil Service Law
    D. he should evaluate the performance of Jones and Doe before making any determination as to which accountant to lay off

3. An employee who has been on the job for a number of years became a problem drinker during the past year. The supervisor and this employee are good friends.
Because this problem has been affecting the work of the unit adversely, it would be BEST for the supervisor to

A. attempt to cover up the problem by moving the subordinate's desk to a corner of the office where he would not be noticed so readily
B. refer the employee for counseling to the employee counseling service
C. reassign some of the problem drinker's responsibilities to other employees
D. send the employee home in a tactful manner whenever he reports for duty in an unfit condition

4. In a strike situation, a member of the striking union reports for work but abstains from the full performance of his duties in his normal manner. According to the state civil service law, it is ACCURATE to say that the
    A. employee should be presumed to have engaged in a strike
    B. employee should not be presumed to have engaged in a strike
    C. city must bear the burden of proving that the employee engaged in a strike
    D. city may deny the employee the opportunity to rebut any charge that he engaged in a strike

4._____

5. Assume that, as a manager in a health agency which is establishing a *management-by-objective* program, you are asked to review and make recommendations on the following goals set by the agency head for the coming year.
Which one of these objectives should you recommend dropping because of difficulty in verifying the degree to which the goal has been attained?
    A. Establishing night clinics in two preventive health care centers
    B. Informing more people of available health services
    C. Preparing a training manual for data-processing personnel
    D. Producing a 4-page health news bulletin to be distributed monthly to employees

5._____

6. The MAIN purpose of the *management-by-objectives* system is to
    A. develop a method of appraising the performance of managerial employees against verifiable objectives rather than against subjective appraisals and personal supervision
    B. decentralize managerial decision-making more effectively by setting goals for personnel all the way down to each first-line supervisor as well as to staff people
    C. increase managerial accountability and improve managerial effectiveness
    D. enable top level managerial employees to impose quantitative goals which will focus attention on the relevant trends that may affect the future

6._____

7. Certain city and state employees are on one year's probation for violating the strike provisions of the state civil service law.
According to a ruling by the state attorney general, in the event of layoffs during their year of probation, the status of these employees should be considered
    A. *permanent*, with retention rights based on original date of appointment
    B. *probationary*, subject to layoff before permanent employees

7._____

C. *permanent*, to be credited with one year less service than indicated by the original date of appointment
D. *probationary*, subject to layoff before other employees in the layoff unit except for those with one year's seniority

8. Assume that, as a senior supervisor conducting a training course for a group of newly assigned first-line supervisors, you emphasize that an effective supervisor should encourage employee suggestions. One member of the group dissents, asserting that many employees come up with worthless, time-wasting ideas.
The one of the following which would be the MOST appropriate response for you to make is that
   A. the supervisor's attitude is wrong, because no suggestion is entirely without merit
   B. the supervisor must remember that encouragement of employee suggestions is the major part of any employee development program
   C. even if a suggestion seems worthless, the participation of the employee helps to increase his identification with the agency
   D. even if a suggestion seems worthless, the supervisor may be able to save it for future use

8.____

9. The *grapevine* is an informal channel of communication which exists among employees in an organization as a natural result of their social interaction, and their desire to be kept posted on the latest information. Some information transmitted through the grapevine is truth, some half-truth, and some just rumor.
Which one of the following would be the MOST appropriate attitude for a member of a management team to have about the grapevine?
   A. The grapevine often carries false, malicious, and uncontrollable rumors and management should try to stamp it out by improving official channels of communication.
   B. There are more important problems; normally only a small percentage of employees are interested in information transmitted through the grapevine.
   C. The grapevine can give management insight into what employees think and feel and can help to supplement the formal communication systems.
   D. The grapevine gives employees a harmless outlet for their imagination and an opportunity to relieve their fears and tensions in the form of rumors.

9.____

10. Although there are no formal performance appraisal mechanisms for non-managerial employees, managers nevertheless make informal appraisals because some method is needed to measure progress and to let employees know how they are doing.
The MOST import recent trend in making performance appraisals is toward judging the employee primarily on the extent to which he has
   A. tried to perform his assigned tasks
   B. demonstrated personal traits which are accepted as necessary to do the job satisfactorily

10.____

C. accomplished the objectives set for his job
D. followed the procedures established for the job

11. The proof of a successful human relations program in an organization is the morale crises that never happen.
Of the following, the implication for managers that follows MOST directly from this statement is that they should
    A. review and initiate revisions in all organization policies which may have an adverse effect on employee morale
    B. place more emphasis on ability to anticipate and prevent morale problems than on ability to resolve an actual crisis
    C. see that first-line supervisors work fairly and understandingly with employees
    D. avoid morale crises at all costs, since even the best resolution leaves scar, suspicions, and animosities

11.____

12. Suppose that you are conducting a conference on a specific problem. One employee makes a suggestion which you think is highly impractical.
Of the following, the way for you to respond to this suggestion is FIRST to
    A. be frank and tell the employee that his solution is wrong
    B. ask the employee in what way his suggestion will solve the problem under discussion
    C. refrain from any comment on it, and ask the group whether they have any other solutions to offer
    D. ask another participant to point out what is wrong with the suggestion

12.____

13. Suppose that a manager notices continuing deterioration in the work, conduct, and interpersonal relationships of one of his immediate subordinates, indicating that this employee has more than a minor emotional problem. Although the manager has made an attempt to help this employee by talking over his problems with him on several occasions, the employee has shown little improvement.
Of the following, generally the MOST constructive action for the manager to take at this point would be to
    A. continue to be supportive by sympathetic listening and counseling
    B. show tolerance toward the performance of the disturbed employee
    C. discuss the employee's deteriorating condition with him and suggest that he seek professional help
    D. consider whether the need of this employee and the agency would be best served by his transfer to another division

13.____

14. A manager has a problem involving conflict between two employees concerning a method of performing a work assignment. He does not know the reasons for this conflict.
The MOST valuable communications method he can use to aid him in resolving the problem is
    A. a formal hearing for each employee
    B. a staff meeting

14.____

C. disciplinary memoranda
D. an informal interview with each employee

15. As a training technique, role-playing is generally considered to be MOST successful when it results in
    A. uncovering the underlying causes of conflict so that any recurrences are prevented
    B. recreating an actual work situation which involves conflict among people and in which members of the group simulate specific personalities
    C. freeing some people from patterns of rigid thinking and enabling them to look at themselves and others in a new way
    D. increasing the participants' powers of logic and reasoning

15.____

16. In conducting a disciplinary interview, a supervisor finds that he must ask some highly personal questions which are relevant to the problem at hand.
The interviewer is MOST likely to get truthful answers to these questions if he asks them
    A. early in the interview, before the interviewee has had a chance to become emotional
    B. in a manner so that the interviewee can answer them with a simple *yes* or *no*
    C. well into the interview, after rapport and trust have been established
    D. just after the close of the interview, so that the questions appear to be off the record

16.____

17. Suppose that, as a newly assigned manager, you observe that a supervisor in your division uses autocratic methods which are causing resentment among his subordinates.
Of the following, the MOST likely reason for this supervisor's using such methods is that he
    A. was probably exposed to this type of supervision himself
    B. does not have an intuitive sense of tact, diplomacy, and consideration and no amount of training can change this
    C. received approval for use of such method from his former subordinates
    D. does not understand the basic concept of rewards and punishment in the practice of supervision

17.____

18. A newly appointed employee, Mr. Jones, was added to the staff of a supervisor who, because of the pressure of other work, turned him over to an experienced subordinate by saying, *Show Mr. Jones around and give him something to do.*
On the basis of this experience, Mr. Jones' FIRST impression of his new position was most likely to have been
    A. *negative*, mainly because it appeared that his job was not worth his supervisor's attention
    B. *negative*, mainly because the more experienced subordinate would tend to emphasize the unpleasant aspects of the work
    C. *positive*, mainly because his supervisor wasted no time in assigning him to a subordinate
    D. *positive*, mainly because he saw himself working for a dynamic supervisor who expected immediate results

18.____

19. An employee who stays in one assignment for a number of years often develops a feeling of possessiveness concerning his knowledge of the job which may develop into a problem.
Of the following, the BEST way for a supervisor to remedy this difficulty is to
    A. give the employee less important work to do
    B. point out minor errors as often as possible
    C. raise performance standards for all employees
    D. rotate the employee to a different assignment

19._____

20. A supervisor who tends to be supportive of his subordinates, in contrast to a supervisor who relies upon an authoritarian style of leadership, is more likely, in dealing with his staff, to have to listen to complaints, to have to tolerate emotionally upset employees, and even have to hear unreasonable and insulting remarks.
Compared to the authoritarian supervisor, he is MORE likely to
    A. be unconsciously fearful of failure
    B. have an overriding interest in production
    C. have subordinates who are better educated
    D. receive accurate feedback information

20._____

KEY (CORRECT ANSWERS)

1.	B	11.	B
2.	B	12.	B
3.	B	13.	C
4.	A	14.	D
5.	B	15.	C
6.	C	16.	C
7.	B	17.	A
8.	C	18.	A
9.	C	19.	D
10.	C	20.	D

TEST 2

DIRECTIONS: Each question or incomplete statement is followed by several suggested answers or completions. Select the one that BEST answers the question or completes the statement. *PRINT THE LETTER OF THE CORRECT ANSWER IN THE SPACE AT THE RIGHT.*

1. Assume that one of your subordinates, a supervisor in charge of a small unit in your bureau, asks your advice in handling a situation which has just occurred in his unit. On returning from a meeting, the supervisor notices that Jane Jones, the unit secretary, is not at her regular work location. Another employee had become faint, and the secretary accompanied this employee outdoors for some fresh air. It is a long-standing rule that no employee is permitted to leave the building during office hours except on official business or with the unit head's approval. Quite recently another employee was reprimanded by the supervisor for going out at 10 A.M. for a cup of coffee.
   Of the following, it would be BEST for you to advise the supervisor to
   A. circulate a memo within the unit, restating the department's regulation concerning leaving the building during office hours
   B. overlook this rule violation in view of the extenuating circumstances
   C. personally reprimand the unit secretary since all employees must be treated in the same way when official rules are broken
   D. tell the unit secretary that you should reprimand her, but that you've decided to overlook the rule infraction this time

    1._____

2. Of the following, the MOST valid reason why the application of behavioral modification techniques to management of large organizations is not yet widely accepted by managers is these techniques are
   A. based mainly on research conducted under highly controlled conditions
   B. more readily adaptable to training unskilled employees
   C. incompatible with the validated *management-by-objectives* approach
   D. manipulative and incompatible with the democratic approach

    2._____

3. Because of intensive pressures which have developed since the onset of the city's financial problems, the members of a certain bureau have begun to file grievances about their working conditions. These protests are accumulating at a much greater rate than normal and faster than they can be disposed of under the current state of affairs. Concerned about the possible effect of these unresolved matters on the productivity of the bureau at such a critical time, the administrator in charge decides to take immediate action to improve staff relations.
   With this intention in mind, he should
   A. explain to the staff why their grievances cannot be handled at the present time; then inform them that there will be a moratorium on the filing of additional grievances until the current backlog has been eliminated
   B. assemble all grievants at a special meeting and assure them that their problems will be handled in due course, but the current pressures preclude the prompt settling of their grievances

    3._____

2 (#2)

C. assign the assistant directors of the bureau to immediately schedule and conduct hearings on the accumulated grievances until the backlog is eliminated
D. suggest that the grievants again confer with their supervisors about their problems, orally rather than in writing, with direct appeal to him for such cases as are not resolved in this manner

4. A supervisor is attending a staff meeting with other accounting supervisors during which the participants are to propose various possible methods of dealing with a complex operational problem.
The one of the following procedures which will MOST likely produce an acceptable proposal for solving this problem at this meeting is for the
   A. group to agree at the beginning of the meeting on the kinds of approaches to the problem that are most likely to succeed
   B. conference leader to set a firm time limit on the period during which the participants are to present whatever ideas come to mind
   C. group to discuss each proposal fully before the next proposal is made
   D. conference leader to urge every participant in the meeting to present at least one proposal

4.____

5. Which one of the following types of communication systems would foster an authoritarian atmosphere in a large agency?
A communication system which
   A. is restricted to organizational procedures and specific job instructions
   B. provides information to employees about the rationale for their jobs
   C. informs employees about their job performance
   D. provides information about the relationship of employees' work to the agency's goals

5.____

6. According to most management experts, the one of the following which would generally have SERIOUS shortcomings as a component of a performance evaluation program is
   A. rating the performance of each subordinate against the performance of other subordinates
   B. limiting the appraisal to an evaluation of current performance
   C. rating each subordinate in terms of clearly stated, measurable job goals
   D. interviewing the subordinate to discuss present job performance and ways of improvement

6.____

7. Which of the following is consistent with the management-by-objectives approach as used in a fiscal affairs division of a large city agency?
   A. Performance goals for the division are established by the administrator, who requires daily progress reports for each accounting unit.
   B. Each subordinate accountant participates in setting his own short-term performance goals.
   C. A detailed set of short-term performance goals for each accountant is prepared by his supervisor.
   D. Objectives are established and progress evaluated by a committee of administrative accountants.

7.____

3 (#2)

Questions 8-11.

DIRECTIONS: Questions 8 through 11 are to be answered on the basis of the following information.

Assume that you are the director of a small bureau, organized into three divisions. The bureau has a total of twenty employees: fourteen in professional titles and six in clerical titles. Each division has a chief who reports directly to you and who supervises five employees.

For Questions 8 through 11, you are to select the MOST appropriate training method, from the four choices given, based on the situation in the question:
- A. Lecture, with a small blackboard available
- B. Lecture, with audio-visual aids
- C. Conference
- D. Buddy system (experienced worker is accompanied by worker to be trained)

8. A major reorganization of your department was completed. You have decided to conduct a training session of about one hour's duration for all your subordinates in order to acquaint them with the new departmental structure as well as the new responsibilities which have been assigned to the divisions of your bureau. 8.____

9. Three assistant supervisors, each with one year of service in your department, are transferred to your bureau as part of the process of strengthening the major activity of your bureau. In connection with their duties, if they are required to do field visits to business firms located in the various industrial areas of the city. 9.____

10. The work of your bureau requires that various forms be processed sequentially through each of three divisions. In recent weeks, you have received complaints from the division chiefs that their production is being impeded by a lack of cooperation from the chiefs and workers in the other divisions. 10.____

11. In order to improve the efficiency of the department, your department head has directed that all bureaus hold weekly, thirty-minute-long training sessions for all employees, to review relevant work procedures. 11.____

12. Which one of the following actions is usually MOST appropriate for a manager to take in order to encourage and develop coordination of effort among different units or individuals within an organization? 12.____
    - A. Providing rewards to the most productive employees
    - B. Giving employees greater responsibility and the authority to exercise it
    - C. Emphasizing to the employees that it is important to coordinate their efforts
    - D. Explaining the goals of the organization to the employees and how their jobs relate to those goals

13. The management of time is one of the critical aspects of any supervisor's performance.
    Therefore, in evaluating a subordinate from the viewpoint of how he manages time, a supervisor should rate HIGHEST the subordinate who
    A. concentrates on each task as he undertakes it
    B. performs at a standard and predictable pace under all circumstances
    C. takes shortened lunch periods when he is busy
    D. tries to do two things simultaneously

14. A MAJOR research finding regarding employee absenteeism is that
    A. absenteeism is likely to be higher on hot days
    B. male employees tend to be absent more than female employees
    C. the way an employee is treated as a definite bearing on absenteeism
    D. the distance employees have to travel is one of the most important factors in absenteeism

15. Of the following, the supervisory behavior that is of GREATEST benefit to the organization is exhibited by supervisors who
    A. are strict with subordinates about following rules and regulations
    B. encourage subordinates to be interested in the work
    C. are willing to assist with subordinates' work on most occasions
    D. get the most done with available staff and resources

16. In order to maintain a proper relationship with a worker who is assigned to staff rather than line functions, a line supervisor should
    A. accept all recommendations of the staff worker
    B. include the staff worker in the conferences called by the supervisor for his subordinates
    C. keep the staff worker informed of developments in the area of his staff assignment
    D. require that the staff worker's recommendations be communicated to the supervisor through the supervisor's own superior

17. Of the following, the GREATEST disadvantage of placing a worker in a staff position under the direct supervision of the supervisor whom he advises is the possibility that the
    A. staff worker will tend to be insubordinate because of a feeling of superiority over the supervisor
    B. staff worker will tend to give advice of the type which the supervisor wants to hear or finds acceptable
    C. supervisor will tend to be mistrustful of the advice of a worker of subordinate rank
    D. supervisor will tend to derive little benefit from the advice because to supervise properly he should know at least as much as his subordinate

18. One factor which might be given consideration in deciding upon the optimum span of control of a supervisor over his immediate subordinates is the position of the supervisor in the hierarchy of the organization.
    It is generally considered proper that the number of subordinates immediately supervised by a higher, upper echelon, supervisor
    A. is unrelated to and tends to form no pattern with the number of supervised by lower level supervisors
    B. should be about the same as the number supervised by a lower level supervisor
    C. should be larger than the number supervised by a lower level supervisor
    D. should be smaller than the number supervised by a lower level supervisor

18.____

19. Assume that you are a supervisor and have been assigned to assist the head of a large agency unit. He asks you to prepare a simple, functional organization chart of the unit.
    Such a chart would be USEFUL for
    A. favorably impressing members of the public with the important nature of the agency's work
    B. graphically presenting staff relationships which may indicate previously unknown duplications, overlaps, and gaps in job duties
    C. motivating all employees toward better performance because they will have a better understanding of job procedures
    D. subtly and inoffensively making known to the staff in the unit that you are now in a position of responsibility

19.____

20. In some large organizations, management's traditional means of learning about employee dissatisfaction has been in the *open door policy*.
    This policy USUALLY means that
    A. management lets it be known that a management representative is generally available to discuss employees' questions, suggestions, and complaints
    B. management sets up an informal employee organization to establish a democratic procedure for orderly representation of employees
    C. employees are encouraged to attempt to resolve dissatisfactions at the lowest possible level of authority
    D. employees are provided with an address or box so that they may safely and anonymously register complaints

20.____

KEY (CORRECT ANSWERS)

1.	B	11.	A
2.	A	12.	D
3.	D	13.	A
4.	B	14.	C
5.	A	15.	D
6.	A	16.	C
7.	B	17.	B
8.	B	18.	D
9.	D	19.	B
10.	C	20.	A

PRINCIPLES AND PRACTICES, OF ADMINISTRATION, SUPERVISION AND MANAGEMENT

TABLE OF CONTENTS

	Page
GENERAL ADMINISTRATION	1
SEVEN BASIC FUNCTIONS OF THE SUPERVISOR	2
I. Planning	2
II. Organizing	3
III. Staffing	3
IV. Directing	3
V. Coordinating	3
VI. Reporting	3
VII. Budgeting	3
PLANNING TO MEET MANAGEMENT GOALS	4
I. What is Planning	4
II. Who Should Make Plans	4
III. What are the Results of Poor Planning	4
IV. Principles of Planning	4
MANAGEMENT PRINCIPLES	5
I. Management	5
II. Management Principles	5
III. Organization Structure	6
ORGANIZATION	8
I. Unity of Command	8
II. Span of Control	8
III. Uniformity of Assignment	9
IV. Assignment of Responsibility and Delegation of Authority	9
PRINCIPLES OF ORGANIZATION	9
I. Definition	9
II. Purpose of Organization	9
III. Basic Considerations in Organizational Planning	9
IV. Bases for Organization	10
V. Assignment of Functions	10
VI. Delegation of Authority and Responsibility	10
VII. Employee Relationships	11

DELEGATING		11
I.	WHAT IS DELEGATING:	11
II.	TO WHOM TO DELEGATE	11
REPORTS		12
I.	DEFINITION	12
II.	PURPOSE	12
III.	TYPES	12
IV.	FACTORS TO CONSIDER BEFORE WRITING REPORT	12
V.	PREPARATORY STEPS	12
VI.	OUTLINE FOR A RECOMMENDATION REPORT	12
MANAGEMENT CONTROLS		13
I.	Control	13
II.	Basis for Control	13
III.	Policy	13
IV.	Procedure	14
V.	Basis of Control	14
FRAMEWORK OF MANAGEMENT		14
I.	Elements	14
II.	Manager's Responsibility	15
III.	Control Techniques	16
IV.	Where Forecasts Fit	16
PROBLEM SOLVING		16
I.	Identify the Problem	16
II.	Gather Data	17
III.	List Possible Solutions	17
IV.	Test Possible Solutions	18
V.	Select the Best Solution	18
VI.	Put the Solution into Actual Practice	19
COMMUNICATION		19
I.	What is Communication?	19
II.	Why is Communication Needed?	19
III.	How is Communication Achieved?	20
IV.	Why Does Communication Fail?	21
V.	How to Improve Communication	21
VI.	How to Determine If You Are Getting Across	21
VII.	The Key Attitude	22
HOW ORDERS AND INSTRUCTIONS SHOULD BE GIVEN		22
I.	Characteristics of Good Orders and Instructions	22
FUNCTIONS OF A DEPARTMENT PERSONNEL OFFICE		23

SUPERVISION	23
I. Leadership	23
A. The Authoritarian Approach	23
B. The Laissez-Faire Approach	24
C. The Democratic Approach	24
II. Nine Points of Contrast Between Boss and Leader	25
EMPLOYEE MORALE	25
I. Some Ways to Develop and Maintain Good Employee Morale	25
II. Some Indicators of Good Morale	26
MOTIVATION	26
EMPLOYEE PARTICIPATION	27
I. WHAT IS PARTICIPATION	27
II. WHY IS IT IMPORTANT?	27
III. HOW MAY SUPERVISORS OBTAIN IT?	28
STEPS IN HANDLING A GRIEVANCE	28
DISCIPLINE	29
I. THE DISCIPLINARY INTERVIEW	29
II. PLANNING THE INTERVIEW	29
III. CONDUCTING THE INTERVIEW	30

PRINCIPLES AND PRACTICES, OF ADMINISTRATION, SUPERVISION AND MANAGEMENT

Most people are inclined to think of administration as something that only a few persons are responsible for in a large organization. Perhaps this is true if you are thinking of Administration with a capital A, but administration with a lower case *a* is a responsibility of supervisors at all levels each working day.

All of us feel we are pretty good supervisors and that we do a good job of administering the workings of our agency. By and large, this is true, but every so often it is good to check up on ourselves. Checklists appear from time to time in various publications which psychologists say tell whether or not a person will make a good wife, husband, doctor, lawyer, or supervisor.

The following questions are an excellent checklist to test yourself as a supervisor and administrator.

Remember, Administration gives direction and points the way but administration carries the ideas to fruition. Each is dependent on the other for its success. Remember, too, that no unit is too small for these departmental functions to be carried out. These statements apply equally as well as to the Chief Librarian as to the Department Head with but one or two persons to supervise.

GENERAL ADMINISTRATION: General Responsibilities of Supervisors

1. Have I prepared written statements of functions, activities, and duties for my organizational unit?

2. Have I prepared procedural guides for operating activities?

3. Have I established clearly in writing, lines of authority and responsibility for my organizational unit?

4. Do I make recommendations for improvements in organization, policies, administrative and operating routines and procedures, including simplification of work and elimination of non-essential operations?

5. Have I designated and trained an understudy to function in my absence?

6. Do I supervise and train personnel within the unit to effectively perform their assignments?

7. Do I assign personnel and distribute work on such a basis as to carry out the organizational unit's assignment or mission in the most effective and efficient manner?

8. Have I established administrative controls by:

    a. Fixing responsibility and accountability on all supervisors under my direction for the proper performance of their functions and duties.

b. Preparations and submitting periodic work load and progress reports covering the operations of the unit to my immediate superior.

c. Analysis and evaluation of such reports received from subordinate units.

d. Submission of significant developments and problems arising within the organizational unit to my immediate superior.

e. Conducting conferences, inspections, etc., as to the status and efficiency of unit operations.

9. Do I maintain an adequate and competent working force?

10. Have I fostered good employee-department relations, seeing that established rules, regulations, and instructions are being carried out properly?

11. Do I collaborate and consult with other organizational units performing related functions to insure harmonious and efficient working relationships?

12. Do I maintain liaison through prescribed channels with city departments and other governmental agencies concerned with the activities of the unit?

13. Do I maintain contact with and keep abreast of the latest developments and techniques of administration (professional societies, groups, periodicals, etc.) as to their applicability to the activities of the unit?

14. Do I communicate with superiors and subordinates through prescribed organizational channels?

15. Do I notify superiors and subordinates in instances where bypassing is necessary as soon thereafter as practicable?

16. Do I keep my superior informed of significant developments and problems?

SEVEN BASIC FUNCTIONS OF THE SUPERVISOR

I. PLANNING
This means working out goals and means to obtain goals. <u>What</u> needs to be done, <u>who</u> will do it, <u>how</u>, <u>when</u>, and <u>where</u> it is to be done.

SEVEN STEPS IN PLANNING

A. Define job or problem clearly.
B. Consider priority of job.
C. Consider time-limit—starting and completing.
D. Consider minimum distraction to, or interference with, other activities.
E. Consider and provide for contingencies—possible emergencies.
F. Break job down into components.

G. Consider the 5 W's and H:
WHY..........is it necessary to do the job? (Is the purpose clearly defined?)
WHAT........needs to be done to accomplish the defined purpose?
..........is needed to do the job? (Money, materials, etc.)
WHO..........is needed to do the job?
..........will have responsibilities?
WHERE......is the work to be done?
WHEN........is the job to begin and end? (Schedules, etc.)
HOW..........is the job to bed done? (Methods, controls, records, etc.)

II. ORGANIZING

This means dividing up the work, establishing clear lines of responsibility and authority and coordinating efforts to get the job done.

III. STAFFING

The whole personnel function of bringing in and <u>training</u> staff, getting the right man and fitting him to the right job—the job to which he is best suited.

In the normal situation, the supervisor's responsibility regarding staffing normally includes providing accurate job descriptions, that is, duties of the jobs, requirements, education and experience, skills, physical, etc.; assigning the work for maximum use of skills; and proper utilization of the probationary period to weed out unsatisfactory employees.

IV. DIRECTING

Providing the necessary leadership to the group supervised. Important work gets done to the supervisor's satisfaction.

V. COORDINATING

The all-important duty of inter-relating the various parts of the work.
The supervisor is also responsible for controlling the coordinated activities. This means measuring performance according to a time schedule and setting quotas to see that the goals previously set are being reached. Reports from workers should be analyzed, evaluated, and made part of all future plans.

VI. REPORTING

This means proper and effective communication to your superiors, subordinates, and your peers (in definition of the job of the supervisor). Reports should be read and information contained therein should be used, not be filed away and forgotten. Reports should be written in such a way that the desired action recommended by the report is forthcoming.

VII. BUDGETING
This means controlling current costs and forecasting future costs. This forecast is based on past experience, future plans and programs, as well as current costs.

You will note that these seven functions can fall under three topics:

Planning) Make a plan	Staffing)	Reporting) Watch it work
Organizing)	Directing) Get things done	Budgeting)
	Controlling)	

PLANNING TO MEET MANAGEMENT GOALS

I. WHAT IS PLANNING?

   A. Thinking a job through before new work is done to determine the best way to do it
   B. A method of doing something
   C. Ways and means for achieving set goals
   D. A means of enabling a supervisor to deliver with a minimum of effort, all details involved in coordinating his work

II. WHO SHOULD MAKE PLANS?

   Everybody!
   All levels of supervision must plan work. (Top management, heads of divisions or bureaus, first line supervisors, and individual employees.) The higher the level, the more planning required.

III. WHAT ARE THE RESULTS OF POOR PLANNING?

   A. Failure to meet deadline
   B. Low employee morale
   C. Lack of job coordination
   D. Overtime is frequently necessary
   E. Excessive cost, waste of material and manhours

IV. PRINCIPLES OF PLANNING

   A. Getting a clear picture of your objectives. What exactly are you trying to accomplish?
   B. Plan the whole job, then the parts, in proper sequence.
   C. Delegate the planning of details to those responsible for executing them.
   D. Make your plan flexible.
   E. Coordinate your plan with the plans of others so that the work may be processed with a minimum of delay.
   F. Sell your plan before you execute it.
   G. Sell your plan to your superior, subordinate, in order to gain maximum participation and coordination.
   H. Your plan should take precedence. Use knowledge and skills that others have brought to a similar job.
   I. Your plan should take account of future contingencies; allow for future expansion.
   J. Plans should include minor details. Leave nothing to chance that can be anticipated.
   K. Your plan should be simple and provide standards and controls. Establish quality and quantity standards and set a standard method of doing the job. The controls will indicate whether the job is proceeding according to plan.
   L. Consider possible bottlenecks, breakdowns, or other difficulties that are likely to arise.

V. Q. WHAT ARE THE YARDSTICKS BY WHICH PLANNING SHOULD BE MEASURED?
   A. Any plan should:
   — Clearly state a definite course of action to be followed and goal to be achieved, with consideration for emergencies.
   — Be realistic and practical.
   — State what's to be done, when it's to be done, where, how, and by whom.
   — Establish the most efficient sequence of operating steps so that more is accomplished in less time, with the least effort, and with the best quality results.
   — Assure meeting deliveries without delays.
   — Establish the standard by which performance is to be judged.

   Q. WHAT KINDS OF PLANS DOES EFFECTIVE SUPERVISION REQUIRE?
   A. Plans should cover such factors as:
   — Manpower: right number of properly trained employees on the job
   — Materials: adequate supply of the right materials and supplies
   — Machines: full utilization of machines and equipment, with proper maintenance
   — Methods: most efficient handling of operations
   — Deliveries: making deliveries on time
   — Tools: sufficient well-conditioned tools
   — Layout: most effective use of space
   — Reports: maintaining proper records and reports
   — Supervision: planning work for employees and organizing supervisor's own time

MANAGEMENT PRINCIPLES

I. MANAGEMENT
   Q. What do we mean by management?
   A. Getting work done through others.

   Management could also be defined as planning, directing, and controlling the operations of a bureau or division so that all factors will function properly and all persons cooperate efficiently for a common objective.

II. MANAGEMENT PRINCIPLES

   A. There should be a hierarchy—wherein authority and responsibility run upward and downward through several levels—with a broad base at the bottom and a single head at the top.

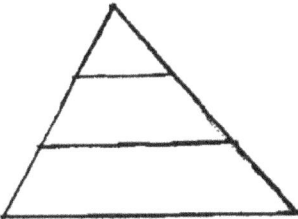

   B. Each and every unit or person in the organization should be answerable ultimately to the manager at the apex. In other words, *The buck stops here!*

C. Every necessary function involved in the bureau's objectives is assigned to a unit in that bureau.

D. Responsibilities assigned to a unit are specifically clear-cut and understood.

E. Consistent methods of organizational structure should be applied at each level of the organization.

F. Each member of the bureau from top to bottom knows: to whom he reports and who reports to him.

G. No member of one bureau reports to more than one supervisor. No dual functions.

H. Responsibility for a function is matched by authority necessary to perform that function. Weight of authority.

I. Individuals or units reporting to a supervisor do not exceed the number which can be feasibly and effectively coordinated and directed. Concept of *span of control.*

J. Channels of command (management) are not violated by staff units, although there should be staff services to facilitate and coordinate management functions.

K. Authority and responsibility should be decentralized to units and individuals who are responsible for the actual performance of operations.
Welfare – down to Welfare Centers
Hospitals – down to local hospitals

L. Management should exercise control through attention to policy problems of exceptional performance, rather than through review of routine actions of subordinates.

M. Organizations should never be permitted to grow so elaborate as to hinder work accomplishments.

III. ORGANIZATION STRUCTURE

Types of Organizations
The purest form is a leader and a few followers, such as:

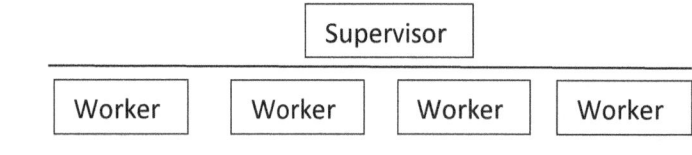

(Refer to organization chart) from supervisor to workers.

The line of authority is direct, The workers know exactly where they stand in relation to their boss, to whom they report for instructions and direction.

Unfortunately, in our present complex society, few organizations are similar to this example of a pure line organization. In this era of specialization, other people are often needed in the simplest of organizations. These specialists are known as staff. The sole purpose for their existence (staff) is to assist, advise, suggest, help or counsel line organizations. Staff has no authority to direct line people—nor do they give them direct instructions.

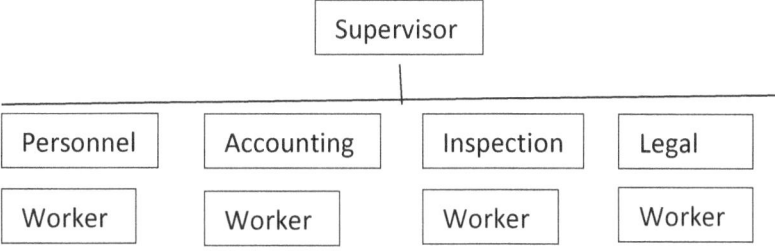

Line Functions
1. Directs
2. Orders
3. Responsibility for carrying out activities from beginning to end
4. Follows chain of command
5. Is identified with what it does
6. Decides when and how to use staff advice
7. Line executes

Staff Functions
1. Advises
2. Persuades and sells
3. Staff studies, reports, recommends but does not carry out
4. May advise across department lines
5. May find its ideas identified with others
6. Has to persuade line to want its advice
7. Staff: Conducts studies and research. Provides advice and instructions in technical matters. Serves as technical specialist to render specific services.

Types and Functions of Organization Charts
An organization chart is a picture of the arrangement and inter-relationship of the subdivisions of an organization.

A. Types of Charts:
   1. Structural: basic relationships only
   2. Functional: includes functions or duties
   3. Personnel: positions, salaries, status, etc.
   4. Process Chart: work performed
   5. Gantt Chart: actual performance against planned
   5. Flow Chart: flow and distribution of work

B. Functions of Charts:
   1. Assist in management planning and control
   2. Indicate duplication of functions
   3. Indicate incorrect stressing of functions
   4. Indicate neglect of important functions
   5. Correct unclear authority
   6. Establish proper span of control

C. Limitations of Charts:
   1. Seldom maintained on current basis
   2. Chart is oversimplified
   3. Human factors cannot adequately be charted

D. Organization Charts should be:
   1. Simple
   2. Symmetrical
   3. Indicate authority
   4. Line and staff relationship differentiated
   5. Chart should be dated and bear signature of approving officer
   6. Chart should be displayed, not hidden

ORGANIZATION

There are four basic principles of organization:
1. Unity of command
2. Span of control
3. Uniformity of assignment
4. Assignment of responsibility and delegation of authority

I. UNITY OF COMMAND

Unity of command means that each person in the organization should receive orders from one, and only one, supervisor. When a person has to take orders from two or more people, (a) the orders may be in conflict and the employee is upset because he does not know which he should obey, or (b) different orders may reach him at the same time and he does not know which he should carry out first.

Equally as bad as having two bosses is the situation where the supervisor is bypassed. Let us suppose you are a supervisor whose boss bypasses you (deals directly with people reporting to you). To the worker, it is the same as having two bosses; but to you, the supervisor, it is equally serious. Bypassing on the part of your boss will undermine your authority, and the people under you will begin looking to your boss for decisions and even for routine orders.

You can prevent bypassing by telling the people you supervise that if anyone tries to give them orders, they should direct that person to you.

II. SPAN OF CONTROL

Span of control on a given level involves:
A. The number of people being supervised
B. The distance
C The time involved in supervising the people. (One supervisor cannot supervise too many workers effectively.)

Span of control means that a supervisor has the right number (not too many and not too few) of subordinates that he can supervise well.

III. UNIFORMITY OF ASSIGNMENT

In assigning work, you as the supervisor should assign to each person jobs that are similar in nature. An employee who is assigned too many different types of jobs will waste time in going from one kind of work to another. It takes time for him to get to top production in one kind of task and, before he does so, he has to start on another.
When you assign work to people, remember that:

A. Job duties should be definite. Make it clear from the beginning <u>what</u> they are to do, <u>how</u> they are to do it, and <u>why</u> they are to do it. Let them know how much they are expected to do and how well they are expected to do it.
B. Check your assignments to be certain that there are no workers with too many unrelated duties, and that no two people have been given overlapping responsibilities. Your aim should be to have every task assigned to a specific person with the work fairly distributed and with each person doing his part.

IV. ASSIGNMENT OF RESPONSIBILITY AND DELEGATION OF AUTHORITY

A supervisor cannot delegate his final responsibility for the work of his department. The experienced supervisor knows that he gets his work done through people. He can't do it all himself. So he must assign the work and the responsibility for the work to his employees. Then they must be given the authority to carry out their responsibilities.

By assigning responsibility and delegating authority to carry out the responsibility, the supervisor builds in his workers initiative, resourcefulness, enthusiasm, and interest in their work. He is treating them as responsible adults. They can find satisfaction in their work, and they will respect the supervisor and be loyal to the supervisor.

PRINCIPLES OF ORGANIZATION

I. DEFINITION

Organization is the method of dividing up the work to provide the best channels for coordinated effort to get the agency's mission accomplished.

II. PURPOSE OF ORGANIZATION

A. To enable each employee within the organization to clearly know his responsibilities and relationships to his fellow employees and to organizational units
B. To avoid conflicts of authority and overlapping of jurisdiction.
C. To ensure teamwork.

III. BASIC CONSIDERATIONS IIN ORGANIZATIONAL PLANNING

A. The basic plans and objectives of the agency should be determined, and the organizational structure should be adapted to carry out effectively such plans and objectives.
B. The organization should be built around the major functions of the agency and not individuals or groups of individuals.

C. The organization should be sufficiently flexible to meet new and changing conditions which may be brought about from within or outside the department.
D. The organizational structure should be as simple as possible and the number of organizational units kept at a minimum.
E. The number of levels of authority should be kept at a minimum. Each additional management level lengthens the chain of authority and responsibility and increases the time for instructions to be distributed to operating levels and for decisions to be obtained from higher authority.
F. The form of organization should permit each executive to exercise maximum initiative within the limits of delegated authority.

IV. BASES FOR ORGANIZATION

A. Purpose (Examples: education, police, sanitation)
B. Process (Examples: accounting, legal, purchasing)
C. Clientele (Examples: welfare, parks, veteran)
D. Geographic (Examples: borough offices, precincts, libraries)

V. ASSIGNMENTS OF FUNCTIONS

A. Every function of the agency should be assigned to a specific organizational unit. Under normal circumstances, no single function should be assigned to more than one organizational unit.
B. There should be no overlapping, duplication, or conflict between organizational elements.
C. Line functions should be separated from staff functions, and proper emphasis should be placed on staff activities.
D. Functions which are closely related or similar should normally be assigned to a single organizational unit.
E. Functions should be properly distributed to promote balance, and to avoid overemphasis of less important functions and underemphasis of more essential functions.

VI. DELEGATION OF AUTHORITY AND RESPONSIBILITY

A. Responsibilities assigned to a specific individual or organizational unit should carry corresponding authority, and all statements of authority or limitations thereof should be as specific as possible.
B. Authority and responsibility for action should be decentralized to organizational units and individuals responsible for actual performance to the greatest extent possible, without relaxing necessary control over policy or the standardization of procedures. Delegation of authority will be consistent with decentralization of responsibility but such delegation will not divest an executive in higher authority of his overall responsibility.
C. The heads of organizational units should concern themselves with important matters and should delegate to the maximum extent details and routines performed in the ordinary course of business.
D. All responsibilities, authorities, and relationships should be stated in simple language to avoid misinterpretation.
E. Each individual or organizational unit charged with a specific responsibility will be held responsible for results.

VII. EMPLOYEE RELATIONSHIPS

   A. The employees reporting to one executive should not exceed the number which can be effectively directed and coordinated. The number will depend largely upon the scope and extent of the responsibilities of the subordinates.
   B. No person should report to more than one supervisor. Every supervisor should know who reports to him, and every employee should know to whom he reports. Channels of authority and responsibility should not be violated by staff units.
   C. Relationships between organizational units within the agency and with outside organizations and associations should be clearly stated and thoroughly understood to avoid misunderstanding.

DELEGATING

I. WHAT IS DELEGATING?
Delegating is assigning a job to an employee, giving him the authority to get that job done, and giving him the responsibility for seeing to it that the job is done.

   A. What To Delegate
      1. Routine details
      2. Jobs which may be necessary and take a lot of time, but do not have to be done by the supervisor personally (preparing reports, attending meetings, etc.)
      3. Routine decision-making (making decisions which do not require the supervisor's personal attention)

   B. What Not To Delegate
      1. Job details which are *executive functions* (setting goals, organizing employees into a good team, analyzing results so as to plan for the future)
      2. Disciplinary power (handling grievances, preparing service ratings, reprimands, etc.)
      3. Decision-making which involves large numbers of employees or other bureaus and departments
      4. Final and complete responsibility for the job done by the unit being supervised

   C. Why Delegate?
      1. To strengthen the organization by developing a greater number of skilled employees
      2. To improve the employee's performance by giving him the chance to learn more about the job, handle some responsibility, and become more interested in getting the job done
      3. To improve a supervisor's performance by relieving him of routine jobs and giving him more time for *executive functions* (planning, organizing, controlling, etc.) which cannot be delegated

II. TO WHOM TO DELEGATE
People with abilities not being used. Selection should be based on ability, not on favoritism.

REPORTS

I. **DEFINITION**
A report is an orderly presentation of factual information directed to a specific reader for a specific purpose

II. **PURPOSE**
The general purpose of a report is to bring to the reader useful and factual information about a condition or a problem. Some specific purposes of a report may be:

   A. To enable the reader to appraise the efficiency or effectiveness of a person or an operation
   B. To provide a basis for establishing standards
   C. To reflect the results of expenditures of time, effort, and money
   D. To provide a basis for developing or altering programs

III. **TYPES**

   A. Information Report: Contains facts arranged in sequence
   B. Summary (Examination) Report: Contains facts plus an analysis or discussion of the significance of the facts. Analysis may give advantages and disadvantages or give qualitative and quantitative comparisons
   C. Recommendation Report: Contains facts, analysis, and conclusion logically drawn from the facts and analysis, plus a recommendation based upon the facts, analysis, and conclusions

IV. **FACTORS TO CONSIDER BEFORE WRITING REPORT**

   A. <u>Why</u> write the report?: The purpose of the report should be clearly defined.
   B. <u>Who</u> will read the report?: What level of language should be used? Will the reader understand professional or technical language?
   C. <u>What</u> should be said?: What does the reader need or want to know about the subject?
   D. <u>How</u> should it be said?: Should the subject be presented tactfully? Convincingly? In a stimulating manner?

V. **PREPARATORY STEPS**

   A. Assemble the facts: Find out who, why, what, where, when, and how.
   B. Organize the facts: Eliminate unnecessary information
   C. Prepare an outline: Check for orderliness, logical sequence
   D. Prepare a draft: Check for correctness, clearness, completeness, conciseness, and tone
   E. Prepare it in final form: Check for grammar, punctuation, appearance

VI. **OUTLINE FOR A RECOMMENDATION REPORT**

   Is the report:
   A. Correct in information, grammar, and tone?
   B. Clear?
   C. Complete?

D. Concise?
E. Timely?
F. Worth its cost?

Will the report accomplish its purpose?

MANAGEMENT CONTROLS

I. CONTROL
What is control? What is controlled? Who controls?

The essence of control is action which adjusts operations to predetermined standards, and its basis is information in the hands of managers. Control is checking to determine whether plans are being observed and suitable progress toward stated objectives is being made, and action is taken, if necessary, to correct deviations.

We have a ready-made model for this concept of control in the automatic systems which are widely used for process control in the chemical land petroleum industries. A process control system works this way. Suppose, for example, it is desired to maintain a constant rate of flow of oil through a pipe at a predetermined or set-point value. A signal, whose strength represents the rate of flow, can be produced in a measuring device and transmitted to a control mechanism. The control mechanism, when it detects any deviation of the actual from the set-point signal, will reposition the value regulating flow rate.

II. BASIS FOR CONTROL

A process control mechanism thus acts to adjust operations to predetermined standards and does so on the basis of information it receives. In a parallel way, information reaching a manager gives him the opportunity for corrective action and is his basis for control. He cannot exercise control without such information, and he cannot do a complete job of managing without controlling.

III. POLICY

What is policy?

Policy is simply a statement of an organization's intention to act in certain ways when specified types of circumstances arise. It represents a general decision, predetermined and expressed as a principle or rule, establishing a normal pattern of conduct for dealing with given types of business events—usually recurrent. A statement is therefore useful in economizing the time of managers and in assisting them to discharge their responsibilities equitably and consistently.

Policy is not a means of control, but policy does generate the need for control.

Adherence to policies is not guaranteed nor can it be taken on faith. It has to be verified. Without verification, there is no basis for control. Policy and procedures, although closely related and interdependent to a certain extent, are not synonymous. A policy may be adopted, for example, to maintain a materials inventory not to exceed one million dollars.

A procedure for inventory control could interpret that policy and convert it into methods for keeping within that limit, with consideration, too, of possible but foreseeable expedient deviation.

IV. PROCEDURE

What is procedure?

A procedure specifically prescribes:
A. What work is to be performed by the various participants
B. Who are the respective participants
C. When and where the various steps in the different processes are to be performed
D. The sequence of operations that will insure uniform handling of recurring transactions
E. The paper that is involved, its origin, transition, and disposition

Necessary appurtenances to a procedure are:
A. Detailed organizational chart
B. Flow charts
C. Exhibits of forms, all presented in close proximity to the text of the procedure

V. BASIS OF CONTROL – INFORMATION IN THE HANDS OF MANAGERS

If the basis of control is information in the hands of managers, then reporting is elevated to a level of very considerable importance.

Types of reporting may include:
A. Special reports and routine reports
B. Written, oral, and graphic reports
C. Staff meetings
D. Conferences
E. Television screens
F. Non-receipt of information, as where management is by exception
G. Any other means whereby information is transmitted to a manager as a basis for control action

FRAMEWORK OF MANAGEMENT

I. ELEMENTS

A. Policy: It has to be verified, controlled.

B. Organization is part of the giving of an assignment. The organizational chart gives to each individual in his title, a first approximation of the nature of his assignment and orients him as being accountable to a certain individual. Organization is not in a true sense a means of control. Control is checking to ascertain whether the assignment is executed as intended and acting on the basis of that information.

C. Budgets perform three functions:
1. They present the objectives, plans, and programs of the organization in financial terms.

2. They report the progress of actual performance against these predetermined objectives, plans, and programs.
3. Like organizational charts, delegations of authority, procedures, and job descriptions, they define the assignments which have flowed from the Chief Executive. Budgets are a means of control in the respect that they report progress of actual performance against the program. They provide information which enables managers to take action directed toward bringing actual results into conformity with the program.

D. Internal Check provides in practice for the principle that the same person should not have responsibility for all phases of a transaction. This makes it clearly an aspect of organization rather than of control. Internal Check is static, or built-in.

E. Plans, Programs, Objectives
People must know what they are trying to do. Objectives fulfill this need. Without them, people may work industriously and yet, working aimlessly, accomplish little. Plans and Programs complement Objectives, since they propose how and according to what time schedule the objectives are to be reached.

F. Delegations of Authority
Among the ways we have for supplementing the titles and lines of authority of an organizational chart are delegations of authority. Delegations of authority clarify the extent of authority of individuals and in that way serve to define assignments. That they are not means of control is apparent from the very fact that wherever there has been a delegation of authority, the need for control increases. This could hardly be expected to happen if delegations of authority were themselves means of control.

II. MANAGER'S RESPONSIBILITY

Control becomes necessary whenever a manager delegates authority to a subordinate because he cannot delegate and then simply sit back and forget4 about it. A manager's accountability to his own superior has not diminished one whit as a result of delegating part of his authority to a subordinate. The manager must exercise control over actions taken under the authority so delegated. That means checking serves as a basis for possible corrective action.

Objectives, plans, programs, organizational charts, and other elements of the managerial system are not fruitfully regarded as either controls or means of control. They are pre-established standards or models of performance to which operations are adjusted by the exercise of management control. These standards or models of performance are dynamic in character for they are constantly altered, modified, or revised. Policies, organizational set-up, procedures, delegations, etc. are constantly altered but, like objectives and plans, they remain in force until they are either abandoned or revised. All of the elements (or standards or models of performance), objectives, plans, and programs, policies, organization, etc. can be regarded as a *framework of management*.

III. CONTROL TECHNIQUES

Examples of control techniques:
A. Compare against established standards
B. Compare with a similar operation
C. Compare with past operations
D. Compare with predictions of accomplishment

IV. WHERE FORECASTS FIT

Control is after-the-fact while forecasts are before. Forecasts and projections are important for setting objectives and formulating plans.

Information for aiming and planning does not have to be before-the-fact. It may be an after-the-fact analysis proving that a certain policy has been impolitic in its effect on the relation of the company or department with customer, employee, taxpayer, or stockholder; or that a certain plan is no longer practical, or that a certain procedure is unworkable.

The prescription here certainly would not be in control (in these cases, control would simply bring operations into conformity with obsolete standards) but the establishment of new standards, a new policy, a new plan, and a new procedure to be controlled too.

Information is, of course, the basis for all communication in addition to furnishing evidence to management of the need for reconstructing the framework of management.

PROBLEM SOLVING

The accepted concept in modern management for problem solving is the utilization of the following steps:

A. Identify the problem
B. Gather data
C. List possible solutions
D. Test possible solutions
E. Select the best solution
F. Put the solution into actual practice

Occasions might arise where you would have to apply the second step of gathering data before completing the first step.

You might also find that it will be necessary to work on several steps at the same time.

I. IDENTIFY THE PROBLEM

Your first step is to define as precisely as possible the problem to be solved. While this may sound easy, it is often the most difficult part of the process.

It has been said of problem solving that you are halfway to the solution when you can write out a clear statement of the problem itself.

Our job now is to get below the surface manifestations of the trouble and pinpoint the problem. This is usually accomplished by a logical analysis, by going from the general to the particular; from the obvious to the not-so-obvious cause.

Let us say that production is behind schedule. WHY? Absenteeism is high. Now, is absenteeism the basic problem to be tackled, or is it merely a symptom of low morale among the workforce? Under these circumstances, you may decide that production is not the problem; the problem is *employee morale*.

In trying to define the problem, remember there is seldom one simple reason why production is lagging, or reports are late, etc.

Analysis usually leads to the discovery that an apparent problem is really made up of several subproblems which must be attacked separately.

Another way is to limit the problem, and thereby ease the task of finding a solution, and concentrate on the elements which are within the scope of your control.

When you have gone this far, write out a tentative statement of the problem to be solved.

II. GATHER DATA

In the second step, you must set out to collect all the information that might have a bearing on the problem. Do not settle for an assumption when reasonable fact and figures are available.

If you merely go through the motions of problem-solving, you will probably shortcut the information-gathering step. Therefore, do not stack the evidence by confining your research to your own preconceived ideas.

As you collect facts, organize them in some form that helps you make sense of them and spot possible relationships between them. For example, plotting cost per unit figures on a graph can be more meaningful than a long column of figures.

Evaluate each item as you go along. Is the source material absolutely, reliable, probably reliable, or not to be trusted.

One of the best methods for gathering data is to go out and look the situation over carefully. Talk to the people on the job who are most affected by this problem.

Always keep in mind that a primary source is usually better than a secondary source of information.

III. LIST POSSIBLE SOLUTIONS

This is the creative thinking step of problem solving. This is a good time to bring into play whatever techniques of group dynamics the agency or bureau might have developed for a joint attack on problems.

Now the important thing for you to do is: Keep an open mind. Let your imagination roam freely over the facts you have collected. Jot down every possible solution that occurs to you. Resist the temptation to evaluate various proposals as you go along. List seemingly absurd ideas along with more plausible ones. The more possibilities you list during this step, the less risk you will run of settling for merely a workable, rather than the best, solution.

Keep studying the data as long as there seems to be any chance of deriving additional ideas, solutions, explanations, or patterns from it.

IV. TEST POSSIBLE SOLUTIONS

Now you begin to evaluate the possible solutions. Take pains to be objective. Up to this point, you have suspended judgment but you might be tempted to select a solution you secretly favored all along and proclaim it as the best of the lot.

The secret of objectivity in this phase is to test the possible solutions separately, measuring each against a common yardstick. To make this yardstick try to enumerate as many specific criteria as you can think of. Criteria are best phrased as questions which you ask of each possible solution. They can be drawn from these general categories:

- Suitability – Will this solution do the job?
  Will it solve the problem completely or partially?
  Is it a permanent or a stopgap solution?

- Feasibility – Will this plan work in actual practice?
  Can we afford this approach?
  How much will it cost?

- Acceptability – Will the boss go along with the changes required in the plan?
  Are we trying to drive a tack with a sledge hammer?

V. SELECT THE BEST SOLUTION

This is the area of executive decision.

Occasionally, one clearly superior solution will stand out at the conclusion of the testing process. But often it is not that simple. You may find that no one solution has come through all the tests with flying colors.

You may also find that a proposal, which flunked miserably on one of the essential tests, racked up a very high score on others.

The best solution frequently will turn out to be a combination.

Try to arrange a marriage that will bring together the strong points of one possible solution with the particular virtues of another. The more skill and imagination that you apply, the greater is the likelihood that you will come out with a solution that is not merely adequate and workable, but is the best possible under the circumstances.

VI. PUT THE SOLUTION INTO ACTUAL PRACTICE

As every executive knows, a plan which works perfectly on paper may develop all sorts of bugs when put into actual practice.

Problem-solving does not stop with selecting the solution which looks best in theory. The next step is to put the chosen solution into action and watch the results. The results may point towards modifications.

If the problem disappears when you put your solution into effect, you know you have the right solution.

If it does not disappear, even after you have adjusted your plan to cover unforeseen difficulties that turned up in practice, work your way back through the problem-solving solutions.

> Would one of them have worked better?
> Did you overlook some vital piece of data which would have given you a different slant on the whole situation? Did you apply all necessary criteria in testing solutions? If no light dawns after this much rechecking, it is a pretty good bet that you defined the problem incorrectly in the first place.

You came up with the wrong solution because you tackled the wrong problem.

Thus, step six may become step one of a new problem-solving cycle.

COMMUNICATION

I. WHAT IS COMMUNICATION?
We communicate through writing, speaking, action, or inaction. In speaking to people face-to-face, there is opportunity to judge reactions and to adjust the message. This makes the supervisory chain one of the most, and in many instances the most, important channels of communication.

In an organization, communication means keeping employees informed about the organization's objectives, policies, problems, and progress. Communication is the free interchange of information, ideas, and desirable attitudes between and among employees and between employees and management.

II. WHY IS COMMUNICATION NEEDED?

A. People have certain social needs
B. Good communication is essential in meeting those social needs
C. While people have similar basic needs, at the same time they differ from each other
D. Communication must be adapted to these individual differences

An employee cannot do his best work unless he knows why he is doing it. If he has the feeling that he is being kept in the dark about what is going on, his enthusiasm and productivity suffer.

Effective communication is needed in an organization so that employees will understand what the organization is trying to accomplish; and how the work of one unit contributes to or affects the work of other units in the organization and other organizations.

III. HOW IS COMMUNICATION ACHIEVED?

Communication flows downward, upward, sideways.

A. Communication may come from top management down to employees. This is downward communication.

   Some means of downward communication are:
   1. Training (orientation, job instruction, supervision, public relations, etc.)
   2. Conferences
   3. Staff meetings
   4. Policy statements
   5. Bulletins
   6. Newsletters
   7. Memoranda
   8. Circulation of important letters

   In downward communication, it is important that employees be informed in advance of changes that will affect them.

B. Communications should also be developed so that the ideas, suggestions, and knowledge of employees will flow upward to top management.

   Some means of upward communication are:
   1. Personal discussion conferences
   2. Committees
   3. Memoranda
   4. Employees suggestion program
   5. Questionnaires to be filled in giving comments and suggestions about proposed actions that will affect field operations.

   Upward communication requires that management be willing to listen, to accept, and to make changes when good ideas are present. Upward communication succeeds when there is no fear of punishment for speaking out or lack of interest at the top. Employees will share their knowledge and ideas with management when interest is shown and recognition is given.

C. The advantages of downward communication:
   1. It enables the passing down of orders, policies, and plans necessary to the continued operation of the station.
   2. By making information available, it diminishes the fears and suspicions which result from misinformation and misunderstanding.
   3. It fosters the pride people want to have in their work when they are told of good work.
   4. It improves the morale and stature of the individual to be *in the know*.

5. It helps employees to understand, accept, and cooperate with changes when they know about them in advance.

D. The advantages of upward communication:
1. It enables the passing upward of information, attitudes, and feelings.
2. It makes it easier to find out how ready people are to receive downward communication.
3. It reveals the degree to which the downward communication is understood and accepted.
4. It helps to satisfy the basic social needs.
5. It stimulates employees to participate in the operation of their organization.
6. It encourage employees to contribute ideas for improving the efficiency and economy of operations.
7. It helps to solve problem situations before they reach the explosion point.

IV. WHY DOES COMMUNICATION FAIL?

A. The technical difficulties of conveying information clearly
B. The emotional content of communication which prevents complete transmission
C. The fact that there is a difference between what management needs to say, what it wants to day, and what it does say
D. The fact that there is a difference between what employees would like to say, what they think is profitable or safe to say, and what they do say

V. HOW TO IMPROVE COMMUNICATION

As a supervisor, you are a key figure in communication. To improve as a communicator, you should:
A. Know: Knowing your subordinates will help you to recognize and work with individual differences.
B. Like: If you like those who work for you and those for whom you work, this will foster the kind of friendly, warm, work atmosphere that will facilitate communication.
C. Trust: Showing a sincere desire to communicate will help to develop the mutual trust and confidence which are essential to the free flow of communication.
D. Tell: Tell your subordinates and superiors *what's doing*. Tell your subordinates *why* as well as *how*.
E. Listen: By listening, you help others to talk and you create good listeners. Don't forget that listening implies action.
F. Stimulate: Communication has to be stimulated and encouraged. Be receptive to ideas and suggestions and motivate your people so that each member of the team identifies himself with the job at hand.
G. Consult: The most effective way of consulting is to let your people participate, insofar as possible, in developing determinations which affect them or their work.

VI. HOW TO DETERMINE WHETHER YOU ARE GETTING ACROSS

A. Check to see that communication is received and understood
B. Judge this understanding by actions rather than words
C. Adapt or vary communication, when necessary
D. Remember that good communication cannot cure all problems

VII. THE KEY ATTITUDE

Try to see things from the other person's point of view. By doing this, you help to develop the permissive atmosphere and the shared confidence and understanding which are essential to effective two-way communication.

Communication is a two-way process:
A. The basic purpose of any communication is to get action.
B. The only way to get action is through acceptance.
C. In order to get acceptance, communication must be humanly satisfying as well as technically efficient.

HOW ORDERS AND INSTRUCTIONS SHOULD BE GIVEN

I. CHARACTERISTICS OF GOOD ORDERS AND INSTRUCTIONS

   A. Clear
      Orders should be definite as to
      —What is to be done
      —Who is to do it
      —When it is to be done
      —Where it is to be done
      —How it is to be done

   B. Concise
      Avoid wordiness. Orders should be brief and to the point.

   C. Timely
      Instructions and orders should be sent out at the proper time and not too long in advance of expected performance.

   D. Possibility of Performance
      Orders should be feasible:
      1. Investigate before giving orders
      2. Consult those who are to carry out instructions before formulating and issuing them

   E. Properly Directed
      Give the orders to the people concerned. Do not send orders to people who are not concerned. People who continually receive instructions that are not applicable to them get in the habit of neglecting instructions generally.

   F. Reviewed Before Issuance
      Orders should be reviewed before issuance:
      1. Test them by putting yourself in the position of the recipient
      2. If they involve new procedures, have the persons who are to do the work review them for suggestions.

   G. Reviewed After Issuance
      Persons who receive orders should be allowed to raise questions and to point out unforeseen consequences of orders.

H. Coordinated
Orders should be coordinated so that work runs smoothly.

I. Courteous
Make a request rather than a demand. There is no need to continually call attention to the fact that you are the boss.

J. Recognizable as an Order
Be sure that the order is recognizable as such.

K. Complete
Be sure recipient has knowledge and experience sufficient to carry out order. Give illustrations and examples.

A DEPARTMENTAL PERSONNEL OFFICE IS RESPONSIBLE FOR THE FOLLOWING FUNCTIONS

1. Policy
2. Personnel Programs
3. Recruitment and Placement
4. Position Classification
5. Salary and Wage Administration
6. Employee performance Standards and Evaluation
7. Employee Relations
8. Disciplinary Actions and Separations
9. Health and Safety
10. Staff Training and Development
11. Personnel Records, Procedures, and Reports
12. Employee Services
13. Personnel Research

SUPERVISION

I. LEADERSHIP

All leadership is based essentially on authority. This comes from two sources: It is received from higher management or it is earned by the supervisor through his methods of supervision. Although effective leadership has always depended upon the leader's using his authority in such a way as to appeal successfully to the motives of the people supervised, the conditions for making this appeal are continually changing. The key to today's problem of leadership is flexibility and resourcefulness on the part of the leader in meeting changes in conditions as they occur.

Three basic approaches to leadership are generally recognized:

A. The Authoritarian Approach
   1. The methods and techniques used in this approach emphasize the *I* in leadership and depend primarily on the formal authority of the leader. This authority is sometimes exercised in a hardboiled manner and sometimes in a benevolent

manner, but in either case the dominating role of the leader is reflected in the thinking, planning, and decisions of the group.
2. Group results are to a large degree dependent on close supervision by the leader. Usually, the individuals in the group will not show a high degree of initiative or acceptance of responsibility and their capacity to grow and develop probably will not be fully utilized. The group may react with resentment or submission, depending upon the manner and skill of the leader in using his authority.
3. This approach develops as a natural outgrowth of the authority that goes with the leader's job and his feeling of sole responsibility for getting the job done. It is relatively easy to use and does not require must resourcefulness.
4. The use of this approach is effective in times of emergencies, in meeting close deadline as a final resort, in settling some issues, in disciplinary matters, and with dependent individuals and groups.

B. The Laissez-Faire or Let 'em Alone Approach
1. This approach generally is characterized by an avoidance of leadership responsibility by the leader. The activities of the group depend largely on the choice of its members rather than the leader.
2. Group results probably will be poor. Generally, there will be disagreements over petty things, bickering, and confusion. Except for a few aggressive people, individuals will not show much initiative and growth and development will be retarded. There may be a tendency for informal leaders to take over leadership of the group.
3. This approach frequently results from the leader's dislike of responsibility, from his lack of confidence, from failure of other methods to work, from disappointment or criticism. It is usually the easiest of the three to use and requires both understanding and resourcefulness on the part of the leader.
4. This approach is occasionally useful and effective, particularly in forcing dependent individuals or groups to rely on themselves, to give someone a chance to save face by clearing his own difficulties, or when action should be delayed temporarily for good cause.

C. The Democratic Approach
1. The methods and techniques used in this approach emphasize the *we* in leadership and build up the responsibility of the group to attain its objectives. Reliance is placed largely on the earned authority of the leader.
2. Group results are likely to be good because most of the job motives of the people will be satisfied. Cooperation and teamwork, initiative, acceptance of responsibility, and the individual's capacity for growth probably will show a high degree of development.
3. This approach grows out of a desire or necessity of the leader to find ways to appeal effectively to the motivation of his group. It is the best approach to build up inside the person a strong desire to cooperate and apply himself to the job. It is the most difficult to develop, and requires both understanding and resourcefulness on the part of the leader.
4. The value of this approach increases over a long period where sustained efficiency and development of people are important. It may not be fully effective in all situations, however, particularly when there is not sufficient time to use it properly or where quick decisions must be made.

All three approaches are used by most leaders and have a place in supervising people. The extent of their use varies with individual leaders, with some using one approach predominantly. The leader who uses these three approaches, and varies their use with time and circumstance, is probably the most effective. Leadership which is used predominantly with a democratic approach requires more resourcefulness on the part of the leader but offers the greatest possibilities in terms of teamwork and cooperation.

The one best way of developing democratic leadership is to provide a real sense of participation on the part of the group, since this satisfies most of the chief job motives. Although there are many ways of providing participation, consulting as frequently as possible with individuals and groups on things that affect them seems to offer the most in building cooperation and responsibility. Consultation takes different forms, but it is most constructive when people feel they are actually helping in finding the answers to the problems on the job.

There are some requirements of leaders in respect to human relations which should be considered in their selection and development. Generally, the leader should be interested in working with other people, emotionally stable, self-confident, and sensitive to the reactions of others. In addition, his viewpoint should be one of getting the job done through people who work cooperatively in response to his leadership. He should have a knowledge of individual and group behavior, but, most important of all, he should work to combine all of these requirements into a definite, practical skill in leadership.

II. NINE POINTS OF CONTRAST BETWEEN *BOSS* AND *LEADER*

   A. The boss drives his men; the leader coaches them.
   B. The boss depends on authority; the leader on good will.
   C. The boss inspires fear; the leader inspires enthusiasm.
   D. The boss says I; the leader says *We*.
   E. The boss says *Get here on time*; the leader gets there ahead of time.
   F. The boss fixes the blame for the breakdown; the leader fixes the breakdown.
   G. The boss knows how it is done; the leader shows how.
   H. The boss makes work a drudgery; the leader makes work a game.
   I. The boss says *Go*; the leader says *Let's go*.

EMPLOYEE MORALE

Employee morale is the way employees feel about each other, the organization or unit in which they work, and the work they perform.

I. SOME WAYS TO DEVELOP AND MAINTAIN GOOD EMPLYEE MORALE

   A. Give adequate credit and praise when due.
   B. Recognize importance of all jobs and equalize load with proper assignments, always giving consideration to personality differences and abilities.
   C. Welcome suggestions and do not have an *all-wise* attitude. Request employees' assistance in solving problems and use assistants when conducting group meetings on certain subjects.
   D. Properly assign responsibilities and give adequate authority for fulfillment of such assignments.

E. Keep employees informed about matters that affect them.
F. Criticize and reprimand employees privately.
G. Be accessible and willing to listen.
H. Be fair.
I. Be alert to detect training possibilities so that you will not miss an opportunity to help each employee do a better job, and if possible with less effort on his part.
J. Set a good example.
K. Apply the golden rule.

II. SOME INDICATIONS OF GOOD MORALE

A. Good quality of work
B. Good quantity
C. Good attitude of employees
D. Good discipline
E. Teamwork
F. Good attendance
G. Employee participation

MOTIVATION

DRIVES

A drive, stated simply, is a desire or force which causes a person to do or say certain things. These are some of the most usual drives and some of their identifying characteristics recognizable in people motivated by such drives:

A. Security (desire to provide for the future)
Always on time for work
Works for the same employer for many years
Never takes unnecessary chances
Seldom resists doing what he is told

B. Recognition (desire to be rewarded for accomplishment)
Likes to be asked for his opinion
Becomes very disturbed when he makes a mistake
Does things to attract attention
Likes to see his name in print

C. Position (desire to hold certain status in relation to others)
Boasts about important people he knows
Wants to be known as a key man
Likes titles
Demands respect
Belongs to clubs, for prestige

D. Accomplishment (desire to get things done)
   Complains when things are held up
   Likes to do things that have tangible results
   Never lies down on the job
   Is proud of turning out good work

E. Companionship (desire to associate with other people)
   Likes to work with others
   Tells stories and jokes
   Indulges in horseplay
   Finds excuses to talk to others on the job

F. Possession (desire to collect and hoard objects)
   Likes to collect things
   Puts his name on things belonging to him
   Insists on the same location

Supervisors may find that identifying the drives of employees is a helpful step toward motivating them to self-improvement and better job performance. For example: An employee's job performance is below average. His supervisor, having previously determined that the employee is motivated by a drive for security, suggests that taking training courses will help the employee to improve, advance, and earn more money. Since earning more money can be a step toward greater security, the employee's drive for security would motivate him to take the training suggested by the supervisor. In essence, this is the process of charting an employee's future course by using his motivating drives to positive advantage.

EMPLOYEE PARTICIPATION

I. WHAT IS PARTICIPATION

Employee participation is the employee's giving freely of his time, skill, and knowledge to an extent which cannot be obtained by demand.

II. WHY IS IT IMPORTANT?

The supervisor's responsibility is to get the job done through people. A good supervisor gets the job done through people who work willingly and well. The participation of employees is important because:

A. Employees develop a greater sense of responsibility when they share in working out operating plans and goals.
B. Participation provides greater opportunity and stimulation for employees to learn, and to develop their ability.
C. Participation sometimes provides better solutions to problems because such solutions may combine the experience and knowledge of interested employees who want the solutions to work.
D. An employee or group may offer a solution which the supervisor might hesitate to make for fear of demanding too much.

E. Since the group wants to make the solution work, they exert pressure in a constructive way on each other.
F. Participation usually results in reducing the need for close supervision.

II. HOW MAY SUPERVISORS OBTAIN IT?

Participation is encouraged when employees feel that they share some responsibility for the work and that their ideas are sincerely wanted and valued. Some ways of obtaining employee participation are:

A. Conduct orientation programs for new employees to inform them about the organization and their rights and responsibilities as employees.
B. Explain the aims and objectives of the agency. On a continuing basis, be sure that the employees know what these aims and objectives are.
C. Share job successes and responsibilities and give credit for success.
D. Consult with employees, both as individuals and in groups, about things that affect them.
E. Encourage suggestions for job improvements. Help employees to develop good suggestions. The suggestions can bring them recognition. The city's suggestion program offers additional encouragement through cash awards.

The supervisor who encourages employee participation is not surrendering his authority. He must still make decisions and initiate action, and he must continue to be ultimately responsible for the work of those he supervises. But, through employee participation, he is helping his group to develop greater ability and a sense of responsibility while getting the job done faster and better.

STEPS IN HANDLING A GRIEVANCE

1. Get the Facts
   a. Listen sympathetically
   b. Let him talk himself out
   c. Get his story straight
   d. Get his point of view
   e. Don't argue with him
   f. Give him plenty of time
   g. Conduct the interview privately
   h. Don't try to shift the blame or pass the buck

2. Consider the Facts
   a. Consider the employee's viewpoint
   b. How will the decision affect similar cases
   c. Consider each decision as a possible precedent
   d. Avoid snap judgments—don't jump to conclusions

3. Make or Get a Decision
   a. Frame an effective counter-proposal
   b. Make sure it is fair to all
   c. Have confidence in your judgment
   d. Be sure you can substantiate your decision

4. Notify the Employee of Your Decision
   Be sure he is told; try to convince him that the decision is fair and just.

5. Take Action When Needed and If Within Your Authority
   Otherwise, tell employee that the matter will be called to the attention of the proper person or that nothing can be done, and why it cannot.

6. Follow through to see that the desired result is achieved.

7. Record key facts concerning the complaint and the action taken.

8. Leave the way open to him to appeal your decision to a higher authority.

9. Report all grievances to your superior, whether they are appealed or not.

DISCIPLINE

Discipline is training that develops self-control, orderly conduct, and efficiency.

To discipline does not necessarily mean to punish.

To discipline does mean to train, to regulate, and to govern conduct.

I. THE DISCIPLINARY INTERVIEW

Most employees sincerely want to do what is expected of them. In other words, they are self-disciplined. Some employees, however, fail to observe established rules and standards, and disciplinary action by the supervisor is required.

The primary purpose of disciplinary action is to improve conduct without creating dissatisfaction, bitterness, or resentment in the process.

Constructive disciplinary action is more concerned with causes and explanations of breaches of conduct than with punishment. The disciplinary interview is held to get at the causes of apparent misbehavior and to motivate better performance in the future.

It is important that the interview be kept on an impersonal a basis as possible. If the supervisor lets the interview descend to the plane of an argument, it loses its effectiveness.

II. PLANNING THE INTERVIEW

Get all pertinent facts concerning the situation so that you can talk in specific terms to the employee.

Review the employee's record, appraisal ratings, etc.

Consider what you know about the temperament of the employee. Consider your attitude toward the employee. Remember that the primary requisite of disciplinary action is fairness.

Don't enter upon the interview when angry.

Schedule the interview for a place which is private and out of hearing of others.

III. CONDUCTING THE INTERVIEW

   A. Make an effort to establish accord.
   B. Question the employee about the apparent breach of discipline. Be sure that the question is not so worded as to be itself an accusation.
   C. Give the employee a chance to tell his side of the story. Give him ample opportunity to talk.
   D. Use understanding—listening except where it is necessary to ask a question or to point out some details of which the employee may not be aware. If the employee misrepresents facts, make a plain, accurate statement of the facts, but don't argue and don't engage in personal controversy.
   E. Listen and try to understand the reasons for the employee's (mis)conduct. First of all, don't assume that there has been a breach of discipline. Evaluate the employee's reasons for his conduct in the light of his opinions and feelings concerning the consistency and reasonableness of the standards which he was expected to follow. Has the supervisor done his part in explaining the reasons for the rule? Was the employee's behavior unintentional or deliberate? Does he think he had real reasons for his actions? What new facts is he telling? Do the facts justify his actions? What causes, other than those mentioned, could have stimulated the behavior?
   F. After listening to the employee's version of the situation, and if censure of his actions is warranted, the supervisor should proceed with whatever criticism is justified. Emphasis should be placed on future improvement rather than exclusively on the employee's failure to measure up to expected standards of job conduct.
   G. Fit the criticism to the individual. With one employee, a word of correction may be all that is required.
   H. Attempt to distinguish between unintentional error and deliberate misbehavior. An error due to ignorance requires training and not censure.
   I. Administer criticism in a controlled, even tone of voice, never in anger. Make it clear that you are acting as an agent of the department. In general, criticism should refer to the job or the employee's actions and not to the person. Criticism of the employee's work is not an attack on the individual.
   J. Be sure the interview does not destroy the employee's self-confidence. Mention his good qualities and assure him that you feel confident that he can improve his performance.
   K. Wherever possible, before the employee leaves the interview, satisfy him that the incident is closed, that nothing more will be said on the subject unless the offense is repeated.

www.ingramcontent.com/pod-product-compliance
Lightning Source LLC
Chambersburg PA
CBHW081808300426
44116CB00014B/2287